W9-AQO-664

THE CLASSICS
OF **WESTERN**
SPIRITUALITY

THE CLASSICS OF WESTERN SPIRITUALITY
A Library of the Great Spiritual Masters

President and Publisher
Lawrence Boadt, C.S.P.

EDITORIAL BOARD

Editor-in-Chief
Bernard McGinn—Naomi Shenstone Donnelly Professor of Historical Theology and the History of Christianity, Divinity School, University of Chicago, Chicago, Ill.

Editorial Consultant
Ewert H. Cousins—Professor of Theology, Fordham University, Bronx, N.Y.

John E. Booty—Professor of Anglican Studies, School of Theology, University of the South, Sewanee, Tenn.

Joseph Dan—Professor of Kabbalah, Department of Jewish Thought, Hebrew University, Jerusalem, Israel.

Louis Dupré—T. L. Riggs Professor of Philosophy of Religion, Yale University, New Haven, Conn.

Rozanne Elder—Executive Vice-President, Cistercian Publications, Kalamazoo, Mich.

Michael Fishbane—Nathan Cummings Professor, Divinity School, University of Chicago, Chicago, Ill.

Anne Fremantle—Teacher, Editor, and Writer, New York, N.Y.

Karlfried Froehlich—Professor of the History of the Early and Medieval Church, Princeton Theological Seminary, Princeton, N.J.

Arthur Green—Professor of Jewish Thought, Brandeis University, Waltham, Mass.

Stanley S. Harakas—Archbishop Iakovos Professor of Orthodox Theology, Holy Cross Greek Orthodox Seminary, Brookline, Mass.

Moshe Idel—Professor of Jewish Thought, Department of Jewish Thought, Hebrew University, Jerusalem, Israel.

Bishop Kallistos of Diokleia—Fellow of Pembroke College, Oxford, Spalding Lecturer in Eastern Orthodox Studies, Oxford University, England.

George A. Maloney—Spiritual Writer and Lecturer, Seal Beach, Calif.

Seyyed Hossein Nasr—Professor of Islamic Studies, George Washington University, Washington, D.C.

Raimon Panikkar—Professor Emeritus, Department of Religious Studies, University of California at Santa Barbara, Calif.

Jaroslav Pelikan—Sterling Professor of History and Religious Studies, Yale University, New Haven, Conn.

Sandra M. Schneiders—Professor of New Testament Studies and Spirituality, Jesuit School of Theology, Berkeley, Calif.

Michael A. Sells—Emily Judson Baugh and John Marshall Gest Professor of Comparative Religions, Haverford College, Haverford, Penn.

Huston Smith—Thomas J. Watson Professor of Religion Emeritus, Syracuse University, Syracuse, N.Y.

John R. Sommerfeldt—Professor of History, University of Dallas, Irving, Tex.

David Steindl-Rast—Spiritual Author, Benedictine Grange, West Redding, Conn.

David Tracy—Greeley Professor of Roman Catholic Studies, Divinity School, University of Chicago, Chicago, Ill.

The Rt. Rev. Rowan D. Williams—Bishop of Monmouth, Wales.

BM
495
,R29
2002

RABBINIC STORIES

TRANSLATED AND INTRODUCED BY
JEFFREY L. RUBENSTEIN

PREFACE BY
SHAYE J. D. COHEN

MAY 14 2002

PAULIST PRESS
NEW YORK • MAHWAH, N.J.

Cover art: Haggadah. Germany, 1732. Ms. 4446, folio 3b. Courtesy of the Library of the Jewish Theological Seminary of America.

Earlier versions of several translations appeared in the following journals: "Elisha ben Abuya: Torah and the Sinful Sage," *Journal of Jewish Thought and Philosophy* 7 (1998): 141–222 (=chapter 38); "Bavli Gittin 55b–56b: An Aggada and Its Halakhic Context," *Hebrew Studies* 38 (1997): 21–45 (=chapter 4A). Versions of chapters 9, 13, and 17B appeared in my book *Talmudic Stories: Narrative Art, Composition, and Culture* (Baltimore, Md.: Johns Hopkins University Press, 1999.) I thank the editors for permission to reprint them here.

Book design by Theresa M. Sparacio

Cover and caseside design by A. Michael Velthaus

Copyright © 2002 by Jeffrey L. Rubenstein

The Classics of Western Spirituality® is a registered trademark of Paulist Press.

All rights reserved. No part of this book may be reproduced or transmitted in any form or by any means, electronic or mechanical, including photocopying, recording or by any information storage and retrieval system without permission in writing from the Publisher.

Library of Congress Cataloging-in-Publication Data

Rabbinic stories / translated and introduced by Jeffrey L. Rubenstein.
    p. cm.—(The classics of Western Spirituality®)
    Stories from the major works of classical Rabbinic literature produced between 200 and 600 C.E.
    Includes bibliographical references and index.
    ISBN 0-8091-0533-0 (alk paper)—ISBN 0-8091-4024-1 (pbk.: alk. paper)
    1. Rabbinical literature—Translations into English. I. Rubenstein, Jeffrey L. II. Series.

BM495 .R29 2001
296.1'20521—dc21

2001050019

Published by Paulist Press
997 Macarthur Boulevard
Mahwah, New Jersey 07430

www.paulistpress.com

Printed and bound in the
United States of America

Contents

Part I:
Historical Memories and the Lessons of History

CONTENTS

Part II:
Rabbinic Authority, Rabbinic Character

Part III:
Life and Death in the Rabbinic Academy

CONTENTS

CONTENTS

Part VI:
Romans, Gentiles and Others

Part VII:
The Life of Piety:
Charity, Commandments, Virtues

CONTENTS

Part VIII:
Suffering, Martyrdom and Theodicy

Part IX:
Sin and Repentance

CONTENTS

Translator of This Volume

JEFFREY L. RUBENSTEIN is an associate professor in the Skirball Department of Hebrew and Judaic Studies of New York University. He received his B.A. in religion from Oberlin College, his
M.A. in Talmud from the Jewish Theological Seminary, where he
also received rabbinic ordination, and his Ph.D. from the Department of Religion of Columbia University. He has taught at Columbia University, the University of Pennsylvania, and the Jewish
Theological Seminary in addition to New York University. His
book, *The History of Sukkot in the Second Temple and Rabbinic Periods*,
was published in the Brown Judaica Series (1995). He recently published a book entitled *Talmudic Stories: Narrative Art, Composition
and Culture* with the John Hopkins University Press (1999). Dr.
Rubenstein has written numerous articles on the festival of Sukkot,
Talmudic stories, the development of Jewish law, and topics in Jewish liturgy and ethics.

Author of the Preface

SHAYE J. D. COHEN is the Littauer Professor of Hebrew Literature and Philosophy in the Department of Near Eastern Languages
and Civilizations of Harvard University. This is one of the oldest and
most distinguished professorships of Jewish studies in the United
States. Before arriving at Harvard in July 2001, Professor Cohen was
for ten years the Samuel Ungerleider Professor of Judaic Studies and
professor of religious studies at Brown University. Professor Cohen
began his career at the Jewish Theological Seminary, where he was
ordained, and for many years was the dean of the graduate school and
Shenkman Professor of Jewish History. He received his Ph.D. in
ancient history, with distinction, from Columbia University in 1975.
The focus of Professor Cohen's research is the boundary between
Jews and Gentiles and between Judaism and its surrounding cultures.
What makes a Jew a Jew, and what makes a non-Jew a non-Jew? Can
a non-Jew become a Jew, and can a Jew become a non-Jew? How
does the Jewish boundary between Jew and non-Jew compare with
the Jewish boundary between male Jew and female Jew? The Jewish
reaction to Hellenism in antiquity and to Christianity from ancient to
modern times consisted of both resistance and accommodation, and
both stances had far-reaching influence on the history of Judaism. On
these and other subjects Professor Cohen has written or edited nine

books and over fifty articles. He is currently working on a study of circumcision and gender in Judaism. He is perhaps best known for *From the Maccabees to the Mishnah* (1987), which is widely used as a textbook in colleges and adult education, and his recent *The Beginnings of Jewishness* (1999). He has also appeared on educational television, including *From Jesus to Christ* and *Nova* on PBS, and *Mysteries of the Bible* on A&E. Professor Cohen has received several honors for his work, including an honorary doctorate from the Jewish Theological Seminary and various fellowships. He has been honored by appointment as Croghan Distinguished Visiting Professor of Religion (Williams College), the Louis Jacobs Lecturer (Oxford University), the David M. Lewis Lecturer (Oxford University), Lady Davis Visiting Professor of Jewish History (Hebrew University of Jerusalem), and the Block Lecturer (Indiana University).

Acknowledgments

I am happy to acknowledge the contribution of my colleagues who read portions of this work and offered many helpful suggestions: Lawrence Schiffman, Michael Satlow, Robert Chazan, Jay Rovner, Yaron Eliav and Jonathan Klawans. I am particularly grateful to Seth Schwartz for his careful reading and copious annotations, and in general for countless hours of fertile discussion on a wide range of scholarly topics. Willis Johnson, who read the manuscript on behalf of Paulist Press, provided many helpful observations. I would also like to thank my colleagues in the Skirball Department of Hebrew and Judaic Studies, New York University, for their encouragement and support. Professor David Weiss Halivni, my teacher, has continued to be an invaluable resource.

Earlier versions of several of the translations appeared in my book, *Talmudic Stories: Narrative Art, Composition, and Culture* (Baltimore, Md.: Johns Hopkins University Press, 1999), and in the following articles: "Elisha ben Abuya: Torah and the Sinful Sage," *Journal of Jewish Thought and Philosophy* 7 (1998), 141–222; "Bavli Gittin 55b–56b: An Aggada and Its Halakhic Context," *Hebrew Studies* 38 (1997), 21–45. I thank the editors for permission to reprint them here. Translations of biblical verses are from the New Jewish Publication Society edition, although I have freely modified them when needed.

I am grateful to all of my family, relatives and friends for their encouragement: Denise, Arthur, Errol, Evelyn, Milton, Ronald, Miriam, Shulie, Rena, Talia, Sarah, Gili, Dani, Racquel, Miri, Tracey, Ivor, Maureen and (even) Ezra.

My wife, Mishaela, has been an unceasing source of love and devotion. Sharing my ideas with her has made this project all the more exciting. It has been a true joy to complete this work over the year when our daughter, Ayelet Isabel, was born.

Among my happiest memories from earliest childhood are those of my mother, Dr. Denise Rubenstein, reading to me on the sofa. She instilled in me a love of literature and a passion for stories, and deserves credit for much of what is of virtue in my work. This book is dedicated to her.

PREFACE

The rabbis of antiquity did not write theology or history, biography, or autobiography. Instead they told stories. If we seek to understand the rabbis and their world, we need to understand their stories.

The rabbis of antiquity composed no treatises on theology and its attendant subjects: the creation of the world and the nature of humankind, divine providence and revelation, the reward of the righteous and the punishment of the wicked, heaven and hell, the messiah and the world to come. For rabbinic reflection on these matters we need to turn to scriptural exegesis and to rabbinic story-telling. Just as the Torah tells stories about God, so too the rabbis.

The rabbis of antiquity were not historians. They composed no treatises on history or historiography, and no commentaries on the events of the day. Our guide to the history of the second temple period is Josephus, not rabbinic literature. The rabbis tell us little about the Roman and Parthian Empires in which they lived. Even momentous events such as the conversion of Constantine to Christianity or the attempt of the emperor Julian to rebuild the Jerusalem temple are barely noticed in rabbinic literature. Instead of sustained reflection on the past and the present, the rabbis give us anecdotes about King Yannai and Herod, Vespasian and Hadrian, Shapur and Diocletian.

Schools, not named individuals, produced all of the rabbinic literature of antiquity. Not a single work is ascribed to a named author.[1] In no rabbinic work does the anonymous editor step forward from behind the authorial curtain to speak about his work or to address the reader. All the rabbinic works are large compendia or anthologies, put together by large numbers of people (or "schools") over protracted periods. Further, rabbinic literature is paradoxically uninterested in the rabbis themselves; it provides no history of the rabbinic movement, no description of how one becomes a rabbi or what it means to be a rabbi, and no biographies. Rabbinic literature has almost no historical self-consciousness. If we seek rabbinic reflection on who they are, whence they have come, what they are doing, and how they fit into Jewish society and indeed the world at large, we need to turn to rabbinic stories. The rabbinic self-image is expressed in rabbinic storytelling.

Rabbinic stories are of many different types, and no one has yet established a definitive typology. By focusing on the content of these stories, Jeffrey Rubenstein, in the introduction to this anthology, observes that rabbinic stories, like rabbinic literature itself, can be divided into the legal ("halakhic") and the nonlegal ("aggadic"). The former report a rabbinic ruling or action that can serve as a legal precedent: What a given rabbi said or did on a given day might be significant for the determination of law generations later. In contrast, aggadic stories, explains Rubenstein, usually have as their purpose the depiction of sages as moral exemplars. Virtually all of the stories in this anthology are aggadic stories. A different and more nuanced classification scheme is advanced by Catherine Hezser. She studied in great detail all the stories that appear in one section of the Talmud of the Land of Israel and by focusing on their literary form classified them as follows: case-stories, example-stories, pronouncement stories, anecdotes, etiological tales, and legends.[2] Ofra Meir has written a wonderful book in Hebrew on the "exegetical story" in Genesis Rabbah, that is, a story spun out of, or illustrating, a biblical verse.[3] No doubt other corpora and other studies will yield other story-types and other classification schemes.

Halakhic stories, as befits their character, are somber and straightforward. Extraneous details are absent, and action (or plot) is at a minimum. Aggadic stories, in contrast, are often elaborate and colorful, fantastic and picaresque. They are filled with detail, real and imagined, extraneous and essential. Here are three examples. The first is from a series of traveler's tales attributed to the sage Rabbah bar Bar Hanah:[4]

Rabbah bar Bar Hanah said: Once, while traveling on a ship, we saw a bird standing up to its ankles in water, while its head reached the sky. Supposing that the water was not deep, we were about to go down into it to cool ourselves, but a divine voice called out, "Do not go down here, for seven years ago a carpenter's adze was dropped [here] and it has not yet reached the bottom."

Here is a remarkable story about the sages Rabbah and R. Zera:[5]

Rava said: On Purim a person is obligated to become so drunk that he does not know the difference between "Cursed be Haman" and "Blessed be Mordecai."

Rabbah and R. Zera joined together in a Purim feast. They became drunk. Rabbah rose up and slaughtered R. Zera. On the morrow he (Rabbah) besought mercy (from God) and revived him. But the following year, when Rabbah said to R. Zera, "Let the master come and we will celebrate Purim together," R. Zera replied, "(Sorry, but) one cannot expect a miracle on every occasion."

A long and extraordinary cycle of stories about the sage R. Elazar b. R. Simeon includes this amazing piece:[6]

When R. Yishmael the son of R. Yosi and R. Elazar b. R. Simeon happened to meet each other, (they were so fat that) a pair of oxen could pass between them without touching them.

A certain Roman matron said to them, "Your children cannot be yours; (you are so fat that you cannot have had sexual relations with your wives)."

They responded to her, "Theirs are even bigger than ours."

(The matron responded, "if that is so), all the more so (do I question the paternity of your children)."

Some say that they answered her thus, "As the man is, so is his strength." (Just as our waists are large, so are our other limbs, and thus we are able to have sex with our wives.)

Some say that they answered her thus, "Love presses the flesh." (We love our wives so much that we are able to have sex with them in spite of our obesity.)

These stories, and hundreds of others like them, puzzle modern readers no less than they puzzled medieval readers. Should they be understood as allegorical or symbolic? Are they written in code? Are they simply "popular" stories told by the rabbis in order to entertain the masses, to keep them awake in synagogues and study halls? Or are these "foreign" intrusions into the otherwise sober and respectable pages of the Talmud? All of these approaches, and yet others, have found advocates among medieval and modern scholars.[7]

Jeffrey Rubenstein had the pleasant but unenviable task of selecting Talmudic stories for this anthology. For every story that he included there are dozens of others, equally interesting and revealing, that he had to exclude. But Rubenstein has given us more than a bare anthology. Every story is provided with illuminating introductions and comments. This anthology, text, and commentary is a fine introduction not only to rabbinic narative but also to the world of rabbinic Judaism, its values, culture, and ideals. Many of these stories are so rich and so thickly textured that they deserve analysis on a scale inappropriate to a volume of this sort; Rubenstein himself has met this need, at least for some of these stories, with his own *Talmudic Stories: Narrative Art, Composition, and Culture*.[8] And now, dear reader, in the immortal words of Hillel (see chapter 29 below), go and study.

NOTES

1. The Talmud assumes that the Mishnah was "edited" by R. Judah the Prince, but the Mishanh itself nowhere advances this claim. The first rabbinic writer to claim authorship of a book was R. Saadya Gaon in the tenth century.

2. Catherine Hezser, *Form, Function, and Historical Significance of the Rabbinic Story in Yerushalmi Neziqin,* Texte und Studien zum Antiken Judentum 37 (Tübingen: Mohr-Siebeck, 1993) 283–320.

3. Ofra Meir, *Hasippur hadarshani bivreishit rabbah* (=The Darshanic Story in Genesis Rabbah) (Israel: Hakibbutz hameuchad, 1987).

4. B. Bava Batra 73b, as translated in H. N. Bialik and Y. H. Ravnitzky, *The Book of Legends Sefer Ha-Aggadah*, translated by William G. Braude (New York: Schocken, 1992) 785, no. 257.

5. B. Megillah 7b. I have modified the bowdlerized translation of Braude, *Book of Legends* 501, no. 126.

6. B. Bava Metzia 84a, as elucidated by *The Talmud: The Steinsaltz Edition Volume V Tractate Bava Metzia Part V* (New York: Random House, 1992) 119–20. I have modified Steinsaltz's translation.

7. A wonderful anthology (in Hebrew) of medieval reflections on the interpretation of Talmudic aggadah, including Talmudic stories, is Jacob Elbaum, *Medieval Perspectives on Aggadah and Midrash* (Jerusalem: Bialik Institute, 2000).

8. Jeffrey Rubenstein, *Talmudic Stories: Narrative Art, Composition, and Culture* (Baltimore: Johns Hopkins University Press, 1999).

INTRODUCTION

RABBINIC JUDAISM AND RABBINIC LITERATURE

The stories translated in this book come from the main works of classical rabbinic literature, the texts produced by Jewish sages between 200–600 CE. In two major centers, one located in the Galilee, the northern region of the Land of Israel, the other located in the Babylonian region of the Persian Empire, the rabbis (from *rav*, master) shaped a distinct form of Judaism. Rabbinic Judaism gradually spread among Jewish communities in North Africa, Egypt, Asia Minor and Europe, and become the dominant form of Judaism until modern times.

Rabbinic Judaism developed out of the Pharisaic movement and other expressions of Jewish piety that flourished in the Second Temple Period (539 BCE–70 CE). After the destruction of the Jerusalem Temple by the Romans in 70 CE, the rabbis responded by reshaping Judaism so that it became less dependent on the temple and sacrificial worship. While the rabbis both preserved a significant body of tradition from earlier times and hoped for the resumption of biblical religion, they gradually forged a new vision of Judaism based on Torah. *Torah*, meaning "instruction, learning, study," ultimately came to refer to wisdom, tradition, interpretation and a complete way of life. The rabbis sought to study God's Torah and to live a life of Torah, a life dedicated to mastering tradition, fulfilling the commandments and infusing the world with sanctity.

The fundamental tenet of rabbinic theology is that God revealed his will to Moses on Mt. Sinai in two Torahs, a "Written Torah" and an "Oral Torah." The Written Torah (the Bible) began

1

with the Pentateuch and includes the books of the Prophets and Writings. As the name implies, the books of the Written Torah were transmitted in writing from generation to generation. The Oral Torah, the rabbis believed, was passed down orally from Moses to Joshua to other prophets and religious authorities throughout the ages, and ultimately to the sages themselves. The two Torahs are interdependent and complementary. The Written Torah contains the basis for much of the Oral Torah, and the Oral Torah in turn explains how the Written Torah should be understood. In addition, the Oral Torah contains many laws and institutions omitted from the much briefer Written Torah. A paradoxical theological statement asserts that all opinions uttered by sages in the future were already revealed to Moses on Mt. Sinai.[1] Thus the rabbis were aware that new Torah was produced in each generation but simultaneously maintained that this Torah was included in the original revelation.

As time passed the quantity of rabbinic traditions expanded tremendously. Eventually the traditions had to be arranged and organized so as to facilitate memorization. Gradually various rabbis or perhaps rabbinic schools devoted themselves to this project and produced edited compilations of rabbinic traditions. Although we refer to these compilations as "literature" and "texts," it is important to realize that they were oral texts, transmitted by word of mouth from master to disciple.[2] It was not until the Middle Ages that scribes wrote down rabbinic texts so that they could be studied from manuscripts. The main works of rabbinic literature are as follows:

Mishna: The earliest rabbinic work, the Mishna is primarily a compendium of legal traditions attributed to sages who lived before 200 CE. According to tradition, Rabbi Yehuda HaNasi edited the Mishna by selecting rabbinic traditions and organizing them topically.[3] Although the Mishna bears some affinity to a law code, it also includes scriptural interpretations, wisdom sayings and a few stories. The term *Mishna* comes from the Hebrew verb *shana*, which means "to repeat" and refers to the process of orally repeating traditions in order to memorize them. The Mishna contains six major divisions or orders, which in turn are divided into

2

sixty-three tractates. Thus Mishna Shabbat 6:4 refers to the Mishna, tractate Shabbat ("the Sabbath") chapter 6, paragraph 4.

Tosefta: The Tosefta, meaning "supplement," is a companion to the Mishna. It follows the Mishna's structure, comprising the same six orders and sixty-three tractates. It too contains traditions attributed to sages who lived prior to 200 CE. Many traditions that Rabbi Yehuda HaNasi decided not to include in the Mishna were collected in the Tosefta. Some Toseftan traditions appear to be variants of those found in the Mishna, while others comment upon, complement or supplement the Mishna's rulings. The Tosefta is about four times the size of the Mishna and was edited during the third century CE.

Tannaitic Midrashim: The term *midrash* (from the root *darash,* "search," hence also "interpret") refers both to individual scriptural interpretations (a midrash on Exodus 2:3) and to compilations of scriptural interpretations (books of midrash). The Tannaim (singular, Tanna) are the rabbis who lived prior to 200 CE, whose traditions are contained in the Mishna and Tosefta. Tannaitic midrashim are those volumes of midrash containing the scriptural interpretations attributed to the Tannaim, although the editing of these compilations took place much later. There are seven extant Tannaitic midrashim, which comment on substantial portions of Exodus, Leviticus, Numbers and Deuteronomy. The Tannaitic midrashim include interpretations of both the legal and narrative portions of these biblical books. Among our collection of stories are selections from the *Sifre* to Numbers and the *Mekhilta d'Rabbi Ishmael* to Exodus.

Amoraic Midrashim: The Amoraim (singular, Amora) are the rabbis who lived from 200–400 CE, whose traditions are contained in the Talmuds and in later midrashic compilations. As opposed to the Tannaitic midrashim, which include a great deal of legal exegesis, the Amoraic midrashim comment almost exclusively on the narrative portions of the biblical books. Many Amoraic midrashim originated as sermons preached to audiences in synagogues. Our collection of stories includes selections from the Amoraic midrashim known as *Genesis Rabbah*, *Leviticus Rabbah* and *Song of*

Songs Rabbah. These works were edited in the Land of Israel in the fifth and sixth centuries.

Yerushalmi: The Yerushalmi or Jerusalem Talmud (also known as the Palestinian Talmud) was the exposition to the Mishna produced by the sages who lived in the Land of Israel from 200–400 CE. *Talmud*, which means "study, instruction, teaching," follows the Mishna's structure and primarily consists of explanations and discussions of its rulings. However, the Yerushalmi also includes biblical interpretation (midrash), records of court cases, stories and sayings. Like the Mishna and Tosefta, the Yerushalmi is divided into orders and tractates. Thus Yerushalmi Peah 8:9, 21b designates the Yerushalmi's commentary to Mishna Tractate Peah, chapter 8, paragraph 9, found on folio 21, column b in the first edition (Venice, 1523). There is Yerushalmi to thirty-nine of the Mishna's sixty-three tractates.

Bavli: The Bavli or Babylonian Talmud was the great commentary on the Mishna produced by the rabbinic sages of Babylonia from 200–600 CE. The Bavli too contains a variety of materials, including scriptural interpretations, records of court cases, folklore, liturgical texts and stories. Jewish communities in the Middle Ages considered the Bavli to be the authoritative source of Jewish law and made study of the Bavli the cornerstone of the rabbinic curriculum. Consequently, the stories of the Bavli are generally among the best known stories of Jewish tradition. The Bavli too follows the order of the Mishna but is simply referred to by the folio number of the standard printed edition, for example, Bavli Shabbat 34a. There is Bavli to thirty-six of the Mishna's tractates.

TYPES OF RABBINIC STORIES

While the rabbis composed no texts exclusively devoted to stories, every ancient rabbinic compilation included numerous stories, legends, anecdotes and other narrative traditions. These narratives can be divided into two categories: stories about sages and biblical expansions. Stories about sages—the subject of this book—tell of the lives and deeds of rabbis and early masters. A few stories feature historical figures such as Alexander the Great, Vespasian and King Herod, but these stories typically center on the figure's encounter with a famous sage. Biblical expansions, on the other hand, are based on biblical narratives and feature biblical characters. These stories derive, in large part, from processes of biblical exegesis.[4] Storytellers sought to fill gaps in the biblical record and to expand the frustratingly brief biblical narratives by extrapolating from hints in the text, embellishing details, drawing on allusions found in other biblical books and imaginatively reconstructing the exploits of biblical characters. Biblical expansions are therefore a type of midrash in the technical sense of the term—rabbinic biblical interpretation.

Most stories about sages are brief, recounting one or two events in the rabbi's life. They can be characterized as biographical anecdotes rather than biographies or comprehensive accounts of rabbinic lives. Rabbinic texts themselves do not use technical terms to classify different types of stories.[5] But as a first step, we can adopt the standard categorization of rabbinic literature as Halakha (law) or Aggada (lore). Halakha includes law; legal commentary, analysis and exegesis; accounts of court cases and any legally oriented material. Halakhic stories, accordingly, are stories about sages that focus on legal questions and figure primarily in the study of law. Aggada encompasses rabbinic teachings of a nonlegal nature, including moral and ethical instruction, theology, maxims, proverbs, sermons, folklore and biblical exegesis (other than exegesis of biblical law).[6] Aggadic stories deal with ethics, character and general aspects of the rabbinic way of life.

Halakhic Stories

The majority of stories about sages are halakhic. They function as legal precedents, reporting a rabbi's actions when confronting an unclear situation. The very first paragraph of Mishna in fact contains an example of such a story:

Once the sons [of Rabban Gamaliel] returned from a wedding feast. They said to him, "We have not yet recited

5

the *Shema*." He said to them, "If dawn has not broken yet, you are obligated to recite it."[7]

This brief anecdote bears on the question of how late into the night the prayer known as the *Shema* may be said. This prayer must be recited "when you lie down," as prescribed by Deuteronomy 6:7. Does that mean before a certain hour in the evening, or prior to midnight, or whenever one happens to lie down, even until daybreak? To help answer this question, the Mishna reports that the sons of Rabban Gamaliel once neglected to recite the prayer, apparently due to a night of hearty eating and drinking. Their father, an eminent sage, instructed them to recite the prayer provided it was not yet dawn, at which point night ends and day begins. By relating this story the Mishna suggests that the *Shema* may be recited at any time during the night, at least according to the opinion of Rabban Gamaliel.

The assumption behind such stories is that the actions of rabbis are sources of law. A rabbi not only studied Torah but embodied it, hence succeeding generations of sages could shed light on difficult legal questions by studying their predecessors' behavior. Where the sages lacked a specific legal tradition and could not derive the answer from biblical exegesis, they turned to rabbinic practice. In most societies precedent is an important consideration in the determination of law. For the rabbis, precedents could be found not in legal casebooks but in the ways of their masters. They were careful, therefore, to pass down reports—stories—of rabbinic practices.

Aggadic Stories

Stories that depict sages as moral exemplars and character models are found in every rabbinic compilation. Just as a disciple learned the fine points of Jewish law by observing his master's conduct, so he learned moral behavior by emulating the master's interactions with others. And just as students transmitted accounts of their masters' ritual practices, so they preserved stories of their masters' pious deeds, ethical practices and outstanding character traits. Similarly, rabbinic teachers and preachers used such stories to instruct their pupils and congregations. While halakhic stories figured prominently in the rabbinic legal tradition, aggadic stories played a critical role in transmitting rabbinic ethics and teaching rabbinic spirituality throughout the ages. Let us look at a standard example of such a story:

> In Mar Uqba's neighborhood there lived a poor man. He would send him 400 zuzim [each year] on the afternoon before Yom Kippur [the Day of Atonement]. Once he sent his son to give it to him. He [the son] returned and said, "He doesn't need it." He [Mar Uqba] said, "What did you see?" He said, "I saw that he was pouring himself old wine." He said, "Is he so delicate? Let us double the amount and send that to him!"[8]

This is one of many stories about the charitable activities of the sages. Mar Uqba, a prominent third-century Babylonian rabbi, annually made an extremely generous gift to an indigent man. Since the man seemed to have enough money to splurge on expensive wine, Mar Uqba's son believed that he did not deserve alms. But Mar Uqba drew the opposite conclusion: a man with such expensive tastes in fact required more charity to sustain a tolerable existence! The audience—which probably shared the son's assessment initially—learns a striking and certainly counter-intuitive lesson from Mar Uqba's answer. Not only is it proper to give large amounts of charity, but one must sustain the needy at their usual standard of living. It is not enough to keep the poor from starving; one must preserve their dignity and ensure that they are reasonably content.

Perhaps the most engaging stories of this type address fundamental tensions of rabbinic life and rabbinic culture. How should a rabbi strike a balance between his devotion to Torah study, an all-encompassing activity, and his responsibilities to his wife and family? What percent of a sage's time should be dedicated to Torah study and what percent to other good deeds or community service? What are the appropriate ways to confront suffering and death? How should the rabbis relate to the local secular authorities? Such questions have no simple answers and cannot be resolved by turning to a prescriptive guidebook or collection of maxims. But tales of great sages who faced similar situations provided rabbis with a means to ponder and meditate on these challenges. Consider the following story about two sages who decided to leave their studies to provide for themselves:

> [A] Ilfa and R. Yohanan were in extreme need. They said, "Let us rise, go and busy ourselves with commerce, and we will fulfill [the verse], *There shall be no needy among you* (Deut 15:4)." They went. They sat down beneath a certain rickety wall. While they were eating their meal, R. Yohanan heard one angel say to his fellow, "Let us cast it down upon them and kill them,[9] for they abandon eternal life and busy themselves with temporal life."[10] His fellow said to him, "Leave them be. One of them is destined for important things."
>
> [B] R. Yohanan said to Ilfa, "Did you hear anything?" He said to him, "No." He said [to himself], "This means that I am the one. I will go and return [to my studies], and I will fulfill the verse, *For there will never cease to be needy ones in your land* (Deut 15:11)."
>
> [C] By the time Ilfa came [back to the academy], R. Yohanan was leading [the academy]. When Ilfa came, they [the students] said to him, "If you had sat and studied, he would not be leading [but you would]."[11]

The story concludes with Ilfa challenging anyone to fault his knowledge of tradition, an assertion that he too achieved great erudition despite engaging in a trade.

This story addresses a problem faced by those rabbis whose parents or in-laws could not support them: at what point should they give up their studies and earn a living wage? On the one hand, a man must eat and provide for his family. No one could criticize a rabbi who had to work in order to survive. On the other hand, to abandon Torah study, the highest value in the rabbinic worldview, for a mundane job could be seen as selling out. Was the sage really in such need or was he pursuing earthly riches at the expense of spiritual values? To earn enduring merit required a life of dedication and self-sacrifice, and personal hardships were to be expected.

The story does not offer a facile solution to the problem. That the angels consider killing the sages because they "abandon eternal life"—the study of Torah—certainly indicates a negative view of their decision. Similarly, R. Yohanan's rise to glory as head of the academy proves that he chose the right path, while the students' remark that Ilfa could have achieved such stature implies that he made a poor choice. Yet at the outset of the story the angels foresee a great future for but one of the two sages. That R. Yohanan alone hears the angelic talk leads to the conclusion that he, not Ilfa, is destined for greatness. So it is far from clear that Ilfa made the wrong decision, or that he could have become head of the academy, despite the students' comment. Moreover, the continuation of the story suggests that Ilfa was no slouch but had mastered a great deal of Torah despite engaging in business. How R. Yohanan managed to support himself must also be considered. The verse he cites implies that he accepted alms and was maintained from the community's funds for the poor. But this option would be viable only in reasonably prosperous communities and only for a limited number of sages. In these ways the story expresses the tensions that confront sages and offers several perspectives on the various possible choices. It encourages the sages to appreciate the different sides of the problem without clarifying exactly what should be done.

Many stories of this type, especially those found in the two Talmuds, focus on aspects of life in the rabbinic academy. Who should be the head of the academy and on what grounds should he be chosen? How should academic ranks and honors be distributed? What are the mechanisms by which conflicts can be resolved? To what extent should dissenting opinions be tolerated or encouraged, and on what points must there be unanimity? How are decisions to be made: by majority vote or by the decree of the head of the academy? What will be the ultimate rewards for choosing the life of Torah and giving up so many earthly comforts? Storytellers addressed these questions by telling stories of the conflicts and struggles of earlier sages. And as the stories were incorporated into the works that became part of the rabbinic curriculum, they provided students with a set of texts with which to study, discuss and ponder these issues.

Some aggadic stories bear a strong affinity to folktales.[12] Stories of the common dimensions of human experience—the rich and the poor, the wisdom of children, the perils of greed, the danger of pride—found their place in the rabbinic moral tradition. Such stories pass easily from culture to culture and are routinely translated from one language to another. Tales of Alexander the Great and his exploits, for example, which spread through all parts of the Hellenistic world, appear in rabbinic texts.[13] So too do stories of riddling competitions, magical snakes, mysterious strangers, seventy-year naps and pious robbers.

Seldom, however, did folktales and stories of foreign provenance enter rabbinic literature without undergoing significant change. Just as every culture alters elements of the stories it adopts to conform to its particular idiom, so rabbinic storytellers "rabbinized" the tales they adopted. Wise men, philosophers and other sage-like characters were transformed into rabbis in rabbinic texts, and instead of quoting aphorisms and proverbs they cite biblical verses. The morals of such rabbinized folktales are typically rabbinic sayings or biblical principles rather than popular adages.

Even the tales that filtered into rabbinic literature from earlier strands of Judaism—which we might call traditional Jewish folktales—were refracted through rabbinic eyes. The first-century historian Josephus, for example, who began his career as a leader of the Jewish forces who fought the Romans during the first revolt (66–73 CE), relates that he predicted to the Roman general Vespasian that Vespasian would be selected emperor of Rome.[14] This "prophecy" eventually proved true, and Vespasian rewarded Josephus for his prophetic talents and for divulging this good fortune. Rabbinic literature contains a similar tale in which Rabbi Yohanan b. Zakkai encounters Vespasian and demonstrates by interpreting scripture that Vespasian will soon be crowned emperor (see chapter 4A, 4B herein). Similarly, Josephus tells a story of a holy man named Onias who once prayed for rain in the midst of a drought and successfully caused a downpour.[15] In an early rabbinic version of this story, Honi (the Hebraized form of the Greek name Onias) successfully brings rain but is subsequently rebuked by a famous sage. And some later rabbinic versions portray Honi as a sage who studies in the rabbinic academy (see chapters 16 and 18 herein).

In sum, while there are a variety of types of rabbinic stories that serve a spectrum of ends, their common denominator is their didactic character. Some of these stories originated in homilies delivered before a popular audience attending synagogue or ritual gatherings. Others derive from the rabbinic academy, intended for an audience of aspiring rabbinic students and relating to aspects of the rabbinic way of life. In all cases they served to instruct the audience on points of law, proper ethics, ideal character, folk wisdom and rabbinic self-definition. Stories were thus an indispensable element of the spiritual lives of Jews in late antiquity.

Most of the stories translated in this book are aggadic. Halakhic stories essentially form part of the rabbinic legal tradition. In subsequent centuries they were included in legal responsa, talmudic commentaries and law codes. Aggadic stories came to form a distinct component of Jewish spirituality. They were often included in rabbinic sermons and in books of moral and ethical literature. Aggadic stories had great appeal on a popular level for those seeking moral and spiritual inspiration. In the sixteenth century, for example, Rabbi Yaakov ibn Habib (d. 1516) excerpted almost all of the aggadic portions of the Babylonian Talmud.[16] He called this anthology of stories, lore and biblical interpretation the *Ein Yaakov*. Completed by his son and first published in 1522, this work became one of the most popular Jewish books, republished more than one hundred times between the sixteenth and nineteenth centuries and still studied in Jewish homes to this day.[17]

RABBINIC STORIES: FICTIONAL AND BIOGRAPHICAL ASPECTS

Although rabbinic stories tell of the lives and acts of sages and occasionally refer to historical events such as the building of the Herodian temple and the rebellion against Rome, they should not be classified as biographical in our sense of the term. The story-tellers were not attempting to document "what actually happened" out of a dispassionate interest in the objective historical record, or to transmit biographical facts in order to provide pure data for posterity. This type of detached, impartial writing of a biography is a distinctly modern approach. Nowadays we distinguish biography from fiction. The former involves scholarly research, examination of sources, verification of facts, testing of hypotheses and presentation of evidence. In principle the enterprise is replicable: another scholar should be able to analyze the evidence and arrive at similar conclusions. Fiction makes no claims to veracity and involves none of these constraints. In pre-modern cultures, however, the distinction between biography and fiction was blurred. Ancient authors saw themselves as teachers, and they were more concerned with the didactic point than historical accuracy.[18]

Biographical writing in late antiquity, the culture in which much of rabbinic literature took shape, involved a weighty fictional component.[19] The purpose of Roman biographers was overwhelmingly didactic: to use the lives of their subjects to model character, teach virtue and provide lessons. They endeavored to portray their heroes as great, virtuous, brilliant and noble even when the truth was rather different. Biographers made little effort to verify their sources of information or to distinguish rumor, hearsay and legend from eye-witness accounts and accurate reports. Plutarch, the celebrated Roman biographer and author of *Lives of the Greeks and Romans*, explained to his audience, "We are not writing history but lives."[20] By this he meant that he should not be accountable even to the standards of classical history-writing, for the genre of biography worked according to different conventions. Readers should expect a great deal more truth-bending and outright fiction, for his purpose was to educate, not to provide a record of real events. Sometimes we find that Roman anecdotes told of a certain figure in one biography are reported of another figure by a different author. If the anecdote effectively taught an important lesson, a biographer had little compunction to relate it to his protagonist and incorporate it into his work. Many biographies also include stock themes such as a hero's miraculous birth, childhood portents of future greatness, sudden arrival at a scene in a time of crisis, discovery of true identity and suchlike. Moreover, scholars have noted that Roman historiography underwent a "degeneration" during imperial times, in the very period when rabbinic traditions were formed. The authors placed less emphasis on the accurate recording of history than on achieving their literary aims. Rabbinic stories share much in common with the Roman biographical tradition and contain many of these characteristics of fiction. Indeed, the fact that rabbinic stories circulated orally made them more malleable than the written sources of classical literature.[21]

Several other factors contribute to our understanding of rabbinic stories as didactic fiction rather than accurate history. Many rabbinic stories appear in multiple versions in the various rabbinic works. The Bavli, for example, often reports a biographical incident in a way that differs substantially from the version preserved in the Yerushalmi. Storytellers clearly felt free to shape the material according to their own needs and to introduce changes that they deemed appropriate. Moreover, when we compare the versions contained in later texts, such as the Bavli or Yerushalmi, with the versions in earlier texts, such as the Mishna and Tosefta, we find that the later versions are consistently more elaborate and literarily developed. As stories were handed down from generation to generation, storytellers embellished and added to received traditions. Similarly, as noted above, the rabbinic versions of stories with parallels in the writings of the historian Josephus and other non-rabbinic sources have been altered significantly. By "rabbinizing" the story, by transforming some of the characters into rabbis and refracting the story through the prism of the rabbinic world, the storytellers communicated their message more effectively.

Another reason to recognize rabbinic stories as fiction is the hefty component of supernatural material. The sages routinely perform miracles, such as curing the ill, bringing rain and resuscitating the dead. They have supernatural powers, such as the ability to look at an enemy and transform him or her into a heap of bones (see chapter 17 herein). Some stories tell of angels, demons, speaking snakes, gargantuan creatures and other mythic beasts (see chapter 38A herein). In some stories rabbis travel down to Hell or up to Heaven, where they encounter God teaching in the heavenly academy.[22]

These elements obviously mark the imaginative and fictional nature of the rabbinic story.

This is not to say that most rabbinic stories lack a historical kernel. The sages about whom the stories are told were real historical figures, as were the subjects of Roman biographical writing. Some stories relate to historical events such as the journeys of Alexander the Great, the Roman siege of Jerusalem and the Bar Kokhba revolt. But the presence of core historical material does not alter the story's fundamental fictional character any more than in the case of modern historical or biographical fiction. A modern author might write a fictional novel about Christopher Columbus, for example, that incorporated some of the facts we know about Columbus's life in an imaginative account whose sole goal was to entertain the audience. Moreover, to isolate a rabbinic story's historical kernel from the fictional embellishment is in most cases an impossible task. There is no accurate way to decide between contradictory versions or to determine which sections are legendary and which are "true." Furthermore, to strip away parts of the story in a search for the historical core does serious injustice to the story. The storyteller included the supernatural and fictive elements for a reason, so to ignore them is to miss important keys to understanding the message. That a rabbi turns his opponent into a heap of bones teaches us a great deal about the storyteller's view of the powers of a rabbi and about the rabbinic image he wished to convey to his audience. Consider a relatively modern example: the famous story in which George Washington's father asks him whether he cut down the cherry tree, and George replies, "Yes, Father, I cannot tell a lie." Whether completely true, completely fictive, or containing a historical kernel, the story's point lies in the moral. The proper questions to ask of this story are *not:* Did it really happen? Where was Washington residing when his father discovered the deed? What type of cherry tree was it? Rather one should ask: Why did the storyteller tell this story of Washington? What ethical quality was he trying to teach? So too the proper questions to ask of rabbinic stories are: Why did the storyteller tell this story? What lessons did he wish to impart to his audience? What does the story teach us about rabbinic beliefs, virtues and ethics?

INTRODUCTION

LITERARY CHARACTERISTICS
OF THE RABBINIC STORY

Rabbinic stories often strike the modern ear as raw and unpolished. In part the problem is that they derive from a distant time and place and have been translated from their original language to a foreign idiom. More significant is their oral provenance: not only were the stories originally spoken by the storyteller to his audience, but they were preserved in oral form in rabbinic literature. When we read them today, whether in the original Hebrew and Aramaic or in a translation to another language, we apprehend from a page words that were originally verbalized and heard. Oral literature, however, works by conventions that differ from those that govern written texts. First and foremost, oral narratives tend to be extremely brief so as to facilitate memorization. In most cultures the transmitters memorize only the skeleton of the story with the essential information necessary to understand the action. Thus one finds in the rabbinic story little description of a character's appearance, personal qualities or past experiences unless that information is indispensable to the plot. Typical protagonists include "a certain man," "a certain woman," "a righteous man," "an evil woman," and so forth, without further detail. A great deal of the background information that we would expect an author to provide is lacking. Apparently the sages who transmitted and received the memorized versions within the rabbinic academies filled in part of the missing background by drawing on their knowledge of tradition and deduced the rest from the context or narrative dynamic. Most likely, when they performed the story, that is, when they recited it before a live audience, they embellished the skeletal narratives with rich descriptions and supplied the requisite background. Performances probably varied considerably according to the talents of the storyteller, the particular setting and the type of audience. At all events, we have received only the terse outlines that were formulated for memorization and preserved in the rabbinic corpus. To make the translations comprehensible to the reader I have supplied the necessary information in square brackets (and occasionally in endnotes) in order to distinguish it from the actual text of the stories. In this way readers can both appreciate the true texture of the rabbinic narrative and understand what is going on. Other standard characteristics of the rabbinic story, some of which typify oral literature in many cultures, include the following:[23]

A preference for dialogue over narration: Rabbinic stories make heavy use of dialogue, as we might expect of oral literature. Many stories begin with a brief narrational introduction to set the scene followed primarily by interchanges among the characters.[24] These interchanges are usually introduced by simple quotation formulas: "He said....He said to him....He said to him....He said to him...." Sometimes even these quotation markers are omitted so that the story consists of an uninterrupted dialogue; only the context informs us when one character's words end and the other's begin. The rapid back-and-forth dialogue makes the stories more dramatic.

Interior monologues: Together with the high density of dialogue, rabbinic stories typically use interior monologues to communicate a character's thoughts. Instead of reporting the thought in indirect discourse ("R. So-and-so thought that..."), the stories use the standard quotation formula, "R. So-and-so said...," where "said" means "said to himself" or "thought." Some scholars suggest that the ancients did not fully distinguish thought from speech or that they understood thought as an inner type of speech. Be that as it may, this rhetorical device contributes to the dramatic quality of the rabbinic story by allowing characters to express their thoughts and feelings directly, not through the narrator's voice. Thus a story of a bitter rabbinic conflict relates, "R. Yaakov b. Qudshai heard them. He said, 'Perhaps, God forbid, it will result in shame!'" (see chapter 13 herein). We gain a better sense of R. Yaakov's state of alarm than if the narrator had reported, "R. Yaakov b. Qudshai was very worried because he thought that someone would be publicly embarrassed."

Questions directed to the audience: Rabbinic stories often contain rhetorical questions directed to the audience, such as: "What did he do?" "What did he see?" (chapter 38A herein). "What did Israel do at that time?" (chapter 18B herein). Here one must picture a storyteller speaking to a live audience. To engage the audience and to keep it attentive, an effective storyteller periodically poses direct questions. This rhetorical device involves the audience by making it more of a participant in the encounter. Such addresses are rare in written narratives, although occasionally an author will turn to the reader in the second person ("You might wonder, dear reader,…") to similar effect.

Wordplay: Many rabbinic stories involve wordplay or paronomasia. Words that rhyme, alliterate or resemble each other in some respect are juxtaposed. Wordplay has aesthetic appeal as a literary device, a hallmark of the narrative art of the storyteller. It also contributes to the content by creating a connection between parts of the story. For example, a story about a rabbi named Rav Rahumei who caused his wife great anguish concludes: "She became distressed and a tear fell *(ahit)* from her eye. He was sitting on a roof. The roof collapsed *(ifhit)* under him and he died" (chapter 20 herein). The rhyme *ahit/ifhit* emphasizes the cause-and-effect relationship. *Because* of the pain Rav Rahumei caused his wife, the roof fell under him. Wordplay frequently appears in poetry and occasionally in written prose. It is particularly common in oral literature, where the audience hears the sounds of the words and thus senses the play immediately.

Symbolic names of characters: The characters in rabbinic stories frequently have names that relate to their role or to some aspect of the plot. One rabbinic story features a sinner named Pantokakos, which means "completely evil" (chapter 40 herein). In another story Imma Shalom, meaning "Mother Peace," attempts to keep her husband from causing the death of another sage (chapter 9 herein). Symbolic names are a very economical means of characterization, since little additional effort need be spent on sketching the character. Once we hear a name like Pantokakos, we know the character's essential qualities. In this way symbolic names contribute to the brevity of the rabbinic story. Symbolic names are often found in folktales and are particularly prominent in the Bible.[25]

Threefold repetitions: Rabbinic stories often repeat the description of an event or the pattern of a dialogue three times with minor variations, as is common in folklore, children's stories and other oral genres. Anyone familiar with the story of "The *Three* Little Pigs" or of "Goldilocks and the *Three* Bears" has encountered this phenomenon. Thus in the famous story of the "Oven of Akhnai" (chapter 9 herein), R. Eliezer tries to prove his case to the sages by appealing to miracles of nature: "He said to them, 'If the law is as I say, let the carob [tree] prove it.' The carob uprooted itself....They said to him, 'One does not bring proof from the carob.'" He proceeds to appeal to the water of the aqueduct, which flows backward, and to the walls of the academy, which begin to fall, and the story narrates the events with the same words apart from the varied items. Now in written prose it is considered poor style to repeat the same words or phrases in close proximity. In oral communication, however, repetition makes it easier for the audience to follow the action and allows it to anticipate what will happen. Unlike readers, who can reread a passage to grasp the meaning fully and pick up what they missed at first sight, an audience to an oral performance has no means of going back. It must follow the speaker closely and comprehend as the words are spoken, and repetition facilitates this task.

Structure: Many rabbinic stories display a well-defined structure, dividing easily into two halves or into three or four parts. Sometimes the structure is created by a repeated phrase that introduces each section (chapter 24 herein). In other cases the content creates the divisions, such as an account of the character's advent, encounter and departure. A few highly crafted stories display a chiastic structure, in which the first section corresponds to the last, the second section to the second-to-last, the third to the third-to-last, and so forth (chapters 12B, 38B herein).[26] A precise structure serves a mnemonic function. It is much easier to memorize a story with a familiar pattern than a text lacking clear organization. Similarly, it is easier for the audience to follow the oral recitation of a story with a defined pattern.

The use of biblical verses: The Bible, for the rabbis, was much more than an eternally relevant source of insight and inspiration. It was the lens through which they understood the present. They related biblical passages not only to the larger, history-making events of their times but to their mundane experiences. The sages knew the biblical text by heart; its verses were constantly on their lips. To incorporate a pertinent biblical verse or phrase into their everyday speech was a type of art. Just as we might quote an apt line of Shakespeare in ordinary conversation and thereby please our friends with the familiar phrase brought into a new context, so the rabbis integrated biblical passages into their informal talk. Similarly, they wove biblical phrases into almost every story they told, including stories about sages and post-biblical events. In some cases the verse serves as the moral of the story, a succinct illustration to summarize the point. In other cases the characters debate the meaning of verses or explain their actions by invoking a particular precept. In yet other cases the storyteller formed the dialogue of the characters out of biblical phrases, modifying them as need be.

Let us look at an example of a character's dialogue that incorporates a biblical verse. A remarkable story relates that a Gentile named Onqelos, son of Qaloniqos, contemplated conversion to Judaism and raised up from the dead Bilaam, the seer mentioned in Numbers 22—24, in order to seek advice (chapter 4A herein). Bilaam tells Onqelos, "You shall never concern yourself with their welfare or benefit as long as you live," which in this context means that Onqelos should have nothing to do with the Jews. A Jewish audience schooled on the Bible immediately would have recognized these words as a direct quotation from Deuteronomy 23:7. The full biblical context is significant: "No Ammonite or Moabite shall be admitted into the congregation of the Lord…because they did not meet you with food and water on your journey after you left Egypt, and because they hired Bilaam son of Beor, from Pethor of Aram-naharaim to curse you….You shall never concern yourself with their welfare or benefit as long as you live" (Deut 23:4–7). In its original context the verse is addressed by God to Israel and comprises a commandment prohibiting certain nations from being "admitted to the congregation," understood by the rabbis as conversion. And the same biblical passage explains that these nations may not convert because they attempted to recruit Bilaam to curse the Israelites. I imagine that the audience would have smiled at the powerful irony created by the storyteller placing the verse in Bilaam's mouth. For Bilaam's answer to Onqelos draws on a passage that implicates himself in evil and forbids conversion on account of that crime. Now the storyteller could have had Bilaam say, "Don't convert," or "Don't waste your time," or suchlike. But this would lack the irony that contributes to the literary art of the story and the enjoyment of the audience.

THE TRANSLATIONS

Translators generally claim that they have remained faithful to the original language while rendering the translation in smooth, idiomatic English. In these translations the English is idiomatic and comprehensible, but I adhere extremely closely to the original Hebrew or Aramaic, even at the expense of an occasional awkward or strained construction. Only in this way can the English reader appreciate the literary features and structure of the original story. Where parts of the story begin with the same Hebrew word or phrase, I replicate that form in the translation, even if the resulting construction sounds stilted. Where an Aramaic word is used in two distinct meanings in the story, I use the same English word in both places, even if the English equivalent may not have the exact semantic field. If the Hebrew repeats language three times, I translate accordingly. This fidelity to the form and literary character of the original distinguishes these translations from most others. For in most translations the translator has endeavored to "improve" the style to conform to modern English standards, such as avoiding the repetition of the same phrase. Unfortunately, such translations do an injustice to rabbinic stories by destroying their literary characteristics and distorting their contours.

Square brackets in the translations indicate words and phrases that are needed to understand the story but that do not appear explicitly in the original. In this way the reader can get a sense of the true content of the story and see how brief and elliptical most stories are. Generally the bracketed information is implied or presupposed by the story, and any well-versed rabbi would have had no trouble supplying it from his knowledge of tradition. Occasionally, however, the data derive from commentators who offer plausible explanations to make sense of what seem to be gaps in the story. In these cases extrinsic information has been "read in" to the story through an interpretive process. Astute readers may wish to consider alternative ways to understand the story that stem from different assumptions and interpretations. Issues that require more detailed explanation than can be supplied in a brief parenthetic comment are addressed in endnotes.

The translations are divided into sections labeled with English letters: A, B, C, and so forth. The divisions provide an easy means to refer to specific parts of the story and thereby to facilitate discussion. They also allow the reader to recognize both the overall structure of the story and the internal structural units created by repetitions. In addition, where the story appears in multiple versions in different rabbinic texts, the marked divisions facilitate the task of comparison and contrast. Some divisions stem from formal criteria such as the repetition of a phrase, while others devolve from explicit anticipatory signs in the text, such as "three types of men have no share in the world to come," followed by the detailing of the three types. In some cases, however, I determined the divisions based on the content and general flow of the action. In these cases the divisions are more subjective, and the reader should feel free to contemplate alternative divisions that would yield different structures.

A brief introduction precedes each translation. The introduction provides both background to the specific issues that figure in the story and a brief analysis of the story's principal themes, meanings and literary character. While the analysis will help the reader appreciate the story, the reader simultaneously must have read the story in order to follow the analysis. The reader, therefore, should work back and forth between the story and the introduction, or should be sure to reread the introduction after studying the story. In no way should the analysis be considered the only possible interpretation or a comprehensive discussion of the story's significance. Readers are encouraged to arrive at their own interpretations and to find additional messages. Most rabbinic stories are extremely rich in meaning, and the introductions are intended as a means to enter the world of the story, not as the final word in its evaluation.

The editions of rabbinic texts used for the translations are listed in the bibliography. However, in many cases the translations are based on versions preserved in manuscripts, which often provide better readings than those of the standard printed editions. For this reason the translations may differ slightly from those found elsewhere and from the standard printings.

PART I:

HISTORICAL MEMORIES AND THE LESSONS OF HISTORY

Chapter 1

HASMONEAN MEMORIES

The Hasmonean dynasty held power in Judea from 153 BCE, when Jonathan (the younger brother of Judah "Maccabee") consolidated his rule, until 37 BCE, when Herod rose to the throne. The rabbis preserved only a few traditions from this time. Many of these provide explanations for events mentioned in *Megilat Taanit*, the "Scroll of Fasts." This document listed the dates of Jewish victories and other significant occasions from the Second Temple Period on which fasting and eulogies were prohibited. The Talmud introduces the famous story of the Hanukka miracle (see story A below) and the account of Nikanor's Day (story B) to explain their inclusion in *Megilat Taanit*.

The story of the miraculous oil burning for eight days is not mentioned in the earliest sources about Hanukka. The Second Book of Maccabees calls the festival "Purification of the Temple" in one passage, and connects it to the eight-day celebration of Sukkot (Tabernacles) in another.[1] The First Book of Maccabees calls the festival "Days of Dedication" *(hanukka)* after the rededication of the altar, but says nothing of lighting ritual lamps.[2] The first-century Jewish historian Josephus Flavius also connects the festival to the Hasmonean rededication of the temple and calls it "the festival of lights." Unfortunately, he provides no description of a ritual.[3] The rabbis preferred a spiritual and supernatural rationale for a festival to a celebration of a military triumph. Moreover, they felt ambivalent toward the Hasmonean dynasty, whose later kings increasingly adopted Hellenistic ways and periodically oppressed the people. They probably hesitated to commemorate the founding

25

victory of the dynasty and shifted the focus to the miraculous resumption of the temple rituals.

Nikanor was the Syrian general sent by King Demetrius to subdue Judah Maccabee (story B). According to the Books of Maccabees, Nikanor insulted the priests who greeted him in Jerusalem and threatened that if they did not deliver Judah to him, he would burn the temple when he returned. Judah's army defeated his forces in 161 BCE, and Nikanor fell in the battle.[4] The identity of the Turyanus mentioned in the same source is unclear. Some scholars identify him with the Roman Emperor Trajan; the martyrdom of the brothers Lulianus and Pappus is indeed mentioned in other rabbinic sources in connection with Roman persecutions. In any case, the significance of the story lies not in the identity of the characters but in the lesson about divine justice. Many rabbinic sources explain that in this world the righteous suffer as punishment for their few sins, and the wicked prosper as reward for their few merits. But in the next world God metes out justice; the righteous exclusively receive reward and the wicked exclusively suffer. Here the brothers' prediction comes to pass even before they expect it: the persecutor is immediately struck down to avenge his crime.

The Hasmonean civil war between Aristobolus and Hyrcanus probably took place in 65 BCE (see story C). In Josephus's account the besieged let down money in a basket in return for animals for Passover sacrifices.[5] But the besiegers took the money and sent no animals. The priests then prayed to God to punish the outrage, and God sent a destructive wind that ruined the crops and caused a famine. The rabbinic tradition transforms the incident to explain the prohibition against raising pigs and to teach a lesson about "Greek wisdom," that is, Hellenistic culture, including what we might today call secular knowledge. While the sacrificial service provides protection and blessing, Greek wisdom shakes the very foundations of Jewish life.

The Yerushalmi contains other traditions of procuring animals for sacrifices under siege conditions (see story D). This version of the pig shaking the land sets the event in Roman times and connects it to the destruction of the temple. Nor does the story polemicize against Greek wisdom: it emphasizes the importance of the temple worship and the disasters caused by sin. The second tradition of a siege attests to a law about the latest time permitted for certain sacrifices. This source comprises a good example of the rabbis preserving historical accounts for legal precedents and moral instruction, not out of inherent interest in history.[6]

A. The Festival of Hanukka (Bavli Shabbat 21a)

[A] What [is the festival of] Hanukka?[7]

[B] For our sages taught [in *Megilat Taanit*]: "On the twenty-fifth of Kislev [begin] the eight days of Hanukka, during which one may not recite a eulogy and one may not fast."

[C] For when the Greeks entered the temple they caused impurity to all the [containers of] oil in the temple.

[D] And when the Hasmonean dynasty triumphed, they searched and found only one vessel of oil that had the seal of the High Priest intact, and it contained sufficient [oil] to light [a lamp] for only one day. A miracle happened and they lit [a lamp] from it for eight days.

[E] The following year they designated them [those days] to be festive days [celebrated] with the Hallel[8] and thanksgiving.

B. Nikanor's Day (Bavli Taanit 18b)

[A] What is [the Day of] Nikanor and what is [the Day of] Turyanus?

[B] For it was taught: Nikanor was one of the Greek lieutenants. Each day he would shake his hand at Judah and Jerusalem and say, "When it falls into my hand I will trample it!"

[C] And when the kings of the Hasmonean dynasty triumphed and defeated him, they penetrated his ranks and cut off his thumbs and his big toes.[9] They hung them in the gates of Jerusalem and said, "The mouth that spoke arrogantly and the hands that shook at Jerusalem—let this vengeance be done to them."[10]

[D] What is [the Day] of Turyanus?

[E] They said: When Turyanus killed Lulianus and his brother Pappus in Laodicea, he said to them, "If you are from the nation of Hananiah, Mishael and Azariah, let your God come and save you from my hand just as he saved Hananiah, Mishael and Azariah from the hand of Nevuchadnezzar."[11]

[F] They said to him, "Hananiah, Mishael and Azariah were pure righteous ones, and Nevuchadnezzar was a legitimate king and deserving that a miracle be done on his behalf. But 'that wicked man' [= you] is a commoner and not deserving that a miracle be done on his behalf. As for us, we are liable to [be punished by] death before the Omnipresent.[12] If you don't kill us, the Omnipresent has many [other] killers—many bears, many leopards and many lions that could attack us and kill us. But the Holy One, blessed be He, has delivered us into your hand only in order that in the future [world] he can exact punishment from your hand for our blood."

[G] They said: He did not move from there before a dispatch came from Rome and they split his skull with clubs.[13]

C. The War of Aristobolus and Hyrcanus (Bavli Sotah 49b)

[A] Our sages have taught: When the Hasmonean kings besieged one another, Hyrcanus was outside and Aristobolus was inside. Each day they would lower down to them a basket with coins, and they would send up to them [animals for the] regular sacrifices.[14]

[B] There was a certain old man there who was versed in Greek wisdom.[15] He spoke to them with Greek wisdom. He said to them, "As long as they busy themselves with the [temple] service, they will not be delivered into your hands."

[C] The next day they lowered down coins in the basket, and they sent up a pig.

[D] When it reached halfway up the wall, it stuck its nails into the wall, and the Land of Israel was jolted 400 parasangs by 400 parasangs.[16]

[E] At that time they said: "Cursed be the man who raises pigs, and cursed be the man who teaches his son Greek wisdom."[17]

D. Of Sieges and Sacrifices (Yerushalmi Berakhot 4:1, 7b)

[A] R. Simon [said] in the name of R. Yehoshua b. Levi:

[B] In the days of the kingdom of Greece they would lower down to them two baskets with gold. And they would send up to them two lambs [for the regular sacrifice].[18]

[C] One day they lowered to them two baskets of gold, and they sent up to them two kids [which cannot be used for the regular sacrifice.]

[D] At that time God enlightened their eyes and they found two lambs, [already] inspected [and fit for the sacrifice], in the Hewn Chamber [of the temple].

[E] R. Yuda bar Abba testified of that time that the regular sacrifice was offered at the fourth hour.[19]

[F] R. Levi said: So too in the days of this evil kingdom [Rome], they would lower down to them two baskets of gold, and they would send up to them two sheep.

[G] Ultimately they sent up to them two pigs. They did not manage to get [the basket] halfway up the wall before the pig pressed [against the wall] and jumped 400 parasangs from the Land of Israel.

[H] At that time sins brought it about that the regular sacrifice was annulled and the temple was destroyed.

Chapter 2

THE SAGES AND KING YANNAI: STANDING UP TO AUTHORITY (BAVLI SANHEDRIN 19a–b)

King Yannai (called Alexander or Janneus in Greek sources), who ruled from 103–76 BCE, is the subject of several unflattering rabbinic stories. The sages recalled the Hasmonean kings with ambivalence, preserving traditions about their Hellenizing ways, allegiance to the Sadducees and cruelty to the people.[1]

The Bavli cites the following story to explain the origin of the law in Mishna Sanhedrin 2:1: "A king does not judge [others] and is not judged [in court]." The story suggests that the royal exemption is not the ideal but the consequence of the rabbis' cowardice, of their failure to stand up courageously to authority.[2] Shimon b. Shetah insists that King Yannai take responsibility for the deeds of his slave and that the sages take responsibility for administering God's justice (D, E). But when he summons Yannai to trial and demands that the king stand up, apparently the standard judicial protocol, his colleagues recoil from the king and remain silent.[3] Their immediate punishment at the hands of an angel makes abundantly clear the severity of their sin. As we will see in other Bavli sources, the storytellers do not shrink from portraying the sages unfavorably to achieve their didactic aims.[4]

[A] Why is a king of Israel not [judged]? Because of what once happened. For—

[B] The slave of King Yannai killed someone. Shimon b. Shetah said to the sages, "Set your eyes upon him and let us judge him."

[C] They sent [a message] to him [Yannai], "Your slave killed someone." He [Yannai] sent him to them.

[D] They sent to him, "[It is written,] *And its masters have been warned* (Exod 21:29).[5] The Torah stated, 'Let the master of the ox come and stand by his ox.'" He [Yannai] came and sat down.

[E] Shimon b. Shetah said to him, "King Yannai! Stand on your feet and let them give testimony regarding you. You do not stand before us but before Him-who-spoke-and-the-world-was, as it says, *The two parties to the dispute shall stand before the Lord, [before the priests or magistrates in authority at the time]* (Deut 19:17)."[6] He [Yannai] said to him, "[I will] not [act] as you say but as your colleagues say."

[F] He turned to his right, but they looked down to the ground.[7] He turned to his left, but they looked down to the ground.[8]

[G] Shimon b. Shetah said, "Are you preoccupied with your thoughts? Let the master of thoughts come and punish you." [The angel] Gabriel came and struck them [the sages] to the ground.[9]

[H] At that time they said, *A king does not judge [others] and is not judged [in court]* (Mishna Sanhedrin 2:1).

Chapter 3

HEROD AND BAVA B. BUTA (BAVLI BAVA BATRA 3b–4a)

King Herod the Great ruled Judea from 37 BCE to 4 CE. His father, Antipater, was an aristocrat, opportunist and friend of one of the last Hasmonean rulers, Hyrcanus II (63–40 BCE), who arranged that his two sons, Phasael and Herod, be appointed governors of Judea and Galilee. Antigonus, Hyrcanus's nephew, allied himself with the Parthians and seized the throne when the Parthians briefly overran the Near East in 40 BCE. Herod meanwhile remained loyal to Rome. With Roman backing he defeated Antigonus in 37 BCE, bringing an end to the Hasmonean dynasty. The Romans granted Herod the title King, and he remained their vassal throughout his life.

Herod was descended from Idumeans, the people who lived in the territory south of Judea. John Hyrcanus I (135–104 BCE) had conquered Idumea and forced the inhabitants to accept circumcision and Jewish law, that is, to convert. Herod's Jewishness, as far as we know, was never seriously questioned by his contemporaries, although many Jews probably considered his alien provenance as one factor among many to reject his legitimacy.[1] We know from Josephus that Herod married the Hasmonean Mariamme, granddaughter of Hyrcanus II, clearly an attempt to legitimate his rule.[2]

The rabbinic story exhibits a contemptuous attitude toward Herod's pedigree. He is introduced as a "slave of the Hasmonean House"—apparently a non-Jewish slave is meant (A). The story claims that Herod did not succeed in marrying a Hasmonean, although he desperately attempted to create the impression that he did so. After usurping power Herod kills the rabbis because, as

33

experts in the scriptures, they call attention to the Deuteronomic prohibition against foreign kings (D). The Romans also warn Herod of his lowly lineage and illicit claim on the throne (K). All this discredits Herod's rule in very strong terms. While the rabbis express ambivalence toward the Hasmoneans, they consistently condemn Herod.

The one bright spot, for the rabbis, was Herod's massive building project, the complete reconstruction of the Jerusalem Temple. A master builder, Herod erected fortresses, stadiums, theaters, amphitheaters, pagan temples and new cities, employing the best architects and sparing no expense. The splendor of the rebuilt temple was legendary, as expressed by the saying quoted at the end of the story: "Whoever has not seen the Temple of Herod never saw a glorious building all his days." The story therefore grants him limited credit for this enterprise. But the tradition minimizes his merit by portraying the rebuilding as an attempt to atone for other crimes and by attributing the idea to the sage Bava b. Buta (G-I).

A significant point of rabbinic theology emerges from Bava b. Buta's description of both the temple and the sages as "the light" and "eye" of the world" (H-I). The existence of the cosmos, for the rabbis, depended on the temple service and the study of Torah. Many rabbinic traditions argue that in the present time, after the destruction of the temple, the study of Torah achieves the same functions as the sacrifices. In this story, set in the Second Temple Period, the rebuilding of the temple functions as a surrogate for the destruction of the sages. Thus the Torah, taught by and embodied in the sages, and the temple emerge as the twin foundations of the rabbinic worldview.[3]

[A] Herod was a slave of the Hasmonean house. He set his eyes on a certain girl. One day he heard a heavenly voice that said, "Any slave who rebels now will succeed." He rose up and killed all of his masters and spared [only] that maiden.

[B] When that maiden saw that he wished to marry her, she went up to the roof and lifted her voice and said, "Whoever says

'I am from the Hasmonean house' is a slave. For I alone was spared among all of them." She jumped off and died.

[C] He preserved her in honey for seven years. Some say he had intercourse with her. Some say he did not have intercourse with her. Those who say he had intercourse with her [explain] that he preserved her to satisfy his [sexual] urge. Those who say that he did not have intercourse with her—why did he do that? In order to spread a rumor that he married the daughter of a king.

[D] He [Herod] said, "Who is it who interprets [the verse], *Be sure to set as king over yourself one of your own people; [you must not set a foreigner over you, one who is not your kinsman]* (Deut 17:15)? The rabbis!" He rose up and killed all of the rabbis.

[E] He spared only Bava b. Buta so that he could consult with him. He bedecked him with a wreath of hedgehog [bristles] that poked out his eyes.

[F1] One day he [Herod] came and sat before him [Bava b. Buta]. He [Herod] said to him, "Do you, Sir, see what that wicked slave does?" He said to him, "What can I do to him?" He said to him, "Curse him." He said to him, "It is written, *Don't revile a king even among your intimates* (Qoh 10:20)."

[F2] He [Herod] said to him, "Those words apply to a king. That one is no king." He said to him, "Even if he is simply a rich man, it is written, *[Don't revile] a rich man even in your bed-chamber* (Qoh 10:20). And even if he is simply a leader, it is written, *Do not put a curse upon a chieftain among your people* (Exod 22:27)."

[F3] He [Herod] said to him, "That [applies only to one] who acts according to the ways of your people. That one does not act according to the ways of your people." He said to him, "I am afraid lest someone hear and go and inform him."

[F4] He [Herod] said, "Now, however, you and I are sitting [alone]." He [Bava] said to him, *"For the bird of the air may carry the utterance, and a winged creature may report the word* (Qoh 10:20)."

[G] He [Herod] said to him, "I am he [Herod]. Had I known that the rabbis were so discreet, I would not have killed them. Now, how can I make up for it?"

[H] He [Bava b. Buta] said to him, "You extinguished the light of the world. Go and busy yourself with the light of the world. You extinguished the light of the world—the rabbis, as is written, *For the commandment is a lamp; the Torah is a light* (Prov 6:23). Go and busy yourself with the light of the world—the temple, as is written, *And all the nations shall be illumined by it* [the temple] (Isa 2:2)."[4]

[I] Some say he [Bava b. Buta] said to him, "You extinguished the eye of the world. Go and busy yourself with the eye of the world. You extinguished the eye of the world—the rabbis, as is written, *If this was not known to the eyes of the congregation* (Num 15:24).[5] Go and busy yourself with the eye of the world—the temple, as is written, *I am going to desecrate my sanctuary, your pride and glory, the delight of your eyes* (Ezek 24:21)."

[J] He [Herod] said to him, "I am afraid of the Roman Empire." He said to him, "Send a messenger. He will travel for a year, stay [in Rome] for a year, and return for a year. Meanwhile raze it [the temple] and rebuild it."

[K] He [Herod] did this. They [the Romans] sent to him, "If you haven't razed it, do not raze it. And if you razed it, do not rebuild it. And if you razed it and rebuilt it, [you are] a wicked slave who [first] acts and then asks permission. Although you bear your weapons, the book of your [genealogy] is here. You are neither a king[6] nor the son of a king but Herod, a slave, who made himself a freeman."[7]

[L] Whoever has not seen the Temple of Herod never saw a glorious building all his days. With what did he build it? With alabaster and polished stones. Some say of black marble, alabaster and polished stones. Alternate rows went in and out so that it could be plastered. He considered covering it with gold. The rabbis said to him, "Leave it alone, for it is more beautiful thus, for it looks like the waves of the sea."

Chapter 4

STORIES OF DESTRUCTION

A. The Destruction of the Second Temple (I) (Bavli Gittin 55b-57a)

The lengthy tale of the destruction of the Second Temple found in Bavli Gittin 55b–57a provides a good example of rabbinic historiography. The storytellers included a great deal of accurate historical data in a didactic fictional composition, the main purpose of which was to explain why disasters happen and how the Jewish people best can avoid them. Their goal was not to report "what actually happened" but to impart enduring lessons for future generations of rabbis and Jews.

The first part of the story, sections A-H, shares many elements in common with the account of Josephus, the Jewish general who surrendered to Vespasian and later wrote a detailed history of the conflict entitled *The Jewish War*. Common elements include the refusal to sacrifice an offering, infighting among rival Jewish groups, acute famine, the death of the emperor (Nero), Vespasian's leaving the campaign to claim the throne and the destruction of the temple by Vespasian's son Titus. Yet here too the rabbinic storytellers reworked the historical material with great freedom. For example, according to Josephus the rebels ignored the pleadings of the chief priests, Pharisees and leading aristocrats and stopped the offering sacrificed on behalf of the Roman government each day in the temple. This symbolic act was one stage in a gradual escalation of hostilities that followed a series of Roman assaults and Jewish riots.[1] According to the Bavli, one disgruntled individual simply approached the Roman emperor (!), who then sent a calf with him as a test (A-B) and decided to attack the Jews on that account.

Most intriguing in this regard is the parallel between the roles of Josephus himself and R. Yohanan b. Zakkai (G-H). Josephus claims to have received a prophecy that the Romans would win the war and describes how he approached Vespasian and predicted that Vespasian would soon be emperor, a prediction that was fulfilled two years later. It seems that the rabbinic storytellers transformed oral traditions deriving from Josephus's history such that their hero and founder, R. Yohanan b. Zakkai, encountered the general and predicted his ascent.[2]

Other parts of the composition are less rooted in history or flatly contradict the historical record. Nero's part in the campaign, omen-seeking and conversion (E); Vespasian and his difficulty putting on shoes (H); Titus's outrage in the Holy of Holies, the brain-destroying gnat, and the cremation and scattering of his ashes (L-P) are clearly legendary, to say nothing of the spirits of the dead and their revelations (Q-S).

Among the important messages of the story is the necessity of strong rabbinic leadership and of the sages' responsibility to act as the spiritual, moral, social and political leaders of the community. The crisis begins because the sages witness the host shaming Bar Qamza at the banquet (A), neither objecting to his actions nor leaving the meal in protest. Similarly, they fail to act when confronted with the blemished sacrifice, neither compromising the law nor killing Bar Qamza (B1). R. Yohanan explicitly condemns the "meekness" *(anvetanut)* of R. Zecharia b. Avqulos, who worried so much about the potential consequences of the necessary measures that he paralyzed his colleagues.[3] This censure of *anvetanut* is striking, since the term typically means gentleness, patience and humility, and is one of the highest rabbinic virtues (see chapter 29 herein). While humility or gentleness may be praiseworthy as an individual characteristic, when the rabbis serve as communal leaders, they must act with confidence, resolve and daring. Not to act, not to compromise or emend the law when circumstances demand it, brings disaster.

R. Yohanan b. Zakkai exhibits the leadership characteristics advocated by the story. He recognizes a desperate situation, takes the initiative by summoning the thug leader, escapes the city, confronts Vespasian and impresses the Roman so much that he manages to "save a little" (E-K). He turns to scripture to understand the historical moment and to predict to Vespasian his imminent coronation. Yet the story portrays R. Yohanan with ambivalence, leaving him with no answer to Vespasian's charge that he should have acted earlier (G) and applying to him a verse that characterizes him as foolish (G1, H1). Many Bavli stories, written by and for the sages for their own internal purposes, are self-critical. Even the hero of the saga should have done more to obviate the situation before it spiraled out of control. The version of R. Yohanan b. Zakkai's encounter with Vespasian found in *Avot d'Rabbi Natan* and translated below (story B of this chapter) offers a far more favorable depiction of the sage.

The bizarre account of Titus focuses on the afflictions he endured for the rest of his life and his harsh punishments in the next world (J-Q). His wretched fate offers a message of comfort to the audience: God avenges the destruction of the temple and metes out due punishment to the enemies of Israel (Q-R). Similarly, the traditions of Onqelos b. Qaloniqos conjuring up the dead make it clear that pious Jews hold pride of place in the next world, while their foes and all sinners suffer miserably. However bad the situation appears in this world, in the world to come the righteous will prosper and the wicked suffer. That a lowly gnat, the smallest of God's creatures, kills Titus demonstrates the true power of God. The Roman's outrages in the temple, insults to God and power to destroy Jerusalem demonstrate neither his might nor God's impotence.

This composition exhibits several common characteristics of Bavli stories. The storytellers combined a number of independent sources to construct the extended narrative thread. Not only is this clear from the rapid shifting of protagonists, but other rabbinic compilations preserve those sources independently, albeit in different versions.[4] We also see a number of non-narrative comments, passages that do not narrate additional parts of the story but comment and discuss it (G1, H1, K). These comments offer some insights as to how various sages judged the characters and evaluated the events and thereby influence the audience's perspective.[5]

[A1] R. Yohanan said, "What [is meant] by the scripture, *Happy is the man who is cautious always, but he who hardens his heart falls into misfortune* (Prov 28:14)?" Jerusalem was destroyed because of Qamza and Bar Qamza. Tur Malka was destroyed because of a cock and a hen. Betar was destroyed because of the shaft of a litter.[6]

[A] Jerusalem was destroyed because of Qamza and Bar Qamza. A certain man whose friend was named Qamza and whose enemy was named Bar Qamza held a banquet. He said to his servant, "Go and bring me Qamza." He went and brought Bar Qamza. He [the host] came and found him sitting [at the banquet]. He said, "Since you are my enemy, what are you doing here? Get up and leave." He said to him, "Since I am here, let me be, and I will pay for what I eat and drink." He said to him, "No." [He said,] "I will pay for half the banquet." He said to him, "No." [He said,] "I will pay for the whole banquet." He said to him, "No." He grabbed him, forced him up and threw him out.

[B] He [Bar Qamza] said, "Since the rabbis were sitting and did not intervene,[7] I will go and inform against them at the king's palace." He said to the emperor, "The Jews are rebelling against you." He said, "Who says?" He said to him, "Send them a sacrifice and see if they offer it."

He [the emperor] sent a fine calf with him [Bar Qamza]. While he was traveling he made a blemish in it, in the upper lip, and some say in the withered spots of its eye, a place that we [Jews] consider a blemish, but they [Romans] do not consider a blemish. The rabbis considered offering it for the sake of maintaining peace with the [ruling] kingdom.[8] R. Zecharia b. Avqulos said to them, "Should they say that blemished animals may be offered on the altar?"[9] The rabbis considered killing him [Bar Qamza] in case he should go and tell him [the emperor].

41

R. Zecharia b. Avqulos said to them, "Should they say that one who causes a blemish [to sacrifices] is killed?"

[B1] R. Yohanan said, "The meekness *(anvetanut)* of Zecharia b. Avqulos destroyed our temple and burned our sanctuary and exiled us from our land."[10]

[C] He [the emperor] went and sent Nero the [future] emperor against them. When he arrived, he shot an arrow to the East. It went and fell in Jerusalem. To the West. It went and fell in Jerusalem. To all four directions. It went and fell toward Jerusalem. He said to a child, "Recite your study-verse to me."[11] He said to him, *"I will wreak my vengeance on Edom through My people Israel [and they shall take action against Edom in accordance with My blazing anger; and they shall know My vengeance—declares the Lord God]* (Ezek 25:14)." He said, "The Holy One, blessed be He, wants to destroy his house and He wants to wipe clean his hands with that man [= me]!"[12] He fled and converted, and R. Meir descended from him.

[D] He [the emperor] sent Vespasian the [future] emperor against them. He came and besieged it for three years. There were three rich men there—Naqdimon b. Gurion, Ben Kalba Savua and Ben Tsitsit Hakeset. Naqdimon b. Gurion [was so called] because the sun cut through *(naqda)* [the clouds] for him. Ben Kalba Savua [was so called] because whoever entered his house hungry as a dog *(kalba)* departed full *(sava)*. Ben Tsitsit Hakeset [was so called] because his fringes *(tsitsit)* dragged on pillows *(kesatot)*. And some say because his seat *(kisato)* was among the Roman notables.

One said to them, "I will supply you with wheat and barley." One said to them, "I [will supply you] with wine and oil." And one said to them, "I will supply you with wood." (The rabbis praised the wood since Rav Hisda gave all his keys to his servant except for the key to the wood bin. For Rav Hisda said, "[To bake] one load of bread requires sixty loads of wood.")

They had [enough] to sustain [them] for twenty-one years.

There were these thugs among them. The rabbis said to them, "Let's go out and make peace with them [the Romans.]" They [the thugs] would not let them. They said, "Let's go out and make war against them." The rabbis said to them, "It won't help." They [the thugs] rose up and burned the stores of wheat and barley, and there was famine.[13]

[E] Marta the daughter of Baitos was the richest woman in Jerusalem. She sent her servant and said, "Go and bring me [bread of] fine flour from the market." While he was going, it sold out. He came and said to her, "There is no [bread of] fine flour. There is good bread." [She said to him,] "Go and bring it to me." While he was going, it sold out. He came and said to her, "There is no good bread. There is coarse bread." [She said to him,] "Go and bring it to me." While he was going, it sold out. He returned and said to her, "There is no coarse bread. There is [bread of] barley flour." [She said to him,] "Go and bring it to me." While he was going, the barley sold out.

[Although] she had taken off her shoes, she said, "I will go out and see whether I can find anything to eat." A piece of dung stuck to her foot and she died.[14] R. Yohanan b. Zakkai applied to her the verse, *And she who is most tender and dainty among you, [that she would never venture to set a foot on the ground, shall begrudge the husband of her bosom, and her son and daughter, the afterbirth that issues from between her legs and the babies she bears]* (Deut 28:56).[15]

Some say she ate a fig of R. Zadoq and became ill [and died]. For R. Zadoq fasted for forty years so that Jerusalem would not be destroyed. When he ate anything it could be seen from outside [because he was so thin.] And when he recovered [from his fasts], they would bring him dried figs. He would suck out the juice and throw them away.[16]

While she was dying she threw all her gold and silver into the market. She said, "What do I need this for?" Thus it is written, *They shall throw their silver into the streets, and their gold shall be treated as something unclean. [Their silver and gold shall not avail to*

43

save them in the day of the Lord's wrath—to satisfy their hunger or to fill their stomachs] (Ezek 7:19).

[F] Abba Siqra,[17] the leader of the thugs in Jerusalem, was the son of R. Yohanan b. Zakkai's sister.[18] He [R. Yohanan] sent to him, "Come secretly to me." [He came.] He said, "How long will you act this way and kill everyone with starvation?" He said to him, "What can I do? If I say anything to them [the thugs], they will kill me." He said to him, "Figure out a remedy for me so that I can get out. Perhaps it will save a little." He said to him, "Pretend you are sick, and let everyone come to visit you. Bring something rotten and place it with you and they will say that you died. Let [only] your students attend to you, for they [the thugs] know that a living person is lighter [than a corpse]."[19] He did this. R. Eliezer went on one side and R. Yehoshua on the other side. When they reached the gate they [the thug sentries] wanted to stab him [to make sure he was dead]. He [Abba Siqra] said to them, "Should they [the Romans] say that they stabbed their master?" They wanted to push him. He said to them, "Should they say that they pushed their master?"[20] They opened the gate for them.

[G] When he reached him [Vespasian], he said to him, "Peace to you, O King. Peace to you, O King." He said to him, "You deserve death on two [counts]. First, I am not a king.[21] Second, if I am a king, why did you not come to me until now?" He said to him, "As for what you said, 'I am not a king,' in truth you are a king. For if you were not a king, Jerusalem would not be delivered into your hands, for it says, *Lebanon shall fall to the mighty one* (Isa 10:34) and 'mighty one' refers to a king, as it says, *His mighty one shall come from his midst* (Jer 30:21),[22] and 'Lebanon' refers to the temple, as it says, *That good hill country and the Lebanon* (Deut 3:25).[23] And as for what you said, 'If I am a king, why did you not come to me?'—the thugs among us would not let me." He said to him, "If there is a jar of honey and a snake wound around it, would they not break the jar on account of the snake?"[24] He was silent.

[G1] Rav Yosef [and some say R. Akiba] applied to him the verse, "*[God] turns sages back and makes nonsense of their knowledge* (Isa

44:25). He should have answered him, 'We take tongs and take away the snake and kill it. And we leave the jar.'"

[H] Just then a messenger came from Rome. He said to them, "Rise, for the emperor has died and the notables of Rome voted to make you the leader." He [Vespasian] had put on one shoe. He tried to put on the other but it would not go on. He tried to take off the first, but it would not come off. He said, "What is this?" He [R. Yohanan b. Zakkai] said to him, "Do not worry. You received good news, [as it says], *Good news puts fat on bones* (Prov 15:30)." He said to him, "What is the remedy?" [He said,] "Bring someone who annoys you and have him pass before you, as it says, *Despondency dries up the bones* (Prov 17:22)." He did this. It [the shoe] went on. He said to him, "Since you are so wise, why did you not come to me before now?" He said to him, "Have I not told you?" He said, "I also told you."

He [Vespasian] said to him, "I am going and I will send someone else. Ask something of me and I will give it you." He said, "Give me Yavneh and its sages and the line of Rabban Gamaliel and doctors to heal Rabbi Zadoq."[25]

[H1] Rav Yosef, and some say R. Akiba, applied to him the verse, *"[God] turns sages back [and makes nonsense of their knowledge]* (Isa 44:25). He should have said, 'Let them off this time.'"

[H2] But he thought that perhaps he [Vespasian] would not do so much, and he would not even save a little.

[I] What [was the treatment prescribed by] the doctors who healed Rabbi Zadoq? The first day they gave him bran water to drink; the next day, coarse flour water; the next day, flour water, until his stomach expanded little by little.[26]

[J] He [Vespasian] went and sent Titus, who said, *"Where is their God, the rock in whom they sought refuge?* (Deut 32:37)." This verse refers to Titus the Wicked, who outraged and blasphemed Heaven.[27] What did he do? He took a prostitute by the hand, entered the Holy of Holies, spread out a Torah and committed a sin upon it. He took a knife and slit the curtain [of the Holy of Holies].[28] A miracle occurred and blood burst forth and he thought that he killed [God],[29] as it says, *[All the outrages of the enemy in the sanctuary]; Your foes inside Your meeting-place; they take their signs for true signs* (Ps 74:3–4).

[K] Abba Hanan says, "It says, *Who is strong like You, O Lord* (Ps 89:9). Who is strong and hardened like you, that you hear the reviling and blasphemy of that wicked man and keep silent?" The school of R. Ishmael taught, "*Who is like you, O Lord, among the mighty (ʾeilim)?* (Exod 15:11). Who is like you among the mute (ʾilmim)?*"

[L] What did he [Titus] do? He took the curtain and fashioned a type of net. He gathered all the vessels of the temple and put them in it, and he placed them on a boat and went [intending] to be celebrated in his city, as it says, *And I saw wicked men coming from the Holy Site and being buried, and those who had acted thusly were forgotten in the city* (Qoh 8:10). Do not read "being buried" *(qevurim)* but rather "gathering" *(qevutsim)*. Do not read "forgotten" *(veyishtakekhu)* but rather "be celebrated" *(veyishtabehu)*.[30] Some say "buried" should be taken literally, since even their [the Jews'] hidden things [treasures] were revealed to them [the Romans].[31]

[M] A storm of the sea rose up against him to drown him. He said, "It seems to me that the God of this nation has power only over the water. When Pharaoh came, he drowned him in water. When Sisera came, he drowned him in water.[32] Now he stands against me too to drown me in water. If he is powerful, let him go up on land and wage war against me."

A heavenly voice went forth and said to him, "O Wicked Man son of Wicked Man, descendant of Esau the Wicked,[33] I have an insignificant creature in my world called a gnat. (Why is it called an 'insignificant creature'? Since it has an entrance [for food] but not an egress [for excretion].) Go up to the land and wage war against it."

[N] He went up to the land. A gnat came and entered his nose and bored at his brain for seven years. One day he was passing by the entrance of a blacksmith. It [the gnat] heard the sound of the hammer and settled down.[34] He [Titus] said, "There is a remedy." Each day they brought a smith and he hammered before him. They gave four *zuz* to a Gentile [smith], but to a Jewish [smith] he said, "Let it suffice for you that you see your enemy thus." He did this for thirty days. After that, having grown accustomed [to the sound], it [the gnat] became accustomed to it [and resumed boring.]

[O] It was taught: R. Pinhas b. Aruva said, "I was among the Roman notables. When he died they split open his skull and found there [a gnat as big] as a wild bird weighing two *sela*." It was taught in a Tannaitic tradition,[35] "It [the gnat] was [as big] as a year-old chick weighing two *litra*." Abaye said, "We have [a tradition] that it had a brass beak and iron talons."

[P] When he [Titus] was dying he said to them, "Cremate me and scatter my ashes upon the seven seas in order that the God of the Jews not find me and bring me to judgment."

[Q] Onqelos son of Qaloniqos, the son of Titus's sister, wished to convert.[36]

[R1] He went and raised up Titus by necromancy. He said to him, "Who is esteemed in that world [the world to come]?" He said to him, "Israel." [He said,] "What about joining them?" He said, "They have many observances and you will not be able to fulfill them. [Rather], go and attack them in that world and you will become a ruler, as it says, *Her enemies become rulers* (Lam 1:5). Whoever oppresses Israel becomes a ruler." He [Onqelos] said to him, "With what are you punished?" He said, "With what I decreed for myself. Every day they collect my ashes and sentence me and burn me and spread them over the seven seas."

[R2] He [Onqelos] went and raised up Bilaam by necromancy. He said to him, "Who is esteemed in that world?" He said to him, "Israel." "What about joining them?" He said, "*You shall never concern yourself with their welfare or benefit as long as you live* (Deut 23:7)."[37] He said, "With what are you punished?" He said, "With boiling semen."

[R3] He went and raised up Jesus by necromancy. He said, "Who is esteemed in that world?" He said to him, "Israel." "What about joining them?" He said, "Seek their welfare. Do not cause them harm. Whoever afflicts them is [considered] as if he afflicts the apple of his [God's] eye."[38] He said to him, "With what are you punished?" He said, "With boiling excrement."

For it was stated: "Whoever mocks the words of the sages is punished with boiling excrement."[39] (Come and see the difference between the sinners of Israel and the prophets of the Gentiles who worship idols!)[40]

[S] It was taught: R. Eleazar said, "Come and see how great is the power of shame. Behold, God assisted Bar Qamza and destroyed his temple and burned his sanctuary."[41]

B. The Destruction of the Second Temple (II) (Avot ∂'Rabbi Natan §4)

A different version of R. Yohanan b. Zakkai's encounter with Vespasian and the destruction of Jerusalem appears in *Avot d'Rabbi Natan*, a commentary to Mishna Tractate Avot edited in the fifth or sixth century CE.[42] This account corresponds with sections D, F, G, H of the Bavli's story, but presents the sage in extremely favorable light. It lacks the dialogue in which R. Yohanan b. Zakkai fails to respond to Vespasian's questions as well as the explicit criticism by later authorities, the application of the derogatory verse and the charge that he asked for the wrong thing (G1, H1). Here Vespasian honors R. Yohanan b. Zakkai from the start and immediately grants him a request, which portrays the rabbi as a great man whom even Vespasian respected.[43]

The message of this version accordingly differs from that of the Bavli. The story appears in the section of *Avot d'Rabbi Natan* that comments on Mishna Avot 1:2, "The world stands on three things: on the Torah, on the temple service and on deeds of lovingkindness." The destruction of the temple therefore creates a theological problem: how will the world continue to endure without one of its three pillars?[44] In this context the story suggests that R. Yohanan b. Zakkai anticipated the destruction and made provisions for Jewish life thereafter by obtaining Yavneh as a surrogate of sorts, a place to perform the commandments, study Torah and pray (e). The Jewish people can survive the loss of Jerusalem and the temple because of leaders like R. Yohanan b. Zakkai, heroes with discernment and foresight. While the sages express acute pain at the destruction (h), they have secured the institutions and dedicated themselves to the practices that allow Jewish life to flourish and the world to endure.

[a] Now, when Vespasian came to destroy Jerusalem he said to them: "Idiots! Why do you want to destroy this city and [why do] you want to burn the temple? What do I want of you except that you send me one bow or one arrow and I will go from you?"[45] They said to him, "Just as we went forth against your two predecessors and killed them, so we will go forth against you and kill you."[46]

[b] When R. Yohanan b. Zakkai heard this he sent for the men of Jerusalem and said to them, "My sons: why are you destroying this city and [why] do you want to burn the temple? What does he ask of you except one bow or one arrow and he will go from you?" They said to him, "Just as we went forth against his two predecessors and killed them, so we will go forth against him and kill him."

[c] Vespasian had men positioned within the walls of Jerusalem. They wrote down every single word they heard on arrows and shot them beyond the walls, saying that R. Yohanan b. Zakkai was among the friends of the emperor.

[d] When R. Yohanan b. Zakkai had spoken to them one day, then a second and a third, but they did not accept [his words], he sent for his students, for R. Eliezer and R. Yehoshua. He said to them, "My sons: arise and take me out of here. Make a coffin for me and I will lie down in it." R. Eliezer grasped its front and R. Yehoshua grasped its back. At twilight they carried him until they reached the gates of Jerusalem. The gatekeepers said to him, "What is this?" They said to them, "It is a corpse. Do you not know that one does not leave a corpse overnight in Jerusalem?" They said to him, "If it is a corpse, take it out."

[e] They took him out and carried him until they reached Vespasian. They opened the coffin and he stood before him. He [Vespasian] said to him, "Are you Yohanan b. Zakkai? Ask, what shall I give you?" He said to him, "I ask nothing of you except that I may go to Yavneh and study with my disciples, and institute prayer there, and perform all the commandments." He said to him, "Go and do everything that you wish." He [R. Yohanan b. Zakkai] said to him, "Would you like me to tell you something?" He said to him, "Speak." He said to him, "Behold, you are about to become emperor." He said to him, "How do you know?" He said to him, "It is our tradition that the temple will not be delivered to the hand of a commoner but to the hand of a king, as it says, *The thickets of the forest shall be hacked away with iron, and Lebanon shall fall to the mighty one* (Isa 10:34)."[47]

[f] It was said: No more than one, two or three days passed before there came to him a messenger from his city that the emperor died and they voted him to be emperor.

[g] They brought him [Vespasian] a catapult and drew it up against the wall of Jerusalem.[48] They brought him boards of cedar and he placed them in the catapult and he struck against the wall until he broke through. They brought him the head of a pig and he put it in the catapult and he shot it toward the entrails that were on the altar. At that time Jerusalem was captured.[49]

[h] R. Yohanan b. Zakkai was sitting and looking and shaking just as Eli sat and looked, as it says, *He found Eli sitting on a seat, waiting beside the road—his heart trembling for the Ark of God* (1 Sam 4:13).[50] When R. Yohanan b. Zakkai heard that Jerusalem was destroyed and the temple burned, he tore his clothes, and his students tore their clothes, and they were sitting and crying and mourning.

C. The Destructions of Tur Malka and Betar (Bavli Gittin 57a)

The following two stories of destruction appear in the same complex of stories in Tractate Gittin as the story of the destruction of Jerusalem. An opening comment links the stories into a conceptual unit: "Jerusalem was destroyed because of Qamza and Bar Qamza. Tur Malka was destroyed because of a cock and a hen. Betar was destroyed because of the shaft of a litter" (see above, story A, section A.) All three contain the theme of someone notifying the emperor, "The Jews are rebelling against you." In all three the report is false: in the story of Jerusalem it is Bar Qamza's slander; in the stories of Tur Malka and Betar it is an exaggeration based on a local disturbance.

These two stories have even more in common, including the same basic structure. Both describe a ceremony related to marriage and birth (B, K). In both, agents of the emperor destroy ritual objects, apparently unaware of their significance, and the Jews riot (C, L). Thereupon the emperor is informed of a rebellion and marches against them (D, M). That ritual preparations for celebrations of future life cause war and death creates particularly sharp irony.

A question worth pondering is, who bears ultimate blame for the outbreak of the wars: the Jews, the Romans or both? Did the Jews overreact by attacking the Romans for taking a few animals or trees, especially since the Romans may not have known their import? Or are the Romans guilty of recklessly plundering Jewish property and then overreacting to an inevitable local outbreak? Or does war result from unfortunate misunderstandings: the Romans do not understand Jewish rituals; the Jews do not understand that the Romans meant no offense; the emperor's informants do not understand that a limited reprisal is not a rebellion; the emperor misunderstands rejoicing as ridicule (G)? If so, then the key to avoiding war is knowledge and appreciation of the culture of the other. The framing comments attributing the destructions to a "cock and a hen" and "the shaft of a litter" suggest that trivial matters snowball into serious violence. But does this imply that wars can be avoided with proper vigilance or that they are unavoidable?

The Bavli's story of the destruction of Jerusalem (story A) differs somewhat in blaming internal social abuses—the public shaming of Bar Qamza—as the cause of the trouble, rather than matters of international relations. There too misunderstandings play a role: Bar Qamza thinks that the rabbis approve of his humiliation at the banquet because they do not protest, and the emperor takes the rejection of his sacrifice as evidence of rebellion, not knowing that the blemish violates Jewish sacrificial law (story A, section B). Yet the story clearly blames the Jews, namely the host for humiliating Bar Qamza, the sages for countenancing it and R. Zecharia b. Avqulos for his failure to act when presented with the blemished sacrifice. The story of Tur Malka blames Bar Daroma's impiety for his defeat, although not for causing the hostilities (E).

The identity of Tur Malka—"King's Mountain" in Aramaic—is unclear. Some scholars understand Bar Daroma, literally "Son of the South," as a reference to Bar Kokhba, leader of the second Jewish revolt against Rome in 132–35 CE. Betar was indeed the site of the major battle and the defeat of Bar Kokhba's forces (see chapter 5 herein). Even if these identifications are correct, the rabbinic traditions yield little historical information about the Bar Kokhba revolt other than a distant memory of its magnitude. The purpose of the stories is to explain the causes of war so that destruction can be avoided in the future.[51]

[A] Tur Malka was destroyed because of a cock and a hen. For—

[B] It was the custom that when they would bring out the groom and bride they would bring out a cock and a hen before them, as if to say, "Reproduce and multiply like chickens."

[C] One day a Roman troop was passing by. They took them [the cock and hen] from them. They [the Jews] fell upon them and smote them.

[D] They went and said to the emperor, "The Jews are rebelling against you." He came against them.[52]

[E] There was among them [the Jews] a certain Bar Daroma, who could leap one mile, and he slaughtered [many] of them. The emperor took his crown and placed it on the ground. He said, "Master of the universe, may it not please you to deliver me and my kingdom into the hands of one man."

[F] Bar Daroma's mouth brought about his undoing. He said, "*But you have rejected us, O God; God You do not march with our armies* (Ps 60:12)."[53] (But David [the author of Psalms] said this too! David said it in astonishment.[54]) He [Bar Daroma] entered an outhouse. A snake came in. He dropped his gut and died.[55]

[G] He [the emperor] said, "Since a miracle happened for me, I will let them [the Jews] off." He let them off and departed. They [the Jews] made merry and ate and drank and lit so many torches that the stone of a signet-ring could be seen at a distance of one mile. He [the emperor] said, "The Jews are mocking me!" He came against them again.

[H] R. Asi said, "Three hundred thousand swordsmen entered Tur Malka and they slaughtered for three days and three nights. On the other side [of the mountain] they were celebrating and rejoicing, and neither knew about the others."

[I] *The Lord has laid waste without pity all the habitations of Jacob* (Lam 2:2). When Ravin came [to Babylonia from Israel] he said that R. Yohanan said, "These [mentioned in the verse] are the 600,000 towns that King Yannai possessed on King's Mountain." For Rav Yehuda said that R. Asi said, "King Yannai had 600,000 villages on King's Mountain, and each had [as many people] as went forth from Egypt, except for three that had double [as many] as went forth from Egypt."

[J] Betar was destroyed because of a shaft of a litter. For—

[K] It was the custom that when a baby boy was born they planted a cedar, and [when a] baby girl [was born they planted] a pine. And when they married, they cut them down and made a canopy [for the marriage ceremony].

[L] One day the daughter of the emperor was passing through. The shaft of her litter broke. They cut down the cedar and brought it for her [litter]. They [the Jews] fell upon them and smote them.

[M] They went and said to the emperor, "The Jews are rebelling against you." He came against them.

Chapter 5

BAR KOKHBA: HUBRIS AND DEFEAT (YERUSHALMI TAANIT 4:8, 68d)

In the years 132–35 CE the Jews rebelled against the Romans under the leadership of a charismatic military commander. Non-Jewish writings call him Bar Kokhba (Son of Star), an allusion to his messianic pretensions, whereas rabbinic traditions call him Bar Koziba (Son of Liar), for the same reason (C2). Recently archeologists discovered his letters in caves in the Judean desert and found his name to be Shimon bar Kosiba. His brief revolt enjoyed some limited success before being crushed by Hadrian's forces. The cruel reprisals, enslavement and devastation of Judea, recalled bitterly in the hyperbolic descriptions of rabbinic sources (E1–E4), are confirmed by Christian and Roman historians.[1]

The extent of rabbinic participation in the revolt is not known with certainty. Rabbinic traditions accuse the great sage Akiba of mistakenly believing that Bar Koziba was the Messiah, which suggests that at least some rabbis supported the revolt or participated in it (C3–C4).[2] Many scholars understand the defeat to have influenced the rabbinic attitude to messianic activity. Henceforth the sages adopted a long-range perspective and insisted that God would send the Messiah when he saw fit.

Various traditions integrated into this complex narrative attempt to explain why God did not support the rebels' cause and to draw lessons from the defeat. The main story blames Bar Koziba's character flaws: he displayed hubris, trusting in his own ability and asking God not to interfere,[3] and murderous rage, killing the pious R. Eleazar of Modiin in a fit of anger (D). A contributing factor was the treachery of the Samaritans, who regarded themselves as remnants of the Northern Israelites and came into periodic conflicts with the Jews. The Samaritans probably did not join the Jews in the revolt and perhaps were thought to have collaborated with the Romans. In any case, rabbinic traditions consistently attribute the ultimate causes of victory and defeat to spiritual and moral factors. The Romans were powerless as long as R. Eleazar fasted and prayed; they succeeded only after his murder (D3, D8). Bar Kosiba and his followers were defeated as punishment for that crime (D7). Other traditions blame sin in general (F), or celebrating the downfall of others (H).[4] At the root of all the traditions is the simple theology that God controls war, no matter what the size of the respective forces. If God wills it, the Jews win. But if the Jews sin, God delivers them into the hands of the enemy.

[A] *Betar was captured* [=Mishna Taanit 4:6].[5]

[B] Rabbi [Yehuda HaNasi] expounded *The Lord has laid waste without pity, all the habitations of Jacob; He has razed in anger fair Judah's strongholds* (Lam 2:2) about twenty-four [disastrous] events. R. Yohanan expounded [it about] sixty. Did R. Yohanan exceed Rabbi? But since Rabbi was closer [in time] to the destruction of the temple, the elders there would remember. When he would expound they cried, and he would quiet them down and stop [the discourse].[6]

[C1] It was taught: R. Yehuda b. R. Ilai says, "My master Baruch, used to expound *The voice is the voice of Jacob, yet the hands are the hands of Esau* (Gen 25:22). The voice of Jacob cries out from what the hands of Esau [=Rome] did to him in Betar."

[C2] R. Shimon bar Yohai taught: My master Akiba used to expound, "*A star* (kokhav) *issues from Jacob* (Num 24:19). A liar *(koziba)* issues from Jacob."

[C3] When R. Akiba [first] saw Bar Koziba he would say, "This is the King Messiah." R. Yohanan b. Torta said to him, "Akiba, grass will sprout from your cheeks and the Son of David will not yet have come."

[C4] R. Yohanan said, "*Voice (Gen 25:22)*—[this refers to] Hadrian the Emperor killing eighty thousand myriads in Betar."

[D1] R. Yohanan said: Eighty thousand pairs of trumpet-sounders besieged Betar, and each one commanded a number of soldiers. Bar Koziba was there with two hundred thousand [men with] amputated fingers.[7] The sages sent to him and said, "How long will you do this and maim [the men of] Israel?" He said to them, "How else can they be tested [to show valor]?" They said to him, "Do not register in your army anyone who cannot ride on his horse and uproot a cedar in Lebanon." He had two hundred thousand [soldiers] like this and two hundred thousand like that.

[D2] When he went into battle he would say, "Master of the Universe! Neither help [us] nor hinder [us]. *But have you rejected us, O God? [At least] do not march with our armies* (Ps 60:12)."[8]

[D3] Hadrian besieged Betar for three and one-half years.[9] R. Eleazar of Modiin was sitting on sackcloth and ashes and praying every day, "Master of the Universe. Do not sit in judgment today. Do not sit in judgment today."

[D4] Hadrian decided to leave. A certain Samaritan said to him, "Do not depart. I see what must be done so that the city may be surrendered to you."

[D5] He entered the city from a sewer. He went and found R. Eleazar of Modiin standing and praying. He pretended to whisper something into his ear. The residents saw him and brought him to Bar Koziba. They said to him, "We saw this old man speaking with your uncle." He said to him, "What did you say to him and what did he say to you?" He [the Samaritan] said to him, "If I tell you, the king will kill me. If I do not tell you, you will kill me. Better that the king kill me and not you." He [the Samaritan] said to him, "He said to me, 'I will surrender my city.'"

[D6] He [Bar Koziba] went to R. Eleazar of Modiin. He said to him, "What did that Samaritan say to you?" He said to him, "Nothing." He said to him, "What did you say to him?" He said to him, "Nothing." He gave him one kick and killed him.

[D7] Immediately a heavenly voice went forth and said, "*Oh, the worthless shepherd who abandons the flock! Let a sword descend upon his arm and upon his right eye....His arm shall shrivel up; his right eye shall go blind* (Zech 11:17). You killed R. Eleazar of Modiin, the arm and right eye of all Israel. Therefore let your right hand shrivel up and your right eye go blind."

[D8] Immediately Betar was captured and Bar Koziba was killed. They went and carried his head to Hadrian. He said to them, "Who killed this one?" The Samaritan said, "I killed him." He [Hadrian] said to him, "Show me his body." They showed him his body. They found a snake wound around it. He said, "Had God not killed him, who would have been able to kill him?" He applied to him the verse, [*How could one have routed a thousand, or two put ten thousand to fight,] unless their Rock had sold them, the Lord had given them up?* (Deut 32:30).

[E1] They went about slaughtering them until a horse sunk in the blood up to its nostrils, and the blood carried away boulders that weighed forty *sela* until it went four miles into the sea. If you should think that it [Betar] was close to the sea, behold, it was forty miles distant from the sea.

[E2] They said: "They found three hundred brains of infants on one stone, and they found three heaps of mutilated phylacteries each the size of nine *seah*, and some say nine [heaps] each of three *seah*."

[F] It was taught: Rabban Shimon b. Gamaliel says, "Five hundred schools were in Betar. The smallest of them had no less than five hundred schoolchildren. They would say, 'If the enemies come upon us, we will poke out their eyes with these quills.' When sins brought about [their punishment], they [the Romans] wrapped each one in his scroll and burned him. I alone remain among all of them." He applied to himself the verse, *Mine eyes have brought me grief over all the maidens of the city* (Lam 3:51).

[G1] Hadrian the Wicked had a great vineyard, eighteen miles by eighteen miles, like the distance from Tiberias to Sepphoris. He encircled it with the corpses from Betar, piled [as high] as a man standing [and as wide as the span of] arms outstretched. He did not permit them to be buried until a new king arose and permitted them to be buried.

[G2] Rav Huna said, "When the casualties of Betar were granted burial, they formulated [the blessing] 'who is good and does good': 'Good'—that they did not decompose. 'And does good'— that they were granted burial."[10]

[H] It was taught. R. Yose said, "Betar lasted for fifty-two years after the destruction of the temple. Why was it destroyed? Because they lit lamps after the destruction of the temple.[11] Why did they light lamps?

Because the councilors of Jerusalem would sit in the center of the city, and when they saw someone come up to Jerusalem [for a pilgrimage], they would say to him, 'We heard that you want to become a magistrate or a councilor.' He would say to them, 'I intend no such thing.' [They would say,] 'We heard that you want to sell your property.' He would say to them, 'I intend no such thing.' Then an associate [of the councilors] would say to them, 'What do you want with this one? Write and I will sign.' He [a councilor] would write and the associate would sign, and they would send the [forged] deed of sale to the steward of his [the pilgrim's] house and say to him, 'If So-and-so comes to enter his property, don't let him because it has been sold to us.' When he [the pilgrim] heard this from them, he would say, 'I wish I had broken my leg and not come up to Jerusalem.' Thus it is written, *Our steps were checked; we could not walk with long strides, [our doom is near, our days are done]* (Lam 4:18).

Our steps were checked. They desolated the ways to that house [the temple].

Our doom is near. The doom of that house is near.

Our days are done. The days of that house are done.

They too [the residents of Betar] did not come to good ends. *He who rejoices over another's misfortune will not go unpunished* (Prov 17:5)."

Chapter 6

REBUILDING THE TEMPLE (GENESIS RABBAH 64:8)

The following story tells how the sages attempted to dissuade the people from rebelling against Rome after the Romans rescinded permission to rebuild the temple. The story sets the events in the time of R. Yehoshua b. Hananiah, the early second century CE. The historical background is completely obscure, but perhaps may be found in the brief reign of Emperor Julian "the Apostate," who wished to reverse the Christianization of the Roman Empire (361–63 CE). Julian commissioned the rebuilding of many Pagan temples and also granted the Jews permission to rebuild the Jerusalem Temple. The work of clearing a space and assembling materials began in 363 CE. The project, however, was soon abandoned for unknown reasons. Julian's untimely death on the battlefield in the next year dashed any hopes of a Pagan revival, and the succeeding emperors had no interest in resuming the project. In such conditions it is possible that some Jews, aroused by messianic fervor, contemplated rebellion. Unfortunately we lack good historical sources; the reactions of the Jews and the role of the rabbis remain conjectures.[1]

The motif of the Samaritans'[2] slandering the Jews and causing the Roman emperor to change his mind has no historical worth (C). It devolves from the biblical account of Ezra 4, where the Samaritans denounce the Jews to the Persian king and delay rebuilding of the walls of Jerusalem in the early Second Temple Period (c. 500 BCE). Here we have a nice example of the rabbinic adaptation of a biblical plot.

R. Yehoshua's fable—one of the few fables found in rabbinic literature—contains the moral of the story (G). The Romans, like the lion, are an unstoppable force and a constant danger. The less contact with them, the better. The Jews should therefore consider themselves lucky that their present dealings with the Romans have caused no great harm and should not press their luck by complaining or rebelling.[3]

[A] In the days of R. Yehoshua b. Hananiah the [Roman] Empire decreed that the temple could be rebuilt.

[B] Pappos and Lulianos set up tables from Acco to Antioch to provide for those returning from the diaspora.[4]

[C] The Samaritans went and said to him [the emperor], "*Be it known to the king...that if this city is rebuilt and the walls completed, they will not pay* minda, belo *or* halakh (Ezra 4:12–13). 'Minda'—this refers to the land tax. 'Belo'—this refers to the gold tax. 'Halakh'—this refers to compulsory service."[5]

[D] He [the emperor] said to them, "What can we do? I issued a decree."[6] They said to him, "Send and tell them that they must move it [the temple] from its place, or enlarge it by five cubits, or reduce it by five cubits, and they will cease of their own accord."[7]

[E] The congregation gathered together in the valley of Beit-Rimon. When that letter arrived they began to cry. They wanted to rebel against the [Roman] Empire.

[F] They [the sages] said, "Let a wise man go and pacify the people." They said, "Let R. Yehoshua b. Hananiah go, for he is a scholar of Torah."[8]

[G] He went up and expounded:

> A lion once killed its prey and had a bone stuck in its throat. He said, "I will reward anyone who comes and removes it." There came a certain Egyptian stork with a long beak. It inserted its beak and removed it. It said to him [the lion],

"Give me my reward." He said to it, "Go and proclaim that you went into a lion's mouth in peace and you came out in peace."

So too it is enough that we engaged this nation [Rome] in peace and came out in peace.[9]

PART II:

RABBINIC AUTHORITY, RABBINIC CHARACTER

Chapter 7

THE BANNING
OF AKAVIA b. MEHALALEL:
A DISSIDENT OPPOSES
THE MAJORITY
(MISHNA EDUYYOT 5:6–7)

The disputes over almost every legal issue found in rabbinic sources presented a grave challenge to the sages. Could the rabbinic community avoid dissolving into numerous groups and sects with each faction holding fast to its own opinions? By what process should these legal disputes be resolved? How could the rabbis create norms and standards without denying the legitimacy of traditions duly passed down from master to disciple and without stifling debate and interpretation?

Some rabbinic sources solved this problem by advocating majority rule: the sages voted and the law followed the majority opinion. Dissenting rulings were tolerated provided that they were recognized as minority positions, as theoretical possibilities, but not advocated as practical, legitimate options. Sages who refused to accept the will of the majority could be banned—a type of excommunication or social ostracism.[1]

The following story grapples with the tensions between the majority and the individual, between communal norms and fidelity to tradition, between a legal system that operates through compromise and the need to believe that the resulting legislation is eternal and divine. Akavia's testimony that he has received authoritative traditions on four issues troubles his colleagues, who dispute his rulings and seem to desire unanimity.[2] They try to persuade him to retract his testimony, first by offering him a high office in the rabbinic hierarchy, then by placing him under a ban. That Akavia rejects their offer demonstrates that he is a man of principle, that he sticks to his position because he believes that it is the truth, not because he is a stubborn troublemaker. Indeed, R. Yehudah offers additional praise of Akavia's character and claims that such a pious sage was never banned (E). But if every sage continues to teach and act according to his own ruling, albeit out of the highest motives, how can a community function?

The story resolves the tension in a surprising and ironic manner (G). Although he suffers the ban rather than renounce his tradition, Akavia instructs his son to accept the majority position—and for the very reason his colleagues initially implored him to retract! Akavia thus subscribes to the principle of majority rule and even acts according to it. The beginning of the story, however, suggests that the sages banned him because he rejected that principle.[3] On the one hand, we now wonder whether majority rule will help the sages, since the identity of the majority seems very much at issue: Akavia rejects the majority of his contemporaries because he received traditions from a majority of sages of an earlier time. On the other hand, we sense that with each generation the majority and its ruling emerges more clearly. Lack of a consensus at any given time will not prevent one from emerging in the future.

The concluding dialogue again emphasizes Akavia's moral character and high standards. This interrelationship of character and ethics to law and authority runs through many rabbinic stories.[4]

[A] Akavia b. Mehalalel testified regarding four issues.

[B] They said to him, "Akavia. Retract those four issues that you stated and we will make you the head of the court for Israel." He said to them, "I would rather be called a fool all my days [for refusing such an offer] than be made a wicked man before the

Omnipresent for even one hour, [and] in order that others not say, 'He retracted for the sake of office.'"

> [C] He declared (1) the residual hair [of a skin discoloration] and (2) the greenish blood [of a vaginal discharge] impure. And the sages declared them pure.[5]
> (3) He permitted the hair of a blemished firstling that fell out, and which they stored in a wall-niche, and later they slaughtered [the animal]. And the sages forbade it.[6]
> (4) He used to say, "One does not make a female convert or an emancipated bondmaiden drink [the waters of bitterness]." And the sages say, "They make [them] drink."[7] They said to him, "Once Karkamit, an emancipated bondmaiden, was in Jerusalem, and Shemaya and Avtalion made her drink." He said to him, "They made her drink a likeness [of the waters]."[8]

[D] They banned him, and he died while under the ban, and the court stoned his coffin.

> [E] R. Yehudah said, "Heaven forbid that Akavia was banned. For the [Temple] Court never closed on a man of Israel as wise and sin-fearing as Akavia b. Mehalalel.[9] But whom did they stone? Eliezer b. Hanokh who questioned the [laws of] the purity of hands.[10] And when he [Eliezer b. Hanokh] died the court instructed that they put a stone on his coffin."

[F] This [that they stoned Akavia's coffin] teaches that they stone the coffin of anyone who dies under a ban.

[G] At the time of his [Akavia's] death, he said to his son, "My son, retract the four issues that I stated." He said to him, "Why did you yourself not retract?" He said to him, "I heard from the mouth of the majority and they [the sages] heard from the mouth of the majority. I stood by my tradition and they stood by their tradition. But you heard from the mouth of the individual and from the mouth of the majority. It is better to leave the words of the individual and hold fast to the words of the majority."

[H] He said to him, "Father, commend me to my colleagues."[11] He said to him, "I will not commend you." He said to him, "Perhaps you have found some fault in me?" He said, "No, but it is your deeds that will bring you near [to them] and your deeds that will distance you [from them]."

Chapter 8

HILLEL AND THE PASSOVER

A. Hillel and the Passover (1): The Sources and Methods of Rabbinic Law (Tosefta Pesahim 4:13-14)

The source of law was a critical issue for the sages. Like all law codes, the Torah does not cover every situation and leaves many questions unanswered. By what means and authority did the sages determine these unknown cases? By what techniques should the Torah be interpreted?

The following story offers models of various methods through which the sages derived law. The question concerns the coincidence of the fourteenth of Nisan, when the Passover sacrifice is offered, and the Sabbath, when labor is forbidden. Should worshipers carry out the Passover sacrifice on the Sabbath despite the prohibition against slaughtering? Or does the Sabbath take precedence and defer or cancel the sacrifice? This issue, of course, would have been settled in the early years of the temple's existence; it could not have cropped up for the first time during Hillel's life in the first century BCE. The story creates a fictional scenario to teach the audience about how one derives law in general, not to provide information about this particular law.

Hillel's four demonstrations in D1–D4 employ four different legal methods. D1 involves reasoning by analogy. D2 employs a type of exegesis known as a *gezeira shava* or "equal ordinance," a type of scriptural analogy. If scripture uses the same word in connection

71

with two different laws, then the particulars of the one can be applied to the other. D3 invokes a rabbinic deductive inference called a *qal va-homer* or *a minori ad maius*. If a rule applies to a "light" or less stringent case, it certainly applies to a "weighty" or more stringent case. These three types of scriptural exegesis appear throughout rabbinic literature. D4 turns to oral tradition. Thus four different methods—casuistic reasoning, biblical exegesis, logical inference and received tradition—all yield the law.

Section E models yet another method—to observe the accepted practice of the community. Hillel suggests that the community acts with an intuition inspired by the "holy spirit": God ensures that the people not violate the law.

The reward for Hillel's valuable instruction, his appointment as patriarch (*nasi*), stakes out a position on rabbinic authority. The sage with the greatest knowledge of Torah should lead the community. As we shall see, not all rabbinic stories accept this principle (see chapters 10 and 13 herein).[1]

[A] Once the fourteenth [day of Nisan] fell on the Sabbath. They asked Hillel the Elder, "Does the Passover[2] [sacrifice] supersede the Sabbath?"[3]

[B] He said to them, "Do we have but one Passover [sacrifice] during the year that supersedes the Sabbath? We have more than 300 Passovers[4] during the year, and they supersede the Sabbath."

[C] The whole courtyard [of the temple] congregated around him.

[D1] He said to them, "The regular sacrifice [offered each morning and twilight] is a communal sacrifice, and the Passover is a communal sacrifice. Just as the regular sacrifice is a communal sacrifice that supersedes the Sabbath, so the Passover is a communal sacrifice that supersedes the Sabbath.[5]

[D2] "Another proof: It [scripture] says in connection with the regular sacrifice, [*Present to me*] *at its appointed time* (Num 28:2), and it says in connection with the Passover, [*Keep the Passover*] *at its appointed time* (Num 9:2). Just as the regular sacrifice, of which it says, *At its appointed time*, supersedes the Sabbath, so the Passover, of which it says, *At its appointed time*, supersedes the Sabbath.

[D3] "Moreover, it [can be deduced] *qal va-homer*.[6] If the regular sacrifice, for which one is not subject to [the punishment of] excision, supersedes the Sabbath, is it not logical that the Passover, for which one is subject to [the punishment of] excision, supersede the Sabbath?[7]

[D4] "In addition, I have received [a tradition] from my masters that the Passover supersedes the Sabbath. Not only the First Passover but even the Second Passover, and not only the communal Passover but even the individual Passover."[8]

[E] They said to him, "What will the people do, for they did not bring their [slaughtering] knives and Passovers to the temple [prior to the Sabbath, since they did not know that they would be sacrificing on the Sabbath]?"[9]

[F] He said to them, "Leave them be. The Holy Spirit is upon them. If they are not prophets, they are the sons of prophets."[10]

[G] What did Israel do at that time? He whose Passover was a lamb hid it [the knife] in its wool. He whose Passover was a kid [goat], tied it [the knife] between its horns, and [thus] they brought their knives and Passovers to the temple, and they slaughtered their Passovers.[11]

[H] On that very day they appointed Hillel patriarch *[nasi]*, and he taught them the laws of the Passover.

❦

B. Hillel and the Passover (II): Mastery of Torah and Arrogance (Bavli Pesahim 66a)

Another version of this story appears in Bavli Pesahim 66a. This version focuses less on the nature of rabbinic law than on the appropriate character of a legal authority. After demonstrating his proficiency and being appointed patriarch (*nasi*), Hillel rebukes his colleagues for their insufficient grasp of the law (G). He then forgets a law himself, apparently a measure-for-measure punishment for his arrogance (H). Hillel therefore has no choice but to determine the law by observing the common practice of the community, a somewhat different use of this part of the story than in the Tosefta's version above.[12] As we find in other stories, the Bavli emphasizes that virtuous character, especially humility, must be combined with knowledge of Torah (see chapter 29 herein).

The Bavli version also highlights the importance of discipleship, of learning Torah from one's master. Hillel knows the law and its multiple derivations because he has "served the two great men of the generation," and he rebukes the Bnei Betera for failing to do so (C, G). The concluding line likewise stresses that the practice of the community in fact corresponds to the tradition that Hillel received from these masters. The Tosefta's version mentions Hillel's teachers only once and does not distinguish tradition from other sources of the law (D4).[13]

[A] Our sages have taught: This law was concealed from the Bnei Betera.[14]

[B] Once the fourteenth [day of Nisan] fell on the Sabbath. They forgot and did not know whether the Passover [sacrifice] supersedes the Sabbath or not. They said, "Is there anyone here who knows whether the Passover supersedes the Sabbath or not?"

[C] They said to them, "There is one man who came up from Babylonia, and Hillel the Babylonian is his name. He served the two great men of the generation, Shemaya and Avtalion, and he knows whether the Passover supersedes the Sabbath or not."

[D] They sent and called for him. They said to him, "Do you know whether the Passover supersedes the Sabbath or not?"

[E1] He said to them, "Do we only have one Passover during the year that supersedes the Sabbath? Do we not have many more than two hundred Passovers during the year that supersede the Sabbath?"

[E2] They said to him, "How do you know this?" He said to them, "It says *At its appointed time* (Num 28:2) in connection with the regular sacrifice, and it says *At its appointed time* (Num 9:3) in connection with the Passover. Just as *At its appointed time* (Num 28:2) [teaches that] the regular sacrifice supersedes the Sabbath, so *At its appointed time* (Num 9:3) [teaches that] the Passover supersedes the Sabbath.

[E3] "Also, it can be deduced *qal va-homer*.[15] If the regular sacrifice, for which one is not punished with excision, supersedes the Sabbath, then the Passover, for which one is punished with excision—is it not logical that it supersedes the Sabbath?"

[F] Immediately they seated him at the head and appointed him patriarch over them, and he expounded the laws of the Passover throughout the day.

[G] He began to rebuke them with words. He said to them, "What caused it that I should come up from Babylonia and that I should be the patriarch over you? Your laziness, that you did not serve the two great men of the generation, Shemaya and Avtalion."

[H] They said to him, "Master: If one forgot and did not bring a knife on the eve of the Sabbath, what [is the law]?" He said to them, "This law I heard and forgot. But leave Israel be. If they are not prophets, they are the sons of prophets."

[I] The next day, he whose Passover was a lamb stuck it [the knife] in its wool. He whose Passover was a kid [goat], stuck it between its horns.[16] He [Hillel] saw the act and remembered the law and said, "Thus I received the tradition from the mouth of Shemaya and Avtalion."

❦

C. Hillel and the Passover (III): The Importance of Tradition (Yerushalmi Pesahim 6:1, 33a)

A third version of the story appears in the Yerushalmi. A striking difference is the rejection of Hillel's proofs (G1–G3). Where the Bnei Betera in the Tosefta and Bavli accept Hillel's demonstrations and appoint him patriarch *(nasi)* on that basis, in the Yerushalmi they refute his scriptural analogies and logical inferences. Only when Hillel falls back on received tradition do they accept the law (H).[17] In this respect the Yerushalmi exhibits a suspicion of rabbinic hermeneutics and exegetical techniques. These methods are inconclusive and potentially mistaken: only received tradition assures accurate knowledge of the law. The importance of learning from a rabbinic master is accordingly emphasized throughout the story (B, I, N)

The Yerushalmi version also makes more evident the causal connections implicit in the Bavli. The term "as soon as" *(keivan she)*, which also has the sense of "Because…" clarifies that Hillel rebuked the people because he was appointed patriarch, and that he forgot the law because he rebuked the people. This story too warns against arrogance and pride in one's knowledge.

The Yerushalmi, like the Bavli, repeats numerous words and phrases. Several tripartite structures appear (D, F, G), as does a fourfold repetition of "as soon as" (H, I, J, N).

[A] This law was concealed from the elders of Betera.

[B] Once the fourteenth [day of Nisan] fell on the Sabbath, and they did not know whether the Passover supersedes the Sabbath or not. They said, "There is here a certain Babylonian named Hillel, who served Shemaya and Avtalion. He knows whether the Passover supersedes the Sabbath or not. Perhaps something good will come from him."

[C] He said to them, "Do we have but one Passover alone throughout the whole year that supersedes the Sabbath? Do not many Passovers throughout the year supersede the Sabbath?"

[D] (1) Some *tannaim*[18] teach "one hundred" [Passovers]. (2) Some *tannaim* teach "two hundred." (3) Some *tannaim* teach "three hundred." (1) The one who says "one hundred" [refers to] regular sacrifices. (2) The one who says "two hundred" [refers to] regular sacrifices and the Additional [sacrifices] for Sabbaths. (3) The one who says "three hundred" [refers to] regular sacrifices and the Additional [sacrifices] for Sabbaths, festivals, new months and appointed times.[19]

[E] They said, "Thus we thought that something good would come from you."

[F] He started to expound [the law] for them based on a *heqesh* [topical analogy], a *qal va-homer* [inference] and a *gezeira shava*.[20]

[F1] "From a *heqesh* [topical analogy]: Since the regular sacrifice is a communal sacrifice that supersedes the Sabbath, so too the Passover is a communal sacrifice that supersedes the Sabbath.

[F2] "From a *qal va-homer*:[21] If the regular sacrifice, for which one is not subject [to the punishment of] excision, supersedes the Sabbath, then the Passover, for which one is [subject to the punishment] of excision,—is it not logical that it supersede the Sabbath?[22]

[F3] "From a *gezeira shava:* Just as the regular sacrifice, in connection with which its says *At its appointed time* (Num 28:2), supersedes the Sabbath, so too the Passover, in connection with which it says *At its appointed time* (Num 9:3), supersedes the Sabbath."

[G] They said to him, "Did we think that something good would come from a Babylonian?"[23]

[G1] "The *heqesh* [topical analogy] that you stated can be refuted: What you say of the regular sacrifice, which has a limit [of two per day], you cannot say of [=apply to] the Passover, which has no limit [in the number that may be offered.]"[24]

[G2] "The *qal va-homer* that you stated can be refuted: What you say of the regular sacrifice, which is of the Most Holy [class of] sacrifices, you cannot say of the Passover, which is of the Lesser Holy sacrifices.[25]

[G3] "The *gezeira shava* that you stated—one may not create a *gezeira shava* from his own study [but only if he received it as a tradition from his masters.]"...[26]

[H] Even though he [Hillel] was sitting and expounding for them the whole day, they did not accept it [the ruling] from him until he said to them, "May [harm] befall me if I did not learn thus from Shemaya and Avtalion." As soon as they heard that from him, they rose and appointed him patriarch over them.

[I] As soon as they appointed him patriarch over them he began to rebuke them with words saying, "What caused your need for this Babylonian [=me]? Is it not that you did not serve the two great men of the world, Shemaya and Avtalion, who were dwelling with you?"[27]

[J] As soon as he rebuked them with words the law was concealed from him.[28] They said to him, "What will we do for the people—they did not bring their knives?"

[L] He said to them, "This law I heard and forgot. But leave Israel be. If they are not prophets, they are the sons of prophets."

[M] Immediately, he whose Passover was a lamb stuck it [the knife] in its hair. He whose Passover was a kid tied it between its horns. It turned out that their Passovers brought their knives with them.

[N] As soon as he saw the event, he remembered the law. He said, "Thus I learned from Shemaya and Avtalion."

Chapter 9

THE "OVEN OF AKHNAI": RABBINIC AUTHORITY AND HUMAN DIGNITY (BAVLI BAVA METSIA 59a–59b)

The "Oven of Akhnai" is one of the most frequently cited rabbinic stories in contemporary discussions of rabbinic theology, biblical interpretation and law. In dramatic fashion the rabbis assert not only that the majority has authority over the minority (see chapter 7 herein), but that the sages have authority over God! The sages reject both miracles supporting the minority opinion of R. Eliezer and a heavenly voice stating explicitly that the law follows his opinion with the famous words, "It is not in Heaven" (Deut 30:12). That is, the Torah is no longer in God's control in Heaven but has been entrusted to the rabbis on earth to interpret and administer. And the Torah itself instructs, "Incline after the majority" (Exod 23:2). Paradoxically, the Torah grants the sages the authority to reject God's intentions so as to render decisions according to the normative legal process. The fact that these verses mean something different in their original biblical contexts adds another layer to the paradox.[1] It turns out that the sages have interpreted the verses to give themselves the authority to reject the divine will. Thus their claim to interpretive authority ultimately rests on the very interpretive authority that it claims! Nevertheless, the story reports that God laughed upon being rebuffed and exclaimed, "My sons have defeated me" (G). Much like a father losing to his son in a sporting competition for the first time, God happily accepts this assertion of human independence.

But all this is only part of the story. The plot continues with the rabbis banning R. Eliezer and burning the objects he had ruled pure (H). Apparently they wished to avenge the fact that he refused to accept their authority or to make an example of him. This cruel and extreme measure—to ostracize a sage and cut him off from the community of Torah—kindles God's wrath. R. Eliezer's tears cause the destruction of crops and food, and a storm almost drowns the patriarch Rabban Gamaliel. He temporarily staves off destruction by arguing that he acted for the sake of the legal process, but he dies shortly thereafter when R. Eliezer pours out his pain in prayer. The suffering, destruction and death that result from the conflict among the rabbis contrast sharply with the happy resolution of the conflict between God and the sages. While God tolerates and even approves of humans defeating their "father," God will not allow the "sons" to cause suffering to one another.

A key to the story is the concluding line, Imma Shalom's explanation of the death of Rabban Gamaliel, "All the gates are locked except for the gates of [verbal] wronging" (L). In its talmudic context, the story appears as the climax to a lengthy discussion concerning the sin of "verbal wronging" *(ona'a)*. This is a broad prohibition against all harmful speech, against any utterance that "whitens the face" (=shames), humiliates or causes pain to another human being. According to one tradition that precedes the story, "It is better for a man to throw himself into a fiery furnace, and let him not whiten the face of his fellow in public." Imma Shalom's tradition means that while God has locked "all the gates" such as prayer and tears following the destruction of the temple, that is, although tears and prayer are no longer effective, God nevertheless hears the pain of one who suffers verbal wrong. When R. Eliezer falls on his face to express his pain at the wrongful ban that the sages pronounced upon him, God listens and immediately responds.

Thus the story is not only about the nature and theory of the rabbinic legal process but about how that process must be conducted. In the course of a heated legal debate it is easy to turn from argument to insult, from rejecting an opponent's opinion to rejecting the opponent, from persuasion to humiliation (see chapters 12–14 herein). Nothing was more important to the sages than to shine in the dialectic thrust-and-parry of academic debate; nothing more painful than to be publicly shamed.[2] The story recognizes the importance of the integrity of the legal system, of the will of the majority and of other principles necessary for the legal process to function. But it warns that these principles and abstractions must never be used to justify the real, concrete suffering of an individual. Somehow the sages must negotiate these straits so as to preserve both the integrity of law and the dignity of the individuals who make it.[3]

[A] We learned there: *If he cut it (an oven) into segments and placed sand between the segments, R. Eliezer rules that it is pure and the sages rule that it is impure. And this is the oven of Akhnai* [=Mishna Kelim 5:10].[4]

[B] What is *Akhnai* (=snake)? Rav Yehuda said Shmuel said, "Since they surrounded him with words like this snake and ruled it impure."[5]

[C] It was taught: On that day R. Eliezer responded with all the responses in the world, but they did not accept them from him.

[C1] He said to them, "If the law is as I say, let the carob [tree] prove it." The carob uprooted itself from its place and went 100 cubits—and some say 400 cubits. They said to him, "One does not bring proof from the carob." The carob returned to its place.

[C2] He said to them, "If the law is as I say, let the aqueduct prove it." The water turned backward. They said to him, "One does not bring proof from water." The water returned to its place.

[C3] He said to them, "If it [the law] is as I say, let the walls of the academy prove it." The walls of the academy inclined to fall. R. Yehoshua rebuked them. He said to them, "When sages defeat each other in law, what is it for you?" It was taught: They did not fall because of the honor of R. Yehoshua, and they did not stand because of the honor of R. Eliezer, and they are still inclining and standing.

[D] He said to them, "If it is as I say, let it be proved from Heaven." A heavenly voice went forth and said, "What is it for you with R. Eliezer, since the law is like him in every place?"

[E] R. Yehoshua stood up on his feet and said, "*It is not in Heaven* (Deut 30:12).*"

[F] What is, "It is not in Heaven"? R. Yirmiah said, "We do not listen to a heavenly voice, since you already gave it to us on Mt. Sinai and it is written there, *Incline after the majority* (Exod 23:2)."

[G] R. Natan came upon Elijah. He said to him, "What was the Holy One doing at that time?" He said to him, "He laughed and smiled and said, 'My sons have defeated me, my sons have defeated me.'"[6]

[H] At that time they brought all the objects that R. Eliezer had ruled were pure and burned them and voted and banned him.

[I] They said, "Who will go and inform him?" R. Akiba said to them, "I will go and inform him lest a man who is not fitting goes and informs him and destroys the whole world."[7] What did he do? He dressed in black and covered himself with black and took off his shoes and went and sat before him at a distance of four cubits and his eyes streamed with tears.[8] He [R. Eliezer] said to him, "Akiba, why is this day different from other days?" He said to him, "It seems to me that your colleagues are keeping separate from you." His eyes too streamed with tears, and he took off his shoes and removed [his seat] and sat on the ground.[9]

[J1] The world was smitten in one third of the wheat, one third of the olives and one half of the barley.[10]

[J2] And some say that even the dough in the hands of women swelled up.[11]

[J3] It was taught: It [the destruction] was so great on that day that every place where R. Eliezer cast his eyes immediately was burned.[12]

[K] Also Rabban Gamaliel was on a ship. A wave of the sea stood upon him to drown him.[13] He said, "It seems to me that this is because of [R. Eliezer] the son of Hyrcanus."[14] He stood up on his feet and said, "Master of the universe. I acted not for my honor, nor did I act for the honor of my father's house, but I acted for your honor, in order that disagreements do not multiply in Israel." The sea immediately rested from its anger.[15]

[L] Imma Shalom, the wife of R. Eliezer, was the sister of Rabban Gamaliel.[16] After that event she never allowed him [Eliezer] to fall on his face.[17] That day was the new month and a poor man came and stood at the door. While she was giving him bread she found that he [Eliezer] had fallen on his face. She said, "Stand up. You have killed my brother." Meanwhile the shofar [blast] went out from the House of Rabban Gamaliel [signaling that he had died]. He said to her, "How did you know?" She said to him, "Thus I have received a tradition from my father's house: 'All the gates are locked except for the gates of [verbal] wronging.'"

Chapter 10

THE NEW MONTH AND THE AUTHORITY OF THE PATRIARCH (MISHNA ROSH HASHANA 2:9–11)

The Jewish calendar was not fixed until the fifth century CE. Each month began with the appearance of the new moon and had twenty-nine or thirty days. If the new moon appeared on the thirtieth day of the previous month, then that day became the first of the new month. If the new moon failed to appear, then that month had thirty days and the new month automatically began the next day. To ensure that no mistakes were made, the Mishna prescribes that witnesses testify before a rabbinic court, which would assess their testimony and proclaim the new month.

The calendar was of critical importance because the beginning of the month determined the days for celebrating Jewish festivals, including the offerings sacrificed in the Jerusalem Temple. Control over the calendar was therefore a sign of authority and prestige: he who determined the calendar determined the festivals for the Jewish world. Throughout the Second Temple Period various calendrical systems were used by different Jewish groups. Bitter disputes broke out among the Pharisees, Sadducees and the Dead Sea Sect over this issue. Such tensions persisted into rabbinic times. Rabbinic traditions tell of opposing Jewish groups sending false witnesses to testify that they had seen the moon in order to fix the calendar according to their system.

The following story tells of a conflict among Tannaitic rabbis over the calendar. The story grapples with various aspects of authority.

Rabbinic traditions considered Rabban Gamaliel II (c. 80 CE) to have been the *nasi* or patriarch, the recognized leader of the sages. The story makes a claim for patriarchal authority over the calendar and illustrates the gravity of challenging his power. A related point, expressed primarily in R. Akiba's midrash, is that God has given human beings the authority to set the calendar and to determine the dates of the festivals (E). The Jewish festivals follow the decrees of the human court, not an objective celestial reality. The story also makes a powerful claim for rabbinic judicial authority. R. Dosa b. Harkinas's midrash contends that the decisions rendered by the recognized court cannot be questioned (F). Behind the story is an awareness of the importance of unity within the rabbinic movement and the dangers of the sages splitting into different groups, as had been the case in earlier times. In order to flourish, a religion requires recognized authorities, a common calendar and accepted mechanisms for making decisions.[1]

[A] Rabban Gamaliel had images of forms of the moon on a tablet and on the wall of his upper-story. He would show them to commoners [who came to give testimony about the new moon] and ask: "Did you see [the moon] like this one or like that one?"

[B] Once two came and said, "We saw it [the moon] in the morning in the East, and in the evening in the West." R. Yohanan ben Nuri said, "They are false witnesses." But when they came to Yavneh, Rabban Gamaliel accepted them.[2]

[C] Another time two came and said, "We saw it at the appropriate time. But the following night it could not be seen"—and Rabban Gamaliel accepted them. R. Dosa b. Harkinas said, "They are false witnesses. How can one testify about a woman who gave birth, and the next day her belly is between her teeth?" R. Yehoshua said to him [Dosa]: "I see your words."[3]

[D] Rabban Gamaliel sent to him [R. Yehoshua], "I decree that you come to me with your staff and your money on the day on which Yom Kippur falls according to your [calendrical] reckoning."[4]

[E] R. Akiba went to him [R. Yehoshua] and found him in distress. He [Akiba] said to him, "I can demonstrate that every decision made by Rabban Gamaliel is valid. For it says, *These are the festivals of the Lord, the sacred occasions, which you shall appoint* (Lev 23:4)— whether at their proper times, whether not at their proper times, I have no festivals other than these ones [that *you* appoint]."

[F] He [R. Yehoshua] approached R. Dosa b. Harkinas. He [Dosa] said to him, "If we go and question the [decisions of the] court of Rabban Gamaliel, we should also question [the decisions of] every single court that existed from the time of Moses until now. For it says, *Moses, Aaron, Nadav, Avihu and seventy of the elders of Israel ascended* (Exod 24:9). Why were the names of the elders not specified? To teach that every group of three who stood as a court for Israel—behold, they are like the court of Moses."[5]

[G] He [R. Yehoshua] took his staff and money in his hand, and he went to Yavneh to Rabban Gamaliel on the day that the Day of Atonement fell according to his reckoning. Rabban Gamaliel stood up and kissed him on his head. He said to him, "Come in peace, my master and my student. My master in wisdom, and my student in that you accepted my words."

Chapter 11

AUTHORITY OVER THE CALENDAR

The Jewish lunar calendar with twelve months of twenty-nine or thirty days produces a year of about 354 days. To coordinate the calendar with the solar year, and to ensure that the seasonal festivals fell in the proper seasons, ancient Jews periodically intercalated an extra month (*intercalate* means to add or insert an additional time period). In the fifth century CE the patriarch Hillel II introduced a fixed calendar in which the extra month, Second Adar, was added seven times in a nineteen-year cycle.[1] Before the fixing of the calendar the sages judged each year whether the signs of spring were too far off such that Second Adar should be added.

Who held the authority for setting the calendar? The following story, which appears in both the Bavli and the Yerushalmi, reflects the tensions between the Babylonian and Palestinian sages over this question. These twin rabbinic centers generally worked in tandem. Sages traveled back and forth exchanging traditions and analysis, bringing queries and sending replies. A few issues, however, including the authority to calculate the calendar, sparked conflicts. The calendar was a marker of authority and a leading source of prestige because the entire Jewish world depended on the calendrical authorities to determine the dates of the festivals. Moreover, whichever rabbinic center possessed this authority enjoyed a measure of control over the other.

The dynamics of this conflict in the talmudic period are obscure. Both the Bavli and Yerushalmi versions of the story suggest that the Babylonians attempted to arrogate the authority to intercalate the year, but Palestinian pressure compelled them to stop. We do know that the issue did not die there. In Geonic times (800–1200 CE), when the Babylonian and Palestinian Gaonate competed for the support of the growing diasporic communities, conflicts erupted once again.[2] A particularly nasty confrontation took place in 922 when Aaron ben Meir, the head of the Jerusalem academy, clashed with the Babylonian authorities over the date of Passover. For several years the two communities celebrated the festivals on different days.

One issue that runs through both versions of the story is to what degree authority over the calendar should be vested in those most learned in Torah. The Palestinian delegation informs Hananiah that "the kids you left behind have become goats," that is to say, his former Palestinian students have grown to be sages and leaders (B, f). In the Yerushalmi, Hananiah complains that he should have the authority because of his superior ability to calculate the calendar (G). The Bavli includes a tradition that R. Akiba intercalated the calendar in the diaspora since at that time there were no sages equal to him in Palestine (e). This suggests that in principle the sage with the greatest knowledge deserves the authority. Hence, if the Babylonians are indeed superior in Torah, they are justified in intercalating the calendar again.

The holiness of the Land of Israel and the centrality of Jerusalem and the temple compete with Torah as sources of authority. Both versions of the story compare the sages who intercalate the calendar outside of Israel to renegade priests and Levites who worship at a temple outside of Jerusalem (B, f). This graphic image of violating such a basic tenet of rabbinic theology essentially accuses the Babylonians of heresy; in the Bavli the delegation indeed threatens to place the Babylonian sage under a ban and calls his supporters heretics (f). Both versions also quote the verse, *For Torah shall come forth from Zion, the word of God from Jerusalem* (Isa 2:3), to justify the Palestinian privilege (B, f). The calendar for all Israel should come from its center, the Land of Israel, not from the diaspora.[3]

A. Palestinian Privilege; Babylonian Challenge (1) (Yerushalmi Sanhedrin 1:2, 19a)

[A] Hananiah the nephew of R. Yehoshua intercalated outside of the Land [of Israel].

[B] Rabbi [Yehuda HaNasi] sent three letters to him with R. Yizhaq and R. Natan.
   (1) In one he wrote, "To his holiness Hananiah."
   (2) And in one he wrote, "The kids you left behind have become goats."
   (3) And in one he wrote, "If you do not accept [that the intercalation must be done in the Land of Israel], then go out to the wilderness of Atad. You be the slaughterer [of sacrifices] and let Nehunyon sprinkle [the blood on the altar]."[4]

[C] (1) He [Hananiah] read the first and honored them [R. Yizhaq and R. Natan.]
   (2) He read the second and honored them.
   (3) He read the third and wanted to dishonor them. They said to him, "You cannot, for you already honored us."

[D] R. Yizhaq rose and read [in the Torah], "These are the set times of Hananiah the son of R. Yehoshua's brother." They [the people] said to him, "[No! It says,] *The set times of the Lord* (Lev 23:4)." He said to them, "[That is the reading] with us [but apparently not with you]."[5]

[E] R. Natan rose and read the *haftarah* [from the Prophets], "For Torah shall come forth from Babylonia and the word of God from Nehar Pekod."[6] They said to him, "[No! It says,] *For Torah shall come forth from Zion, the word of God from Jerusalem* (Isa 2:3)." He said to him, "[That is the reading] with us [but apparently not with you]."[7]

[F] He [Hananiah] went and complained about them to R. Yehuda b. Betera in Nisibis [a city in Babylonia.] He [R. Yehuda b. Betera] said to him, "[The calendar is set] according to them, according to them." He [Hananiah] said to him, "Do I not know what I left behind there? What assures me that they know how to calculate [the calendar] as [accurately] as I do?"[8]

[G] [He said to him,] "And [just] because they do not know [how to calculate as accurately] as he [=you], will they listen to him? [But as it is,] because they do know how to calculate [as accurately] as he, he should listen to them."[9]

[H] He[10] arose and rode on his horse. Those [places which] he reached, he reached [and informed them to follow the Palestinian authorities]. Those places he did not reach observe a corrupt [calendar].

❦

B. Palestinian Privilege; Babylonian Challenge (II) (Bavli Berakhot 63a-b)

[a] When Hananiah the nephew of R. Yehoshua went down to the diaspora [Babylonia], he used to intercalate years and fix new moons outside of the Land [of Israel].

[b] They sent to him two scholars, R. Yose b. Kefar and the grandson of Zecharia b. Qevutal. When he saw them he said to them, "Why have you come?" They said to him, "We have come to study Torah." He announced concerning them, "These men are the luminaries of the generation, and their ancestors served in the temple, as we learned, *Zecharia b. Qevutal said, 'Many times I read to him [the high priest] from the Book of Daniel'* (Mishna Yoma 1:6)."[11]

[c] He began to rule impure and they ruled pure. He forbade and they permitted. He announced concerning them, "These men are fraudulent. [These men] are vacuous." They said to him, "You have already built and you cannot destroy. You have already fenced in and you cannot break apart."[12]

[d] He said to them, "Why do I rule impure and you rule pure, I forbid and you permit?" They said to him, "Because you intercalate years and fix new moons outside of the Land [of Israel]."

[e] He said to them, "Did not Akiba b. Yosef intercalate years and fix new moons outside of the Land [of Israel]?" They said to him, "Leave [the case of] R. Akiba, for he left behind no equal [in Torah] in the Land of Israel."

[f] He said to them, "I too left behind no equal in the Land of Israel." They said to him, "The kids you left have become goats with horns, and they sent us to you. They said to us thus: 'Go and speak to him in our name. If he listens—good. If not, let him be under a ban. Speak also to our brethren in the diaspora. If they listen—good. If not, let them go up the mountain. Let Ahia build an altar, let Hananiah play the lute,[13] and let them all be heretics and say, "We have no share in the God of Israel."'"[14]

[g] Immediately all the people broke out in weeping and said, "God forbid! We have a share in the God of Israel."

[h] Why all this? Because it says, *For Torah shall come forth from Zion, the word of God from Jerusalem* (Isa 2:3).

PART III:

LIFE AND DEATH IN THE RABBINIC ACADEMY

Chapter 12

CONFLICT IN THE ACADEMY:
THE DEPOSITION
OF RABBAN GAMALIEL

We know little about the precise workings of the rabbinic study-houses and academies during talmudic times. Throughout the Amoraic period in Babylonia most rabbinic learning probably took place in small disciple circles (200–400 CE). Students congregated around a local master and studied with him for years before moving on to study with another master or to attract disciples of their own.[1] Toward the end of the Amoraic period, after about 400 CE, the rabbis established permanent institutions of higher learning. These rabbinic academies (*beit midrash* or *yeshiva*) were led by a "head of the academy" (*rosh yeshiva*) who directed official study sessions and presided over numerous sages and students. A rigid hierarchy apparently governed the daily protocol. Members of the academy were seated in rows according to their positions within the hierarchy. Sages and disciples honored the head of the academy and the other high offices by rising when they entered or passed by.[2] The situation in Palestine is less clear, but it seems that here too most rabbinic study took place in small schools directed by one sage.[3] In the fourth century larger institutions (usually called "assembly-houses," *beit vaad*) may have been established in the cities of Sepphoris and Tiberias.

Among the most dramatic rabbinic stories are those that describe conflicts in the academies, especially clashes over the positions of leadership. In the following story the sages rebel against the head of the academy, temporarily depose him and appoint another in his stead. While the story is set in the Tannaitic era and features the patriarch Rabban Gamaliel II (died c. 120 CE) and his contemporaries, the description of the assembly house/academy, language and other motifs indicates that a much later story has been projected back upon earlier times. Later storytellers in both Palestine and Babylonia used Tannaitic sages as characters to represent the conflicts of the contemporary institutions and also used the patriarch to represent the head of the academy in their time.

In both Talmuds the conflict is precipitated by the heavy-handed administration of Rabban Gamaliel, in particular his tendency to humiliate other sages. To cause shame was no light matter in rabbinic culture; we have seen in the story of the "Oven of Akhnai" that God severely punishes the rabbis for shaming R. Eliezer (see chapter 9 herein). Both stories depict Rabban Gamaliel as having little care for the poverty in which the other sages toil. Thus he does not know that R. Yehoshua is a needle-maker (K) or smith (k) until he visits R. Yehoshua's house. One senses in the background a growing distance between the leaders atop the rabbinic hierarchy and the rest of the sages.

The story deals in part with the issue of eligibility for the highest positions in the academic hierarchy. There is a strong emphasis on lineage (see also chapter 13 herein). The sages pass over R. Akiba because he has no illustrious ancestors and choose R. Eleazar, in part because he is "tenth [generation] in descent from Ezra" (D, d). Moreover, when R. Yehoshua instructs the sages to give Rabban Gamaliel his position back, he uses imagery that stresses priestly descent (m, M). "Sprinkler" and "ashes" refer to the priest who sprinkled the ashes of the red heifer in the purification ceremony described in Numbers 19:1–22. When he compares Rabban Gamaliel to "sprinkler son of a sprinkler" he seems to mean that he is of the pedigree and dynasty that rightfully leads the academy. Likewise the robe he invokes is the special garment worn by priests when serving in the temple (L). By suggesting that taking Gamaliel's position is analogous to taking "the robe" from the priest who rightfully wears it, he indicates that Gamaliel too enjoys a hereditary right to his office. This is probably why the ousting is temporary. The storytellers seem to believe that a certain family dynasty deservedly leads the academy, but they wish that the leaders were more sympathetic to the rank and file of the sages.

A prominent theme in the Bavli version is the accessibility of Torah. Rabban Gamaliel had placed a guard at the door of the academy to keep out unworthy students but subsequently realizes that he has "held back Torah from Israel" (f, h). During his demotion 400 or 700 benches of students are added, thus opening the doors of Torah to thousands of students (g).[4] The increased brain-power in turn enables the sages to resolve every "single law pending in the academy," that is, to decide all the previously intractable questions (i). Even the issue they discuss at length, whether an Ammonite may convert to Judaism, deals with the matter of inclusion and exclusion (j).[5] An important message of the story is that Torah study should be as inclusive as possible. It is hard to know what, if any, historical reality lies behind this theme. Perhaps some sages (the leaders of the academy?) saw themselves as an elite social class and attempted to exclude the common people from higher studies of Torah. The Yerushalmi version lacks this concern.

In these and the following stories one sees that the storytellers experienced the academy as a place of conflict—the Bavli even uses the metaphor of "shield-bearers" to describe the sages (b). They waged the "war of Torah," thrusting and parrying in the give and take of dispute, attacking weak arguments and defending their rulings from assault. This kind of metaphoric battle was an inherent part of rabbinic activity within the academy. Yet when sages crossed the line and shamed or insulted others, the conflict turned from legal controversy to the personal struggles represented in the stories. Both versions of the story narrate a transition from conflict to reconciliation and compromise. They instruct the sages that the study of Torah should be pursued in a harmonious environment.[6]

A. Gamaliel the Tyrant
(Yerushalmi Berakhot 4:1, 7c-d)[7]

[A] Once a certain student came and asked R. Yehoshua, "The evening prayer—what is its status?" He said to him, "Optional." He went and asked Rabban Gamaliel, "The evening prayer—what is its status?" He said to him, "Obligatory."[8] He said to him, "And yet R. Yehoshua said to me 'Optional.'" He said to him, "When I enter the assembly house tomorrow, stand up and ask about that law."

[B] The next day that student stood up and asked Rabban Gamaliel, "The evening prayer—what is its status?" He said to him, "Obligatory." He said to him, "And yet R. Yehoshua said to me 'Optional.'" Rabban Gamaliel said to R. Yehoshua, "Are you the one who said 'Optional'?" He said to him, "No." He said to him, "Stand on your feet that they may bear witness against you."

[D] Rabban Gamaliel was sitting and expounding while R. Yehoshua stood on his feet until all the people murmured and said to Hutspit the *meturgeman*, "Dismiss the people." They said to Zenon the *hazzan*, "Say 'Begin.'"[9] He said "Begin," and all the people stood on their feet and said to him [Rabban Gamaliel], *"Who has not suffered from your constant malice? (Nah 3:19)."*[10] They went and appointed R. Eleazar b. Azariah to [lead] the assembly. He was sixteen years old, and his entire head became full of white hair.[11] Rabbi Akiba was sitting and feeling upset [that he was not selected]. He said, "Not that he knows more Torah than I, but he is the descendant of greater men than I. Happy is the man whose ancestors have gained merit for him. Happy is the man who has a peg on which to hang." And what was the peg of R. Eleazar b. Azariah? He was tenth generation [in descent] from Ezra.

[G] And how many benches were there? R. Yaakov b. Sisi said, "Eighty benches of students were there, excluding those standing beyond the fence." R. Yose b. R. Avun said, "Three hundred were there, excluding those standing beyond the fence."

[I]   (This refers to what we have learned elsewhere, *On the day they seated R. Eleazar b. Azariah in the assembly* [Mishna Yadaim 3:5].[12] We learned elsewhere, *R. Eleazar expounded this interpretation to the sages at the vineyard in Yavneh* [Mishna Ketubot 4:6]. But was there a vineyard there? Rather, these are the students who used to assemble in rows like a vineyard.[13])

[K]   Immediately Rabban Gamaliel went and apologized to each and every one in his own house. He went to R. Yehoshua and found him sitting and making needles. He said to him, "From these you make your living?" He said to him, "You did not know this until now? Woe be the generation whose chief you are!" He [Rabban Gamaliel] said to him, "I apologize to you."

[L]   They sent a certain laundryman to R. Eleazar b. Azariah, and some say it was R. Akiba.[14]

[M]   He said to him, "Let a sprinkler, the son of a sprinkler, sprinkle. Should he who is neither a sprinkler nor the son of a sprinkler say to a sprinkler, the son of a sprinkler, your water is cave water and your ashes are common ashes?"[15] He [R. Eleazar b. Azariah] said to them [the sages], "If you are satisfied, let you and me rise early to the door of Rabban Gamaliel."[16]

[N]   Nevertheless, they did not demote him [R. Eleazar b. Azariah] from his high office but appointed him head of the court.[17]

B. Gamaliel the Elitist
(Bavli Berakhot 27b-28a)

[a]   Our sages have taught. Once a certain student came before R. Yehoshua. He said to him, "The evening prayer—optional or

obligatory?" He said to him, "Optional." He came before Rabban Gamaliel. He said to him, "The evening prayer—optional or obligatory?" He said to him, "Obligatory." He said to him, "But did not R. Yehoshua say to me, 'Optional.'" He said to him, "Wait until the shield-bearers [the sages] enter the academy."[18]

[b] When the shield-bearers entered, the questioner stood up and asked, "The evening prayer—optional or obligatory?" Rabban Gamaliel said to him, "Obligatory." Rabban Gamaliel said to the sages, "Is there anyone who disagrees on this matter?" R. Yehoshua said to him, "No." Rabban Gamaliel said to him, "But did not they say to me in your name, 'Optional'?" He said to him, "Yehoshua! Stand on your feet that they may bear witness against you."

[c] R. Yehoshua stood on his feet and said, "If I were alive and he [the student] dead—the living could contradict the dead. Now that I am alive and he is alive—how can the living contradict the living?"

[d] Rabban Gamaliel was sitting and expounding while R. Yehoshua stood on his feet, until all the people murmured and said to Hutspit the *turgeman*,[19] "Stop!" and he stopped. They said, "How long will he [Rabban Gamaliel] go on distressing [R. Yehoshua]?

   (1) He distressed him last year on Rosh HaShana.[20]

   (2) He distressed him in [the matter of] the firstling, in the incident involving R. Zadoq.[21]

   (3) Now he distresses him again.

Come, let us depose him. Whom will we raise up [in his place]?

   (1) Shall we raise up R. Yehoshua? He is involved in the matter.

   (2) Shall we raise up R. Akiba? Perhaps he [Rabban Gamaliel] will harm him, since he has no ancestral merit.

   (3) Rather let us raise up R. Eleazar b. Azariah, for he is wise, and he is wealthy, and he is tenth [in descent] from Ezra.

   (1) He is wise—so that if anyone asks a difficult question, he will be able to solve it.

(2) He is wealthy—in case he has to pay honor to the emperor.

(3) And he is tenth in descent from Ezra—he has ancestral merit and he [Rabban Gamaliel] will not be able to harm him."²²

[e] They said to him, "Would our Master consent to be the head of the academy?" He said to them, "Let me go and consult with the members of my household." He went and consulted his wife.

(1) She said to him, "Perhaps they will reconcile with him and depose you?" He said to her, "There is a tradition, *One raises the level of holiness but does not diminish it* (Mishna Menahot 11:7)."²³

(2) She said to him, "Perhaps he [Rabban Gamaliel] will harm you?" He said, "Let a man use a valuable cup for one day even if it breaks on the morrow."

(3) She said to him, "You have no white hair." That day he was eighteen years old. A miracle happened for him and he was crowned with eighteen rows of white hair. (This explains what R. Eleazar b. Azariah said [elsewhere], *One recites the [paragraph about] the redemption from Egypt at night. R. Eleazar b. Azariah said: Behold I am as seventy years old...* (Mishna Berakhot 1:5), and not "[I am] seventy years old.")²⁴

[f] It was taught: That day they removed the guard of the gate and gave students permission to enter. For Rabban Gamaliel had decreed, "Any student whose inside is not like his outside may not enter the academy."

[g] That day many benches were added. R. Yohanan said, "Abba Yosef b. Dostenai and the sages disagree. One said, 'Four hundred benches were added.' And one said, 'Seven hundred benches were added.'"

[h] Rabban Gamaliel became distressed. He said, "Perhaps, God forbid, I held back Torah from Israel." They showed him in a dream white casks filled with ashes.²⁵ But that was not the case, they showed him [the dream] only to put his mind at peace [but he really had held back Torah.]

[i] It was taught, "They taught [Tractate] Eduyyot on that day." (And anywhere that it says *On that day* [in the Mishna]—[refers to] that day.)[26] And there was not a single law pending in the academy that they did not resolve.

[j] And even Rabban Gamaliel did not hold himself back from Torah. For it was taught:

> *On that day Yehuda the Ammonite proselyte stood before them in the academy. He said to them, "Am I [permitted] to enter the congregation of Israel [= to convert]?" Rabban Gamaliel said to him, "You are forbidden." R. Yehoshua said to him, "You are permitted." Rabban Gamaliel said, "Is it not written,* No Ammonite or Moabite shall be admitted into the congregation of the Lord *(Deut 23:4)"? R. Yehoshua said to him, "And are Ammon and Moab in their [original] places? Sennacherib King of Assyria has since come up and mixed up all the nations, as it says,* I have erased the borders of peoples; I have plundered their treasures and exiled their vast populations *(Isa 10:13). And whatever separates, separates from the majority."[27] Rabban Gamaliel said to him, "Has it not already been said,* I will restore the fortunes of the Ammonites—declares the Lord *(Jer 49:6), and they have already been restored"? R. Yehoshua said to him, "Has it not already been said,* I will restore my people Israel *(Amos 9:14), and they have not yet been restored"? Immediately they permitted him to enter the congregation (Mishna Yadaim 4:4).*

[k] Rabban Gamaliel said, "I will go and appease R. Yehoshua."[28] When he arrived at his house, he saw that the walls of his house were black. He said to him, "From the walls of your house it is evident that you are a smith." He said to him, "Woe to the generation whose chief you are, for you do not know the distress of the scholars, how they earn a living and how they subsist." He said to him, "I apologize to you. Forgive me." He [R. Yehoshua] paid no attention to him. [Rabban Gamaliel said,] "Do it for the honor of my father's house."[29] He said to him, "You are forgiven."

[l] They said, "Who will go and tell the rabbis [that we have reconciled]?" A certain laundryman said, "I will go." R. Yehoshua sent [word] to the academy, "Let him who wears the robe wear the robe. Should one who does not wear the robe say to one who wears the robe, 'Take off your robe and I will wear it'?" R. Akiba said, "Lock the doors so that the servants of Rabban Gamaliel cannot come in and distress the sages."[30]

[m] R. Yehoshua went and knocked on the door. He said, "Let a sprinkler, the son of a sprinkler, sprinkle. Should he who is neither a sprinkler nor the son of a sprinkler say to a sprinkler, the son of a sprinkler, your water is cave water and your ashes are common ashes?" R. Akiba said to R. Yehoshua, "Have you been appeased? We acted only for the sake of your honor. Tomorrow you and I will rise early to his [Gamaliel's] door."

[n] They said, "What shall we do?
(1) Shall we depose him [R. Eleazar b. Azariah]? There is a tradition, *One raises the level of holiness but not does not diminish it* (Mishna Menahot 7:11).
(2) Shall this master expound on one Sabbath and that master on the next? He [Rabban Gamaliel] will not accept that since he will be jealous of him."
(3) Rather, they ordained that Rabban Gamaliel would expound three Sabbaths and R. Eleazar b. Azariah one Sabbath.
(This explains the tradition, *Whose Sabbath was it? It was [the Sabbath] of R. Eleazar b. Azariah* [Tosefta Sotah 7:9].)[31]

[o] And that student [who asked the original question] was R. Shimon bar Yohai.[32]

Chapter 13

LEADERSHIP OF THE ACADEMY: LINEAGE OR TORAH? (BAVLI HORAYOT 13b–14a)

While the previous story tells of a successful, if temporary, deposition of the patriarch, the following story describes a plot that failed. Here too we deal with a late Babylonian tale projected upon Tannaitic times that uses the earlier sages as characters.[1] The story probably took shape in the post-Amoraic academy well into the age of the redaction of the Talmud (fifth to seventh centuries CE).

The fundamental question of the story is the primacy of lineage or knowledge of Torah as the basis for positions of academic leadership and the accompanying honors. Rabbis Meir and Natan, who occupy the second and third positions in the academic hierarchy, plan to depose Rabban Shimon b. Gamaliel from his position of leadership when they find that he has reduced their honors so as to distinguish his status from their own. The two rabbis object that they know more Torah than the patriarch, who probably represents the head of the Babylonian academy, hence they should receive equal, if not greater, honors (D). Rabban Shimon b. Gamaliel's claim to his position as patriarch, in contrast, devolves from his lineage. His rebuke of R. Natan emphasizes that R. Natan's admittedly impressive lineage does not qualify him for the position of patriarch (I). In the next generation Rabban Shimon b. Gamaliel's son, R. Yehuda HaNasi, informs his son, R. Shimon, of how R. Meir threatened "your honor and the honor of your father's house" (J). The challenge was not to Rabban Shimon b. Gamaliel alone, but to their dynasty, by virtue of which each holds the highest office.

The movement of the plot clearly favors Rabban Shimon b. Gamaliel and his family. Not only does he successfully meet the challenge posed by R. Meir and R. Natan, but he turns the tables on the sages and stymies them with his knowledge (G). R. Meir and R. Natan attempt to depose the patriarch and move a step up the academic hierarchy, but they lose their positions and find themselves exiled from the academy. R. Natan humbles himself with an apology, while Meir is not rehabilitated until after his death and even then bears a lasting stigma (I-J). Yet Rabban Shimon b. Gamaliel's triumph is by no means absolute. The students force him to re-admit R. Meir and R. Natan to the academy because they need the sages' knowledge of Torah (H). Even the attenuated punishment, the effacement of the rabbis' names, does not last.

Thus the story offers a warning to sages like R. Meir and R. Natan who may be tempted to stake a claim to the highest academic rank based on their knowing more Torah than the "patriarch," the current head of the academy. They had better tread carefully lest they find themselves banished from the academy due to the "patriarch's" power. At the same time, the story sounds a warning to any head of the academy who lags behind his colleagues in Torah knowledge. Perhaps he should be careful about insisting on displays of honor when around sages more proficient than he. Rabban Shimon b. Gamaliel survived the threat due to the fortunate intervention of R. Yaakov b. Qudshai (E-F), but there is no guarantee that the next "patriarch" (=head of the academy) will be so lucky.

Most surprising about the story is that knowledge of Torah, normally the leading value in Babylonian rabbinic culture, does not determine academic rank. Yet we know from other sources that Babylonian Jewry placed extremely high value on lineage.[2] Priests (kohanim), who enjoyed high status before 70 CE by virtue of their serving in the temple, continued to be respected in the rabbinic period. In the Geonic era (c. 700–1100 CE) rabbinic society became increasingly dynastic as the heads of the academy were selected exclusively from a few leading families. Judging by the story, that situation seems to have started already in late talmudic times. These twin values of Torah and lineage, achievement and birth, create a defining tension of Jewish culture.[3]

The theme of shame in the academy features prominently in this story (see the previous and following stories as well), and in particular, the experience of a loss of face in the course of academic debate. Sages distinguished themselves by shining in the questions, answers and give and take of discussion, and felt deep shame when unable to answer as their colleagues and students looked on. When R. Meir and R. Natan attempt to shame Rabban Shimon b. Gamaliel, they not only aim at measure-for-measure punishment for his promoting his personal honor, but they assault the very basis of academic standing. The shocked reaction of R. Yaakov b. Qudshai and harsh retribution of Rabban Shimon b. Gamaliel should be seen against this background.

To understand the story we must briefly review Tosefta Sanhedrin 7:8, the source prescribing the types of honor shown to the leaders of the rabbinic hierarchy.[4] This Tosefta paragraph appears in the talmudic discussion that precedes the story:

[a] When the patriarch enters all stand and they may not sit until he says to them "sit."

[b] When the head of the court enters, they make a row for him on one side [by standing up], and a row for him on the other side, until he sits in his place.

[c] When the sage[5] enters one stands and one sits until he sits in his place.[6]

The story claims that Rabban Shimon b. Gamaliel instituted this teaching in order to promote his own honor at the expense of his fellows. Prior to this act, so the story runs, all officers were shown equal honor. We thus have another example of a story that supplies an etiology for a rabbinic law (see chapter 2 herein).[7]

[A] R. Yohanan said, "This teaching [=Tosefta Sanhedrin 7:8] was taught in the days of Rabban Shimon b. Gamaliel."

[B] Rabban Shimon b. Gamaliel—patriarch. R. Meir—sage. R. Natan—head of the court. When Rabban Shimon b. Gamaliel would enter [the academy], everyone would rise before him. When R. Meir and R. Natan would enter, everyone would rise before them. Rabban Shimon b. Gamaliel said, "Should there not be a distinction between me and them?" He enacted (taqqen) this teaching [=Tosefta Sanhedrin 7:8].

[C] On that day, R. Meir and R. Natan were not there. On the morrow, when they came, they saw that they [the rabbis of the academy] did not rise before them as usual. They said, "What is this?" They said to them, "Thus Rabban Shimon b. Gamaliel enacted (taqqen)."

[D] R. Meir said to R. Natan, "I am sage and you are head of the court. Let us fix (netaqqen) something for ourselves."[8] R. Natan said to him, "What shall we do (na'aveid)?" [Meir said,] "We will say to him, 'Teach us [Tractate] Uqtsin,' which he does not know.[9] And because he has not learned [it], we will say to him, 'Who can tell the mighty acts of God, make all his praise heard? (Ps 106:2). For whom is it pleasing to tell the mighty acts of the Lord? For him who is able to make all his praise heard.'[10] We will depose him (na'avrei)[11] and then you will be patriarch and I will be head of the court."

[E] R. Yaakov b. Qudshai heard them. He said, "Perhaps, God forbid, it will result in shame?" He went and sat behind the upper-story of Rabban Shimon b. Gamaliel. He repeated and taught [Tractate Uqtsin], repeated and taught.[12]

[F] He [Rabban Shimon b. Gamaliel] said, "What is before me? Perhaps, God forbid, there was some matter in the academy?!" He paid attention, looked into it and repeated it.

[G] The next day they [R. Meir and R. Natan] said to him, "Let the master teach us from [Tractate] Uqtsin." He opened and taught. After he stymied [R. Meir and R. Natan], he said to them,

"Had I not learned it, you would have shamed me."[13] He ordered and they removed them from the academy.[14]

[H] They [R. Meir and R. Natan] would write objections on slips of paper and throw [them into the academy]. That which he [Rabban Shimon b. Gamaliel] solved, he solved. That which was not solved, they [R. Meir and R. Natan] wrote the solutions and threw them [in]. R. Yose said to them [the rabbis], "Torah is outside and we are inside?" Rabban Shimon b. Gamaliel said to them, "We will bring them in. However, we will penalize them such that we do not say traditions in their names." They designated R. Meir "Others" and R. Natan "Some say."[15]

[I] They showed them in their dreams, "Go and appease Rabban Shimon b. Gamaliel."[16] R. Natan went. R. Meir did not go. He said, "Dreams neither help nor hinder."[17] When R. Natan went he [Rabban Shimon b. Gamaliel] said to him, "Perhaps the belt of your father benefited you in making you the head of the court. Shall it benefit you to make you patriarch?"[18]

[J] Rabbi [Yehuda HaNasi] taught his son R. Shimon, "Others say, 'If it had been an exchanged beast, it would not have been offered.'"[19] He said to him, "Who are those ['others'] whose waters we drink and whose names we do not mention?" He said to him, "They are men who tried to uproot your honor and the honor of your father's house." He said to him, "*Their loves, their hates, their jealousies have long since perished* (Qoh 9:6)." He said to him, "*The enemy is no more; the ruins last forever* (Ps 9:7)." He said to him, "This applies only when their actions benefited [them]. As for these, their actions did not benefit [them]." He then taught, "*They said in the name of R. Meir, 'If it had been an exchanged beast, it would not have been offered'* [=Mishna Bekhorot 9:8]."[20]

[K] Rava said, "Even Rabbi [Yehuda HaNasi], who was extremely humble, said, 'They said in the name of R. Meir.' He did not say, 'R. Meir said.'"[21]

Chapter 14

THE SAGA OF RAV KAHANA: THE TORAH OF BABYLONIA VS. THE TORAH OF PALESTINE (BAVLI BAVA QAMA 117a–b)

We have seen that Babylonian and Palestinian rabbis competed for authority over the Jewish calendar (chapter 11). Each rabbinic community believed that its Torah was of higher quality, its traditions purer, its sages brighter. The following story from the Babylonian Talmud makes a strong claim for the superiority of the Torah of the Babylonians. The climax tells how the Babylonian sage Rav Kahana explained to R. Yohanan, head of the Tiberian school and the greatest Palestinian sage of his age (c. 220–50 CE), every point of law that was unclear to him. This prompted R. Yohanan to concede that while he had believed that Torah "was yours," that the Palestinians had mastered it, he now realized that it "was theirs," that the Babylonians were more proficient (K). Besides knowing more law, Rav Kahana is far more brilliant than his Palestinian colleagues. He easily propounds objections to the discourses of Resh Laqish and R. Yohanan, thus demonstrating his superior dialectic ability (D, G). In a scene that would have made any Palestinian sage cringe, R. Yohanan describes himself in relation to Rav Kahana as a student before a teacher (I). And Rav Kahana was by no means the brightest of the Babylonians!

The language, manuscript traditions and motifs of the story suggest that it was composed in Babylonia late in the talmudic period.[1] The word for "cushions" is Persian, and the image of a sage sitting atop six or seven cushions appears frequently in Persian art and literature (G). Most significant, the description of the academy with rows of students sitting before the master represents the arrangement of the Babylonian academy in late talmudic and Geonic times. The story may date to the sixth or seventh centuries CE when the Palestinian rabbinic community experienced a period of decline while the Babylonian academies were flourishing.

Two prominent themes in the story are dialectical argumentation and shame. In late Babylonian rabbinic culture the give and take of talmudic debate was considered the highest form of Torah and the true measure of brilliance. A sage demonstrated his abilities by being able to raise "objections" or "difficulties" and to answer them with responses and solutions. Here Rav Kahana's capacity to make objections and solutions earns him recognition as a "lion," while his apparent inability to do so renders him a mere "fox" (D, E). The images of Rav Kahana moving back and forward through rows of students depending on whether he raises objections or not, and of R. Yohanan moving further down from his mound of cushions each time he fails to provide a solution, give concrete representation to the status conferred by dialectical argumentation (E, G).

To lose a debate, to fail to answer an objection directed against one's teaching, produces shame or embarrassment, one of the most important concerns of the Bavli (see chapter 13 and the other chapters in this part). For this reason Rav warns Rav Kahana that he must not speak up while R. Yohanan speaks. He knows that R. Yohanan will feel ashamed when he cannot answer Rav Kahana's brilliant objections and therefore disaster will result. Sure enough, when R. Yohanan becomes "embarrassed," albeit at the mistaken belief that Rav Kahana laughed at him, Rav Kahana dies.[2] Rav Kahana, for his part, experiences shame at being perceived as an inferior student while refraining from objecting (F). To avoid feeling ashamed when holding back a pointed response, while simultaneously not shaming another sage for fear of severe punishment, was undoubtedly a tricky path to tread.

The story has a highly developed literary character. The seven years of silence, seven cushions and seven rows of students create thematic parallels (C, E, G). The metaphors of the lion and fox, the supernatural snake, the magical opening of the cave and the resurrection contribute to the dramatic force.[3]

[A] A certain man intended to reveal another man's straw [to the Persian tax authorities.] He came before Rav. He [Rav] said to him, "Do not reveal it! Do not reveal it." He said to him, "I will reveal it! I will reveal it!"

[B] Rav Kahana was sitting before Rav. He stood up and tore out his [the man's] windpipe. [He said,] *"Your sons lie in a swoon at the corner of every street, like an antelope caught in a net* (Isa 51:20). Just as they never show mercy to an antelope once it has fallen into a net, so the idolaters never show mercy to the money of Jews once it has fallen into their hands."[4]

[C] Rav said to him, "Kahana, until now there was the kingdom of the Greeks, who were not strict about bloodshed [and allowed us to administer capital punishment]. But now there is the [kingdom of the] Persians, who are strict about bloodshed.[5] Rise and go up to the Land of Israel and accept upon yourself that you do not raise objections to [the teaching of] R. Yohanan for seven years."

[D] He went [there] and came upon Resh Laqish, who was sitting and reviewing the daily lesson before the rabbis. He [Rav Kahana] said to them, "Where is Resh Laqish?" They said to him, "What for?" He told them this objection and that objection, this solution and that solution. They went and told Resh Laqish. Resh Laqish went and said to R. Yohanan, "A lion has come up from Babylonia. Let the master look deeply into the lesson for tomorrow."

[E] The next day they seated him [Rav Kahana] in the first row [of sages]. He [R. Yohanan] said a tradition and he [Rav Kahana] did not object. He said [another] tradition and he did not object. They seated him back through seven rows until he was in the last row. R. Yohanan said to Resh Laqish, "The lion you mentioned has become a fox."

[F] He [Rav Kahana] said, "May it be [God's] will that these seven rows take the place of the seven years that Rav told me [not to raise objections]." He stood up on his feet. He said, "Let the master go back to the beginning."

[G] He [R. Yohanan] said a tradition and he [Rav Kahana] objected [until] they placed him in the first row. He said a tradition and he objected. R. Yohanan was sitting on seven cushions. They removed a cushion from under him. He said a tradition and he objected to him, until they removed all the cushions from under him and he was sitting on the ground.

[H] R. Yohanan was an old man and his eyelids sagged [over his eyes]. He said to them, "Lift up my eyes that I may see him." They lifted up [his eyelids] with a silver stick. He saw that his [Rav Kahana's] lip was split. He thought that he was laughing at him. He became embarrassed, and he [Rav Kahana] died [as divine punishment for causing R. Yohanan to feel ashamed].

[I] The next day R. Yohanan said to the rabbis, "Did you see how that Babylonian acted?" They said to him, "That's the way he is [he has a split lip]." He [R. Yohanan] went to his [burial] cave. He saw that a snake was coiled about it. He said, "Snake! Snake! Open the door and let the master approach his student." It did not open. [He said,] "Let a colleague approach his colleague." It did not open. [He said,] "Let a student approach his teacher." It opened for him.

[J] He prayed and revived him. He said to him, "Had I known that that is the way you are, I would not have felt embarrassed. Now, sir, come with us to the academy." He said, "If you can pray that I will never die again [because of you], I will go with you. If not, I won't go." He said, "I cannot, for when times change, that which changes, changes."[6]

[K] He [R. Yohanan] asked him [Rav Kahana] all his doubts [regarding points of law] and he [Rav Kahana] resolved them for him. This is [the meaning] of what R. Yohanan said, "What I thought was yours [=I thought the Torah was the Palestinians'] was theirs [the Babylonians']."

Chapter 15

THE TRAGEDY OF R. YOHANAN AND RESH LAQISH: GIVE ME DIALECTICS OR GIVE ME DEATH! (BAVLI BAVA METSIA 84a)

This account of the third-century Palestinian sages R. Yohanan and R. Shimon b. Laqish (Resh Laqish) is a fictional composition of the Bavli storytellers. They portray Resh Laqish as a brigand who was so enamored with R. Yohanan's beauty that he gave up his trade and became R. Yohanan's pupil, a devoted student of Torah. (R. Yohanan's great beauty is praised in several talmudic passages.) Rabbinic sources frequently compare the relationship of a rabbinic master and his student to that of a father and child because of the close affinity forged over years of study. Here the physical attraction and implied love suggest that some sages bonded with the deepest of friendships as well.[1]

Yet the disputes and conflicts of the academy could strain even the strongest of friendships. R. Yohanan and Resh Laqish turn from legal dispute to personal insults, a slippage we have seen in other stories (C).[2] And R. Yohanan takes such great offense at the falling out that Resh Laqish dies, divine punishment for his causing R. Yohanan shame or distress.[3] In the intense climate of the academy, the break-ups of colleagues or students and their masters were as painful as the deterioration of marriages or families. Indeed, to stress the closeness of their relationship the story has Resh Laqish marry R. Yohanan's sister (A). The two were not only friends, colleagues and teacher and pupil, but brothers-in-law.

A key theme is the importance of dialectic debate and a study-partner with whom to lock horns. In the later Babylonian academies, the give and take of talmudic debate was considered the highest form of Torah (see chapters 13–14 herein). R. Yohanan finds no comfort in the vast knowledge of R. Eleazar b. Pedat (E). Simply to be informed of other traditions that confirm one's ruling brings little intellectual stimulation and leaves the Torah static. Ideal study involves challenge and dissent: Resh Laqish objected to R. Yohanan's every statement with twenty-four difficulties, which in turn generated numerous responses. Through this dynamic process "traditions expanded"—Torah proliferated as new lines of analysis were added to the corpus. Such study, for the rabbis, was the real stuff of academic life. Its absence, so we learn, meant intellectual death: without a study-partner R. Yohanan descends into such depression that the rabbis pray that God put him out of his misery: Give me dialectics or give me death![4]

[A] One day R. Yohanan was swimming in the Jordan [River]. Resh Laqish saw him and thought he was a woman. He crossed the Jordan after him [by] sticking his spear in the Jordan and vaulting to the other side of the Jordan. When R. Yohanan saw R. Shimon b. Laqish he said to him, "Your strength for Torah." He [Resh Laqish] said to him, "Your beauty for women." He said to him, "If you return [repent] I will give you my sister, who is more beautiful than I."[5] He consented. He tried to return [by vaulting back to the other side] to bring his clothing, but he was not able.[6] He [R. Yohanan] taught him scripture and Mishna and made him a great man.

[B] One day they disagreed in the academy:

"The sword and the knife and the dagger and the saw and the spear—when are they subject to impurity? When their manufacture is complete."[7]

And when is their manufacture complete? R. Yohanan said, "When they temper them in an oven." Resh Laqish said, "When they furbish them in water."

[C] He [R. Yohanan] said to him, "A brigand knows brigandage." He [Resh Laqish] said to him, "So how did you benefit me? There [when I was a brigand leader] they called me 'Master.' Here they call me 'Master.'" He said to him, "I benefited you in bringing you under the wings of the Divine Presence." R. Yohanan felt insulted *(halish daatei)*. Resh Laqish became ill *(halish)* [as punishment for causing R. Yohanan to feel hurt].

[D] His [R. Yohanan's] sister came and wept before him. She said to him, "Look at me!" He paid no attention to her. She said to him, "Look at these orphans." He said to her, "*Leave your orphans with me* (Jer 49:11)." She said to him, "Do it for the sake of my widowhood." He said to her, "*Let your widows rely on me* (Jer 49:11)."

[E] Resh Laqish died, and R. Yohanan grieved for him greatly. The rabbis said, "What can we do to restore his peace of mind? Let us get R. Eleazar b. Pedat and place him before him [R. Yohanan], for his traditions are ready." They brought him and seated him before him. For every issue that R. Yohanan mentioned he said, "There is a teaching that supports you." He [R. Yohanan] said to him, "Do I need this?" When I made a statement, the son of Laqish would object with twenty-four objections and I would solve them with twenty-four solutions, and thus our traditions expanded. But you say, 'There is a teaching that supports you.' Do I not know that my statements are accurate?" He tore his clothes and went crying at the gates, "Where are you, son of Laqish?" He could not be consoled.[8] The sages prayed for him, and he died.

Chapter 16

THE TRAGEDY OF HONI: GIVE ME FELLOWSHIP OR GIVE ME DEATH! (BAVLI TAANIT 23a)

The following story offers a good illustration of how rabbinic storytellers transformed folktales into narratives that incorporate biblical interpretation and relate to rabbinic life. The first half of the story employs the common folk motif of a man who falls asleep for many years and awakes to find the world a changed place (A-D). In this case the protagonist, Honi the Circle-Drawer, learns that one should better the world for the sake of the coming generations even if one will not benefit directly from one's labors. Honi's experience, however, serves not only to teach him this lesson but to help him understand a puzzling biblical verse that compares the seventy-year Babylonian exile to a dream (A). Just as Honi did not sense the passing of time, so the exiles who returned to Zion after seventy years felt as if they had awakened after a brief dream.

The second half of the story portrays Honi as a sage and shifts the focus to the rabbinic study-house (E-G).[1] Indeed, Honi was such a brilliant scholar that the students still recall his ability to solve all the difficult questions encountered by his colleagues. Unfortunately, while the students remember Honi's mastery of Torah, they do not believe that Honi is who he claims to be and do not honor him. As we have seen in several other stories (chapters 9, 13, 14, 15), shame or the lack of appropriate academic honor can be deadly. Rava's application of a popular proverb about the need for companionship—here understood as scholastic fellowship—recalls the importance of a study-partner with whom a rabbi can debate and argue (see chapter 15). Lacking academic honor and a study-partner, two essentials of rabbinic life, Honi prays for death.

[A] R. Yohanan said: All his life that righteous man [Honi the Circle-Drawer] was troubled by the scripture, *When the Lord restored those who returned to Zion we were like dreamers* (Ps 126:1). He thought, "How can seventy years compare to a dream [that lasts] one night?"[2]

[B] One day he was walking along his way when he saw a certain man planting carob trees. He said to him, "A carob tree does not bear [fruit] for seventy years. Are you so sure that you will live seventy years and will eat from it?" He said to him, "I found the world with carob trees. Just as my ancestors planted for me, so I plant for my offspring."

[C] He [Honi] sat down to eat his bread. Sleep came upon him. While he slept, a grotto surrounded him and concealed him from sight.

[D] He slept for seventy years. When he awoke he saw a man gathering carobs from that carob tree and eating them. He said to him, "Do you know who planted that carob tree?" He said to him, "My father's father." He said, "Then seventy years were like a dream!"

[E] He went to his home. He said to them, "Does the son of Honi the Circle-Drawer yet live?" They said to him, "He is no more, but his grandson lives." He said to them, "I am he." They did not believe him.

[F] He went to the study-house. He heard the sages saying, "Our traditions are as clear today as in the years of Honi the Circle-Drawer. For when he entered the study-house, he solved every difficulty that the sages had. He said to them, "I am he." They did not believe him, and they did not treat him with the honor that he deserved. He prayed for mercy and his soul departed.

[G] Rava said, "Thus people say, 'Either fellowship or death.'"[3]

PART IV:

HOLY MEN AND RABBINIC MASTERS

Chapter 17

R. SHIMON BAR YOHAI

In this well-known talmudic story, the mercurial Rabbi Shimon bar Yohai (early second century CE) hides in a cave for thirteen years. Medieval Jewish tradition would claim that he spent this time delving into mystical secrets and writing the Zohar, the primary scripture of Kabbala. To this day his tomb near the town of Sefat is a pilgrimage site for prayer and mystical devotion. But the talmudic stories portray R. Shimon along different lines: in the Yerushalmi he is a miracle-worker; in the Bavli a zealot for Torah.

As usual, the Yerushalmi contains the briefer and earlier form of the story. This version opens with R. Shimon hiding in a cave without explaining why he fled there. Upon leaving he hears a heavenly voice decide the fate of hunted birds, from which he learns a lesson of the inexorability of providence (b). He articulates a second teaching concerning the importance of repaying a kindness: The city of Tiberias provided the baths in which he recuperated, so he purifies the city by miraculously exposing corpses whose precise location was not known (c). When troublemakers object to his purification, he deals with them as miracle-workers often do—by performing miracles that make them disappear. The story, on one level, argues that Tiberias is now free of corpse-impurity. Apparently some traditions circulated that the city was unclean, and the storytellers wished to dispel such notions.[1] The story is also part of a cycle of traditions that tell of the holy R. Shimon bar Yohai and his miraculous powers.

How different the version of the Bavli! Here R. Shimon is a radical who believes in the study of Torah as the only legitimate value. Initially he condemns Roman structures and institutions—markets, bathhouses and bridges—on the grounds that they serve decadent purposes (A). But when he subsequently wreaks destruction on Jewish peasants for working the land, for "abandoning eternal life and busying themselves with temporal life," it becomes clear that he opposes not Roman culture specifically, but all activities other than Torah study (B2). He is portrayed not so much as a miracle-worker (though he has miraculous powers) as a sage single-minded in his devotion to Torah. While the Yerushalmi does not mention what R. Shimon did in the cave, the Bavli relates that he and his son studied Torah incessantly, interrupting their studies only for prayer. When R. Shimon returns to society, the story notes that his dialectical proficiency increased exponentially (B4).

Yet the message of the Bavli is that such an uncompromising emphasis on Torah is not desirable. Without markets, bathhouses and agriculture, society would soon crumble for lack of food, clothing, hygiene and other necessities. The ideal that all Jews devote themselves exclusively to the study of Torah is tenable only if all live in a cave where food and water are miraculously supplied and clothing not needed (B1). The story clearly rejects this perspective, for a heavenly voice rebukes R. Shimon and his son for causing destruction, prompting them to identify themselves with "the wicked in Gehenom (Hell)" and to return to the cave for another year. When they emerge, R. Shimon first visits the bathhouses, one of the structures he had condemned at the outset, and then sets about ameliorating the temporal lives of the people by purifying a certain area (B4). He invokes as his model the patriarch Jacob who built markets and established bathhouses. Ironically, R. Shimon now values the mundane activities and facilities he censured at the outset of the story and even uses his knowledge of "eternal life" to improve the "temporal life" of the people.

For all that, the story does not completely resolve the tension between Torah study and mundane life. The years of constant study in the cave have made R. Shimon bar Yohai and his son consummate masters of Torah, the ultimate ideal of the Bavli. The story perhaps hints at a middle ground when the sages emerge from the cave for the second time. They find comfort upon seeing a man running at twilight bearing myrtles in order to "honor the Sabbath" with a pleasant aroma (B3). Agricultural labor, then, may be used for observing the commandments, for worthy religious purposes, even if it distracts time from Torah study. Yet R. Shimon retains his powers and kills twice more at the end of the story. We sense that his zealousness has been attenuated, not allayed. The storytellers realize that the ideal, that all Jews engage in full-time Torah study, is not practical. They exhibit a grudging endorsement of worldly activity, perhaps a warning to scholars not to denigrate their less learned brethren. But they stop well short of saying that anything else truly compares to Torah study as the end of life.

The Bavli story exhibits several literary features worthy of note. Overall, the structure is carefully worked out. The opening section reports R. Shimon's negative opinion of what the Romans "established" (A); the conclusion describes his favorable attitude to what Jacob "established" and the purification he "fixes/establishes" (C1, C2). R. Shimon withdraws from society in two stages, first to the academy (B1), then to the cave (B2). He reemerges in two stages as well, first with a second stint in the cave (B3), then to the baths (B4). A and C display balanced, tripartite structures. A reports three rabbis sitting, their three perspectives on Roman works, R. Yehuda's praise of three Roman achievements, R. Shimon's threefold denigration and the Roman authorities' three decrees. C quotes Rav's statement that Jacob arrived whole in three things, followed by three opinions of what he established.[2] The story also employs several keywords that point to its crucial tensions, including *tiqqen* (establish, fix; see A, C1) and *olam* (world, life; see B2, B3, C3).[3]

A. R. Shimon bar Yohai, the Miracle-worker (Yerushalmi Sheviit 9:1, 38d)

[a] R. Shimon b. Yohai hid in a cave for thirteen years, in a cave with carobs of *teruma*,[4] until his body broke out in skin disease. After thirteen years he said, "Why don't I go out and see what is going on in the world?"

[b] He went out and sat at the mouth of the cave. He saw a hunter hunting birds. As he spread his net he heard a heavenly voice say "Pardoned"[5] and it escaped. He said, "Even a bird does not perish without Heaven. How much the more so a human being!"

[c] When he saw that matters had calmed down,[6] he said, "Let us go and bathe in the public baths in Tiberias." He said, "We should do a service[7] [for the city] as our patriarchs did. *And he was gracious to the city* (Gen 33:18).[8] They set up stands for selling in markets." He said, "Let us purify Tiberias."

[d] He took lupines, cut them up and threw them down. Wherever there was a corpse, it floated and rose above.

[e] A Samaritan saw him and said, "Why don't I go and make fun of this elder of the Jews?" He took a corpse. He went and buried it where he [R. Shimon] had purified. He came to R. Shimon b. Yohai. He said to him, "Did you not purify such-and-such a place? Come and I will raise up [a corpse] for you from there."

[f] R. Shimon b. Yohai saw with the holy spirit that he had placed it there. He said, "I decree that those above should descend and those below should rise."[9] And thus it happened to him.

[g] When he passed by Migdal he heard the voice of a scribe say [sarcastically], "Here is Bar Yohai who purified Tiberias." He said to him, "May [such-and-such] befall me if I did not hear [a tradition] that Tiberias would someday be purified. And in any case, were you not one of the assembly?"[10] He turned him into a heap of bones.

❦

B. The Education of R. Shimon bar Yohai (Bavli Shabbat 33b-34a)

[A] R. Yehuda and R. Yose and R. Shimon were sitting, and Yehuda b. Gerim[11] was sitting beside them. R. Yehuda opened and said, "How pleasant are the acts of this nation [Rome]. (1) They established (tiqnu) markets. (2) They established (tiqnu) bathhouses. (3) They established (tiqnu) bridges." R. Yose was silent. R. Shimon bar Yohai answered and said, "Everything they established (tiqnu), they established (tiqnu) only for their own needs: (1) They established (tiqnu) markets—to place prostitutes there; (2) bathhouses—to pamper themselves; (3) bridges—to take tolls." Yehuda b. Gerim went and retold their words, and it became known to the government. They said: "(1) Yehuda who extolled—let him be extolled. (2) Yose who was silent—let him be exiled to Sepphoris. (3) Shimon who disparaged—let him be killed."

(B1) He went with his son and hid in the academy. Each day his wife brought him bread and a jug of water and they ate.[12] When the decree became more severe, he said to his son, "Women are simpleminded. They may abuse her and she will reveal [us]."[13]

(B2) He went, and they hid in a cave. A miracle happened for them and a carob tree and a spring were created for them. They sat up to their necks in sand. By day they sat and studied, and they took off their clothes. When the time came to pray, they went out and dressed and covered and went out and prayed and again took off their clothes, in order that they not wear out.[14] They dwelled in a cave for thirteen years. Elijah came to the opening of the cave. He said, "Who will inform Bar Yohai that the emperor died and the decree is annulled?" They went out and they saw men plowing and sowing. They said, "They abandon eternal life [Torah] and busy themselves with temporal life?!" Everywhere they turned their eyes was immediately burned. A heavenly voice went out and said to them, "Did you go out to destroy my world? Return to your cave!"

(B3) They dwelled for twelve months. They said, "The sentence of the wicked in Gehenom [Hell] is twelve months."[15] A heavenly voice went out [and said], "Go out from your cave." They went out. Wherever R. Eleazar smote R. Shimon healed. He said, "My son, you and I are sufficient for the world." They saw a certain old man who was holding two bunches of myrtle running at twilight. They said to him, "Why do you need these?" He said to them, "To honor the Sabbath."[16] [They said,] "Would not one suffice for you?" [He said] "One for *Remember [the Sabbath]* (Exod 20:8) and one for *Observe [the Sabbath]* (Deut 5:12)." He [R. Shimon] said to him [his son], "See how dear is a commandment *(mitzva)* to Israel."[17] Their minds were set at ease.[18]

(B4) R. Pinhas b. Yair, his son-in-law, heard [that R. Shimon bar Yohai had returned] and went out to greet him. He took him into the bathhouse. He was massaging his flesh. He saw that there were clefts in his flesh. He was weeping and the tears were falling from his eyes and hurting him [R. Shimon]. He said to him, "Woe am I that I see you so." He [R. Shimon] said to him, "Happy that you see me so. For if you did not see me so, you would not find me so [learned]."[19] For originally when R. Shimon bar Yohai raised an objection R. Pinhas b. Yair solved it with twelve solutions. Subsequently when R. Pinhas b. Yair objected, R. Shimon bar Yohai solved it with twenty-four solutions.

[C1] He said, "Since a miracle occurred I will go and fix *(atqin)* something, since it says, *And Jacob came whole (shalem)* (Gen 33:18)." And Rav said, "(1) Whole in his body, (2) whole in his money, (3) whole in his Torah."[20] *And he was gracious to the city* (Gen 33:18).[21] (1) Rav said, "He established *(tiqqen)* coinage for them." (2) And Shmuel said, "He established *(tiqqen)* markets for them." (3) And R. Yohanan said, "He established *(tiqqen)* bathhouses for them." He [R. Shimon bar Yohai] said, "Is there something to fix (*letaqonei*)?"

[C2] They said to him, "There is a place of doubtful impurity, and it causes trouble for priests to go around it."[22] He said, "Does anyone know if there was a presumption of purity here?" A certain old man said, "Here Ben Azai cut down lupines of *teruma*."[23] He did the same. Wherever it [the ground] was hard he ruled pure. Wherever it was loose he marked.[24]

[C3] A certain old man said, "R. Shimon bar Yohai made a cemetery pure."[25] He [R. Shimon bar Yohai] said, "If you had not been with us, or even if you had been with us but had not voted with us, you would have spoken well. But now that you were with us and voted among us, should they say, '[Even] prostitutes paint each other. How much the more so [should] scholars!'"[26] He cast his eyes at him and his soul departed. He went out to the market. He saw Yehuda b. Gerim. He said, "Is this one still in the world?" He set his eyes upon him and turned him into a heap of bones.

Chapter 18

HONI THE CIRCLE-DRAWER: THE HOLY MAN AND RAIN

Because the Land of Israel depends almost exclusively on rain as a source of water, drought constituted a threat to crops, cattle and ultimately human life. No rain falls in summer, so the winter rainy season, from late October through April, was critical to survival. The Mishna Tractate Taanit ("Fast") prescribes a series of private and communal rituals when the winter rains fail to fall in their proper time. The rituals begin with prayers and include fasts, signs of mourning, prohibition of public celebrations and the sounding of the shofar. The Tractate also contains rituals for other disasters such as pestilence, locusts and invasions.

This story is set in the time of the late Second Temple Period. Rabbinic tradition recalls Shimon b. Shetah as one of the earliest leaders of the sages (first century BCE). Honi is not a sage but a holy man or miracle-worker. An important aspect of the story is the tension between the sages and rabbinic piety over against other charismatic figures and their religious practices. The end of the story, the message Shimon b. Shetah sends to Honi, exhibits both grudging recognition of Honi's talents and a sense of unease about his methods. The leader of the sages states that the miracle-worker deserves to be put under a ban, apparently for religious offense or on account of the excessive flooding. Yet he cannot actually impose it, for God after all acquiesced to Honi's demands. The rabbinic storytellers appear to be uncomfortable with charismatic holy men who present an alternative and challenge to their authority.

The story therefore depicts Honi in somewhat ambivalent light. He confidently instructs the people to bring their ovens indoors, but his prayers initially fail (B, C). While he subsequently succeeds, he must resort to "impertinent" petitions and somewhat childish behavior. In addition, Honi has trouble accomplishing his true aim: first the rains fall too lightly, then too strongly, then just right—but then they don't stop! The storytellers seem to say: we don't like this type of holy man, we don't like his procedures, but we must acknowledge that they work, at least to a certain extent.

The motif of parents and children runs throughout the story. Honi tells God that the people have turned to him because he is "like a member" of God's household (C). Shimon b. Shetah too recognizes Honi's intimate relationship with God, comparing him to an impertinent son before his father and quoting a verse about the happiness of parents (F). But Honi in turn calls the people God's children and appeals to God as a father to have mercy upon his children (C). In a tractate devoted to the laws of rituals and fasting, the story emphasizes the divine-human relationship, the basis for God's providing his blessing of rain.[1]

A. Honi's Prayers for Rain (I) (Mishna Taanit 3:9-12)

[A] They sound the shofar on account of every disaster that afflicts the community—except for excessive rains.[2]

[B] Once they said to Honi the Circle-Drawer,[3] "Pray that the rains fall." He said to them, "Go and bring your Passover ovens inside [your houses] so that they not become softened [by the coming rain]."

[C] He prayed, but rain did not fall. He drew a circle and stood within it, and said, "Master of the Universe. Your children turned to me, for I am like a member of the household before you. I swear by your great name that I shall not move from here until you have mercy on your children."

[D1] The rains began to drizzle. He said, "I did not ask thus, but rains [that fill] cisterns, pits and caves."

[D2] They began to fall stormily. He said, "I did not ask thus, but rains of goodwill *(ratson)*, blessing and bounty."

[D3] They began to fall as he ordered them—until the Israelites went up from Jerusalem to the Temple Mount because of the rains.

[E] They came and said to him, "Just as you prayed for them to fall, so pray that they go." He said to them, "Go and see if the Stone of the Blunderers⁴ has worn away."⁵

[F] Shimon b. Shetah sent to him and said: "You deserve to be placed under a ban. But what can I do to you? For you are impertinent⁶ before the Omnipresent, just as a son is impertinent before his father and [yet] he grants his desire *(ratson)*. Scripture says of you, *Your father and mother will rejoice; she who bore you will exult* (Prov 23:25)."

B. Honi's Prayers for Rain (II) (Bavli Taanit 23a)

Another version of this story appears in the Bavli and provides a good example of the literary processes with which later rabbinic texts rework earlier sources. The Bavli's story has essentially the same structure as the Mishna's story, as can be seen by comparing the corresponding sections A, B, C with a, b, c, etc. It has also preserved parts of the dialogue and narration verbatim. Yet the Bavli has consistently embellished the corresponding sections with additional dialogue and more detailed descriptions. Each raindrop, for example, becomes the size of a barrel (c), while Shimon b. Shetah offers a detailed analogy describing Honi's relationship to God (f).

Note that a few passages are omitted, especially those that pertain to the geography or specific customs of the Land of Israel, as these references would not have been understood or appreciated in talmudic Babylonia (compare sections B, E with b, e).

The later reworking changes the overall thrust of the story to a certain extent. The Bavli version portrays Honi more favorably: it eliminates his self-assured remark directing the people to bring in the ovens (B *vs.* b) and his sarcastic refusal to pray for the rains to stop (E *vs.* e). Rather Honi explains that he cannot comply with this request because it violates his tradition, a pious and righteous reason, and proceeds to solve the problem anyway (e). Even his method of refusing to move from a circle is legitimated with biblical precedent (c). Thus the tension between rabbis and miracle-workers is less at issue. More emphasis is placed on the question of insufficient, appropriate and excessive blessing, the subject of Honi's long prayer (e).

[a] Our sages have taught: Once the greater part of Adar passed and the rain had not fallen.[7]

[b] They sent to Honi the Circle-Drawer: "Pray that the rains fall."

[c] He prayed, but rain did not fall. He drew a circle and stood within it, in a similar manner to Habakkuk the Prophet, as it says, *I will stand on my watch, set myself at my post [and wait to see what He will say to me, what He will reply to my complaint]* (Hab 2:1). He said before him, "Master of the Universe. Your children turned to me, for I am like a member of the household before you. I swear by your great name that I shall not move from here until you have mercy on your children."

[d1] The rains began to drizzle. They said to him, "Master, may we see you and not die.[8] It seems to us that the rains are falling only to free you from your oath." He said to them, "You have seen me and will not die." He said, "I did not ask thus, but rains [that fill] cisterns, pits and caves."

[d2] They began to fall stormily. Each and every drop was the size of a barrel opening, and the sages estimated that no drop contained less than a *log*.[9] They said to him, "Master, may we see you and not die. It seems to us that the rains are falling only in order to destroy the world." He said to them, "You have seen me and will not die." He said, "I did not ask thus, but rains of good-will *(ratson)*, blessing and bounty."

[d3] They began to fall as he ordered them—until the Israelites went up from Jerusalem to the Temple Mount because of the rains.

[e] They came and said to him, "Just as you prayed for them to fall, so pray that they go." He said to them, "Thus I have received [a tradition]: one does not pray regarding too much good. Nevertheless, bring me a bull for a thanksgiving offering."[10] They brought him a bull for a thanksgiving offering. He placed his two hands upon it and said, "Master of the Universe, your people Israel whom you took out of Egypt cannot stand either too much good or too much suffering. You were angry with them— they could not endure it. You heaped good upon them—they could not endure it. May it be pleasing *(ratson)* before you that there be prosperity in the world." Immediately the wind blew and the clouds scattered and the sun shone, and the people went to the field and gathered for themselves mushrooms and truffles.

[f] Shimon b. Shetah sent to him: "Were you not Honi, I would place you under a ban. If these years were like the years [in the time] of Elijah, would you not have profaned Heaven's Name?[11] But what can I do to you? For you are impertinent before the Omnipresent, just as a son is impertinent before his father and [yet] he grants his desire *(ratson)*. He says to him, 'Bathe me in hot water.' He bathes him in hot water. 'Rinse me with cold water.' He rinses him with cold water. 'Give me nuts, peaches, almonds, pomegranates.' He gives him. Scripture says of you, *Your father and mother will rejoice; she who bore you will exult* (Prov 23:25)."

Chapter 19

R. YEHOSHUA b. LEVI AND THE ANGEL OF DEATH (BAVLI KETUBOT 77b)

A number of rabbinic miracle stories center on the early third-century sage R. Yehoshua b. Levi. The following tales involve the common folkloristic motif of outwitting the Angel of Death. R. Yehoshua b. Levi manages to enter Paradise without the angel taking his life, that is, without suffering death in the standard fashion. R. Hanina bar Papa fails to outwit the angel but nevertheless experiences a miraculous death (H-L). While the holiness of both sages derives in part from their devotion to Torah study (A, H-I), R. Yehoshua b. Levi's superior holiness is attributed to his compassion for the sick. A type of Mother Teresa, he approached those who suffered a highly contagious illness and relied on the protective power of Torah to safeguard himself. In medieval times the story of R. Yehoshua b. Levi became very popular and was frequently retold and embellished.

These stories present the sages not only as outstanding rabbinic masters but as holy men. The Angel of Death is commanded to do their bidding, they encounter supernatural beings, and miracles seem to be a routine part of their lives. Such figures were increasingly common in almost all religions of late antiquity.[1] We find similar depictions of Christian monks, Zoroastrian magi and the priests of Greco-Roman religions.[2] In this respect we see the influence of the ambient religious culture on rabbinic thought.

[A] R. Yohanan proclaimed, "Be careful of the flies of those who suffer from *raatan*."[3] R. Zeira would not sit downwind from them. R. Eleazar would not sit in the same tent. R. Ami and R. Asi would not eat eggs that came from the same cul-de-sac [where the victim lived]. R. Yehoshua b. Levi would draw near them[4] and busy himself with Torah. He said, *"A loving doe, a graceful mountain goat* (Prov 5:19). If she [Torah] bestows grace on those who study her, will she not protect them"?[5]

[B] When he [R. Yehoshua b. Levi] was dying, they [the heavenly court] said to the Angel of Death, "Go and grant him a wish." He [the Angel of Death] went and appeared to him. He [R. Yehoshua b. Levi] said, "Show me my place [in Paradise]." He said to him, "Very well." He said to him, "Give me your knife lest you frighten me on the way." He gave it to him.

[C] When they arrived there he set him down. He was showing him [his place in Paradise]. He [R. Yehoshua b. Levi] said, "Lower me down another handbreadth." He lowered him. He jumped and landed on the other side [of the wall that separates Paradise from the rest of the world].[6] He [the Angel of Death] grasped him by the corner of his robe. He [R. Yehoshua b. Levi] said, "I swear I will not go [back with you]." The Holy One, blessed be He, said, "If he ever asked [to be released from] an oath, he must return. If not, he need not return."[7]

[D] He [the Angel of Death] said, "Give me my knife." He would not give it to him. A heavenly voice went forth and said, "Give it to him, since it is required [to cause death] for mortals."[8]

[E] Elijah proclaimed before him, "Clear a place for the son of Levi. Clear a place for the son of Levi."

[F] He [R. Yehoshua b. Levi] went and found R. Shimon bar Yohai, who was sitting beside thirteen tables of gold.[9] He said to him, "Are you the son of Levi?" He said to him, "Yes." He said to him, "Was the rainbow ever seen during your life?" He said to him, "Yes." He said to him, "Then you are not the son of Levi."[10]

[G] But this was not the case. No such thing happened.[11] But he did not wish to claim the credit for himself.[12]

[H] R. Hanina bar Papa was his [R. Yehoshua b. Levi's] friend. When he was dying they [the heavenly court] said to the Angel of Death, "Go and grant him a wish." He [R. Hanina bar Papa] said to him [the Angel of Death], "Leave me for thirty days until I review my studies, for it is said, 'Happy is he who arrives here [Paradise] in firm grasp of his studies.'"[13]

[I] After thirty days he came and appeared to him. He [R. Hanina bar Papa] said, "Show me my place [in Paradise]." He [the Angel of Death] said to him, "Very well." He said to him, "Give me your knife lest you frighten me on the way." He said to him, "Do you wish to do to me as did your colleague?"[14] He said to him, "Bring me a Torah scroll and see if there is anything written there that I did not fulfill."[15] He said to him, "Did you draw near to those who suffer from *raatan* and study Torah?"[16]

[J] Even so, when he died a pillar of fire [appeared] and interposed itself between him [=his corpse] and the world.[17] And we have a tradition that a pillar of fire interposes for but one man in a generation, or for two in a generation.

[K] R. Alexandrai came to him. He said, "Do it [remove the fire] for the honor of the sages [so that they can bury you]." He paid him no attention, and it did not depart. "Do it for your own honor." It departed.

[L] Abaye said, "This [the pillar of fire] was to exclude one who did not fulfill [the Torah from participating in the burial.]"

PART V:

WOMEN, WIVES AND MARRIAGE

Chapter 20

RABBIS AND WIVES: LOVE, BABYLONIAN STYLE (BAVLI KETUBOT 62b)

Torah study, the primary value in Babylonian rabbinic culture, frequently came into tension with the demands of a sage's domestic responsibilities. The dilemma, for the rabbis, went beyond the calculation that time spent with the wife and family took time away from Torah study. It was exacerbated by the fact that the Torah grants a wife "conjugal rights" from her husband (Exod 21:10). This was a necessary protection in polygamous societies where a man was liable to neglect one wife because of his great passion for another. While polygamy was extremely rare in rabbinic circles, the biblical legislation remained in force. A rabbi thus faced not only competing pressures or desires, but obligations: to study Torah, on the one hand, and to perform his marital duty, as well as the general commandment to procreate, on the other. Sages fortunate enough to live near a rabbinic master or academy could study by day and return home at night. But many aspiring students lived in small towns and villages at considerable distances from a center of Torah. Were they permitted to leave their wives and sojourn for extended periods of study? If so, for how long?

The following text is a superb example of the complex interplay between law and narrative in the Babylonian Talmud. Its point of departure is Mishna Ketubot 5:3, a detailed rabbinic formulation of the law of conjugal duty, which specifies the frequencies that men of different professions must have sex with their wives. The Mishna also grants students of Torah a limited exemption: they may leave home to study Torah for up to thirty days without their wives' consent (A1–A2). This straightforward law would seem to settle the matter and to rule out extended absences from home. Yet the talmudic commentary quickly quotes a statement of Rav Ada b. Ahava (c. 250 CE) claiming that the Mishnaic law is in fact a minority opinion and that the consensus of the sages permits students to spend several years away (B). This surprising marginalization of a clear-cut Mishna clearly satisfied the sages' thirst for Torah by permitting them to travel farther and stay in the academy for longer periods of study. But was it fair to their wives? Rava warned that sages who followed this opinion "did so at the cost of their lives" (C). In other words, God punished them for abandoning their wives and families.

The seven stories that follow provide different perspectives on this practice. As a whole, there is a palpable tension between the two rabbinic values. Torah study is portrayed as seductive: it "captivates" or "draws" (mashakh) the student to it (1, 2), possessing him, consuming his attention and energy. In the final story the father even refers to his son's wife as "his whore" because she draws him away from Torah, as it were, his "legitimate" companion (7)! On the other hand, R. Yehuda HaNasi's son lost some zest for Torah each time he gazed upon his fiancée (3, G2). Rabbinic sources often describe the Torah as feminine and beautiful. These stories go beyond such imagery by eroticizing the Torah and providing vivid illustrations of her appeal.

The first two stories essentially criticize sages who leave their wives. Rav Rahumei dies for the pain he causes his wife (1). Yehuda b. R. Hiyya dies because of a tragic misunderstanding ultimately caused by his not returning home (2). The following three stories express deep sympathy for the wife's situation and warn the sages of the deleterious consequences of extended separation. R. Yehuda HaNasi's daughter-in-law becomes barren (3, G3); R. Hananiah b. Hakhinai's wife dies at his sudden and unexpected return (4); R. Hama b. Bisa does not know his own children (5). Now the Talmud never explicitly rejects Rav Ada b. Ahava's dispensation permitting the sages to leave home for years. Technically, a student of Torah who does so is beyond reproach. But these stories provide rabbinic scholars with a substantially different message: "Sure, you can follow the law. But be aware of the pain you cause your wife. And don't be surprised if your decision comes back to haunt you."

In this context the famous story of R. Akiba must be seen as a rabbinic fantasy (6). Here the wife encourages the husband to leave her and to depart for study. After he spends twelve years away and acquires thousands of students, even though she has been cast off by her father and impoverished, she still wishes that he would spend more time in the academy. The sage returns with thousands more students, at the acme of the rabbinic world, to reclaim his faithful wife and now to inherit half the fortune of her suddenly respectful father. He has it all: years of uninterrupted study, students, status, wealth—and everything with the wife's consent and support. Needless to say, and as the other stories suggest, this story represents the ideal, not the reality. And while R. Akiba graciously acknowledges, "What is mine and yours is hers" (J3), one senses that most rabbinic wives envisioned a different sort of utopia.

The final story artfully comprehends the tensions (7). When a son returns early from years of study his father approaches him with an axe and asks if he "remembered his whore," in one version, or "remembered his dove" in another version. The father considers his son's wife a distraction from Torah study, an illicit outlet of (sexual) energy. The son sees her as a beloved object of affection, a view supported by the version "his dove." What is the ideal object of erotic urges? That the two argue, though it is the eve of Yom Kippur, and neglect to eat the final meal, leaves us with a picture of stalemate. Just as the father and son could not resolve their quarrel and move ahead, so this fundamental cultural tension cannot be resolved completely. The intractable argument is a fitting conclusion to the cycle of stories that grapple with this issue.[1]

[A1] Students [of Torah] may depart for Torah study without permission [from their wives] for thirty days. Laborers—for one week.

[A2] The conjugal duty mentioned in the Torah [Exod 21:10]: Men at leisure—each day. Laborers—twice per week. Ass-Drivers—once per week. Camel-drivers—once per thirty days. Sailors—once per six months. These are the words of R. Eliezer (Mishna Ketubot 5:6).

[B] [Talmud:] Rav Beruna said Rav said: "The law follows R. Eliezer." Rav Ada b. Ahava said Rav said: "Those are the words of R. Eliezer [alone]." But the sages say, "Students [of Torah] may depart for Torah study for two or three years without the consent [of their wives]."

[C] Rava said, "The rabbis relied on the words of Rav Ada b. Ahava and acted accordingly at the cost of their lives."

[1][D] For example: Rav Rahumei frequently [studied] before Rava in Mahoza. He regularly came home every Yom Kippur eve.² One day his studies captivated him. His wife was looking out [for him, saying,] "He is coming now. He is coming now." He did not come. She became distressed and a tear fell (*ahit*) from her eye. He [Rav Rahumei] was sitting on a roof. The roof collapsed (*ifhit*) under him and he died.³

[E] When is the conjugal duty for scholars?⁴ Rav Yehuda said Shmuel said, "Every Friday night."

Which yields its fruit in season (Ps 1:3): Rav Yehuda, and some say Rav Nahman, said: "This is one who has sex every Friday night."

[2][F1] Yehuda b. R. Hiyya, son-in-law of R. Yannai, went and sat in the study-house. He would return home every [Friday at] twilight. Whenever he would come, people would see a pillar of fire [going] before him.⁵

[F2] One day his studies captivated him and he did not come. Because they did not see that sign, R. Yannai said to them, "Overturn his bed,⁶ for were Yehuda alive, he would not violate his conjugal duty." It was *As an error that goes forth from a ruler* (Qoh 10:5), and his [Yehuda's] soul departed.⁷

[3][G1] Rabbi [Yehuda HaNasi] was planning for his son's [marriage] into the family of R. Hiyya. When he was about to write the marriage contract, the girl's soul departed. Rabbi said, "Is there, God forbid, a taint [in her lineage]?" They sat down and investigated the families. [They found that] Rabbi descended from Shefatiah, son of Avital [the wife of King

David]. Rabbi Hiyya descended from Shimi, the brother of [King] David. He [Rabbi] said, "Were there not a problem, she would not have died."[8]

[G2] He [Rabbi Yehuda HaNasi] went and planned for his son's [marriage] into the family of R. Yose b. Zimra. He [R. Yose] agreed [to support the son] so that he could go and study for twelve[9] years in the study-house. They passed her before him [Rabbi's son]. He said, "Let it be six years." They passed her before him again. He said, "Let me consummate the marriage and then I will go." He was ashamed before his father. He said to him, "My son. You have your maker's inclination. At first it is written, *You will bring them and plant them in Your own Mountain, [the place You made to dwell in, O Lord, the sanctuary, O Lord, which Your hands established]* (Exod 15:17). But then it is written, *Let them make me a sanctuary that I may dwell among them* (Exod 25:8)."[10]

[G3] He married her. He went and sat in the academy for twelve years. By the time he came back, his wife had become barren. Rabbi said, "What will we do? Should he divorce her? They will say, 'That poor woman waited in vain.' Should he marry another?[11] They will say, 'This one is his wife. That one is his whore.'"[12] He prayed for her and she recovered.

[4][H1] As R. Shimon b. Yohai's wedding celebration was winding down, R. Hananiah b. Hakhinai got ready to leave for Rav's study-house. He [R. Shimon] said to him, "Wait for me and I will go with you." He did not wait for him.

[H2] He went and sat in the study-house for twelve years. By the time he returned all the streets of his town had changed, and he did not know the way home. He went and sat on the bank of a river. He heard them calling to a certain girl, "Daughter of Hakhinai, daughter of Hakhinai. Fill your pitcher and come along." He said, "That means this girl is ours." He followed after her. His wife was sitting and sifting flour. He attracted her eye. She saw him. Her heart swelled. Her spirit flew away [= she died]. He said before Him, "Master of the Universe. This poor woman—that is her reward?" He requested mercy for her and she revived.[13]

[5][I1] R. Hama b. Bisa went and sat for twelve years in the academy. When he [prepared] to come [home] he said, "I won't do as did the son of Hakhinai." He went and sat in the study-house [of his town] and sent [word] to his home.

[I2] R. Oshaya his son came and sat before him. He [R. Hama] asked him about his studies. He saw that his studies were sharp. He became distressed, thinking, "If I had been here, I could have had a son like this one." He entered his house. His son entered [after him]. He [R. Hama] rose before him, because he thought that he [the son] wanted to question him about his studies. His wife said to him, "Was there ever a father who rises in front of his son?" Rami b. Hami applied to him the verse, "*The threefold cord is not readily broken* (Qoh 4:12).—This applies to R. Oshaya, son of R. Hama b. Bisa."[14]

[6][J1] R. Akiba was the shepherd of Ben Kalba Savua. His daughter saw that he [Akiba] was modest and upright. She said, "If I become betrothed to you, will you go to the study-house?" He said to her, "Yes." She was betrothed to him in secret and sent him off. Her father heard. He threw her out of the house and swore that she should have no benefit from his property.

[J2] He went and sat for twelve years in the study-house. When he returned twelve thousand students came with him. He heard a certain old man say to her, "How long will you lead the life of a widow?" She said to him, "If he listened to me, he would stay another twelve years." He [R. Akiba] said, "Then I am doing this with her consent!" He went back and sat for twelve more years in the study-house.

[J3] When he returned twenty-four thousand students came with him. His wife heard and went forth to greet him. Her neighbors said to her, "Borrow something [nice] to wear and adorn yourself." She said, "*A righteous man knows the life of his beast* (Prov 12:10)." When she approached him she fell on her face and kissed his feet. His attendants pushed her away. He said to them, "Leave her be. What is mine and yours is hers."

[J4] Her father heard that a great man had come to town. He said, "I will go to him. Perhaps he can release me from my oath."[15] He came to him. He [Akiba] said to him, "Did you swear knowing that [your daughter would marry] a great man?" He said to him, "Had he known but one chapter or one law [I would not have sworn]." He said, "I am he." He fell on his face and kissed his feet and gave him half his money.

[J5] The daughter of R. Akiba did the same for Ben Azai. Thus runs the proverb, "Ewe follows ewe. As the ways of the mother so are the ways of the daughter."

[7][K] Rav Yosef b. Rava—his father sent him to the study-house [to study] before Rav Yosef [b. Hiyya]. They [the families] agreed [to support] him for six years. After three years, when the eve of Yom Kippur approached, he [Rav Yosef b. Rava] said, "I will go and see my family." His father heard. He took an axe and went forth to meet him. He said to him, "Did you remember your whore *(zonatkha)*?" Others say that he said, "Did you remember your dove? *(yonatkha)*." They quarreled and neither one ate the last meal before the fast.

Chapter 21

GOD AS MARRIAGE-MAKER (LEVITICUS RABBAH 8:1)

Just as God brought Eve to Adam and thus served as the marriage-maker for the first human couple, so the rabbis believed that God played a role in forging every marital union. Finding a "soulmate" and the love between men and women were understood as products of the divine element in all marriages. This understanding of God's activity also responds to the theological question of the nature of God's participation in the world since creation. If God finished creating the world in six days, as the Bible reports, then how does he continue to be involved? In what way does God still participate in the creation of life? Or does God now remain apart from the world and indifferent to his creations?

The following story addresses these issues with a lighthearted description of an encounter between a sage and an aristocratic Roman woman. When the marriages she arranges among her slaves soon deteriorate into violence, she recognizes how great an accomplishment it is to bring about a successful marriage and praises the wisdom of the Torah. The sage's equation of the difficulty of marriage with that of splitting the Reed Sea suggests that the rabbis considered a loving union to be a near miracle. While this lesson is ostensibly for the benefit of the Gentile, it implies that the rabbinic storytellers were well acquainted with unhappy marriages in their society as well (see chapter 22 herein).

Rabbinic literature contains five or six similar stories of a Roman matron asking questions of various rabbis about troubling theological concepts.[1] These encounters are probably literary fictions; to attribute difficult theological questions to a Gentile allows the rabbinic story-tellers to confront the issues in a less threatening manner than were the rabbis to articulate the problems themselves.[2]

[A] A Roman matron questioned R. Yose b. Halfuta. She said to him, "In how many days did God create his world?" He said to her, "In six days, as is written, *For in six days the Lord made Heaven and earth* (Exod 31:17)." She said to him, "What does he sit and do now?" He said to her, "He sits and arranges marriages: Mr. So-and-so's daughter is for Mr. So-and-so, the wife of So-and-so [who died] is for Mr. So-and-so, the estate of Mr. So-and-so is for Mr. So-and-so."

[B] She said to him, "How many slaves and bondmaidens do I have, and in a moment or two I can marry them off!" He said to her, "Although it is a small thing in your eyes, it is as difficult before God as the parting of the Reed Sea, as is written, *God restores the lonely to their homes, [sets free the imprisoned, safe and sound, while the rebellious must live in a parched land]* (Ps 68:7)."[3] R. Yose b. Halfuta went home.

[C] What did she do? She sent [word] and they brought one thousand slaves and one thousand bondwomen and she lined them up in rows. She said to them, "So-and-so will marry So-and-so, and So-and-so will marry So-and-so."

[D] That night they came to her. This one's head was disheveled. That one's eye was blinded. This one's hand was broken. That one's leg was broken. This one said, "I don't want her." That one said, "I don't want him."

[E] She sent word to him [R. Yose] and said to him, "Your Torah is good, beautiful and praiseworthy." He said to her, "Did I not say to you that 'Although it is a small thing in your eyes, it is as difficult before God as the parting of the Reed Sea'?"

Chapter 22

RABBIS, HUSBANDS AND WIVES

Oaths were much more common in ancient society than they are today. While some swore oaths to inspire themselves to greater spiritual goals, others swore out of anger and impulsiveness, and for no higher purpose at all. Having argued with a friend, a man might become irate and rashly swear that his friend should never derive benefit from him. The friend was then forbidden to eat his food or enter his house or profit from him in any way. Needless to say, many subsequently cooled down and felt deep remorse for making such reckless oaths.

Many rabbinic stories tell of husbands becoming angry with their wives and swearing oaths forbidding their wives to benefit from them unless certain conditions should be met. These oaths constituted dire threats to the marriage; if the stipulations could not be fulfilled then the couple had no choice but to divorce.[1] In this way a rash oath could cause the wife—and sometimes the husband too—terrible suffering.

In the following stories rabbis help wives to satisfy the conditions of their husbands' oaths to allow for the lawful endurance of the marriage. In story A, R. Meir endures public humiliation by encouraging a woman to spit in his face. Interestingly, the husband becomes angry at his wife because she attends synagogue and listens to R. Meir's sermon. In contrast to chapter 20, where men neglect their wives because of their devotion to Torah study, here the wife's love of Torah and absence from the home annoy the husband. In story B, a rabbi uses his cleverness and ingenuity to satisfy the conditions of the husband's oath. Rabbis were not only students of Torah, judges, lawyers, holy men and political leaders, but also, in some respects, marriage counselors.

A. The Pious Wife
(Yerushalmi Sotah 1:4, 16d)

[A] R. Meir used to preach in the synagogue of Hammat[2] every Sabbath eve, and a certain woman there used to listen to his voice. One day he preached for a long time. She went and tried to enter her house but found that the lamp had gone out. Her husband said to her, "Where have you been?" She said to him, "I was listening to the preacher." He said to her, "I swear that you will never enter this house until you go and spit in the face of the preacher."[3]

[B] R. Meir saw [what had happened] by means of the holy spirit and pretended that he had a pain in his eye.[4] He said, "Any woman who knows how to whisper [a charm] for the eye should come and whisper it." Her neighbors said to her. "Here is your chance to return to your house. Pretend that you are whispering [a charm] and spit in his eye."[5]

[C] She went to him. He said to her, "Do you know how to whisper [a charm] for the eye?" She took fright and said, "No." He said to her, "If one spits in it seven times it feels better." After she spit he said to her, "Go and say to your husband, 'You told me once, but behold, I have spit seven times.'"

[D] His students said to him, "Master. Does one degrade the Torah in this way? Had you told us, would we not have brought him and whipped him upon a bench and made him reconcile with his wife?" He said to them, "Should not the honor of Meir be like the honor of his Creator? If scripture instructs to erase the Holy Name, which was written in a state of holiness, in order to restore peace between a man and his wife, how much the more so should the honor of Meir [be debased]?"[6]

B. The Ugly Wife (Bavli Nedarim 66b)

[A] A certain man once said to his wife, "I swear that you will have no benefit from me until you show something of beauty in you to R. Ishmael b. R. Yose."

[B] He [R. Ishmael b. R. Yose] said to them, "Perhaps her face is beautiful?" They said to him, "It is round."

He said to them, "Perhaps her hair is beautiful?" They said to him, "It resembles stalks of flax."

"Perhaps her eyes are beautiful?" —"They are slanted."

"Perhaps her ears are beautiful?" —"They are folded over."

"Perhaps her nose is beautiful?" —"It is swollen."

"Perhaps her lips are beautiful?" —"They are thick."

"Perhaps her neck is beautiful?" —"It is too short."

"Perhaps her belly is beautiful?" —"It is distended."

"Perhaps her legs are beautiful?" —"They are as broad as those of a goose."

"Perhaps her name is beautiful?" —"It is *Likhlukhit* (=little ugly one)."

He said to them, "It is beautiful [=fitting] that you call her *Likhlukhit*, for she is ugly with blemishes."

[C] And he permitted her [to her husband].

Chapter 23

BERURIA
(BAVLI ERUVIN 53b,
BERAKHOT 10a)

Rabbinic traditions tell of but a few women learned in Torah. Beruria, wife of R. Meir, is one exception. Several anecdotes relate how she corrected the behavior of various sages or corrected their understanding of biblical passages, thereby displaying superior knowledge and piety. These anecdotes gave rise to additional legends in medieval sources, where we find two well-known tales. According to the first, her two sons died on the Sabbath, but she did not tell her husband so as not to ruin his Sabbath joy.[1] She waited until he returned from the synagogue on Saturday night and fed him a good meal. Then she asked him if she should return a deposit to someone who left it with her for safekeeping. When R. Meir replied that of course she must return the deposit, she showed him his dead sons. The second story relates that Beruria mocked the rabbinic maxim, "Women are simpleminded."[2] R. Meir warned that she would eventually concede that the rabbis were correct. He instructed one of his students to seduce her. She finally capitulated and strangled herself, and Meir fled in shame.[3] The talmudic figure of a learned women thus sparked different reactions among medieval Jews.[4]

RABBINIC STORIES

(BAVLI ERUVIN 53b)

[A1] Rabbi Yosi the Galilean was walking on his way when he came upon Beruria. He said to her, "Which way should we take to Lod?"

[A2] She said to him, "Stupid Galilean! Did the sages not say, *Do not speak at length with a woman* (Mishna Avot 1:5)?[5] You should have said, 'Which way Lod?'"[6]

[B] Beruria came upon a certain student who was repeating traditions in a whisper.[7] She kicked him and said to him, "Is it not written, *Fixed and secured* (2 Sam 23:5)? If it is fixed in your 248 limbs, then it will be secure [in your memory]. But if not, it will not be secure."

(BAVLI BERAKHOT 10a)

[C1] Some hoodlums lived in the neighborhood of Rabbi Meir, and they were causing him great distress. He prayed that they should die.

[C2] Beruria his wife said to him, "What is [the basis] of your thinking? Because it says, *May sins* (hataim) *disappear [from the earth]* (Ps 104:35)? Does it say 'sinners' *(hotim)?* It says, 'sins' *(hataim)*. Moreover, you should go on to the end of the verse, *And the wicked will be no more* (Ps 104:35). Because *sin disappears, the wicked will be no more.* Rather, pray for them that they repent and then *the wicked will be no more* [since they will now be righteous]."

[C3] He prayed for them and they repented.

[D1] A certain heretic[8] said to Beruria, "It is written, *Celebrate, O barren one, You who bore no child* (Isa 54:1). Because she *bore no child,* should she *celebrate?*"

[D2] She said to him, "Fool! Go on to the end of the verse. It is written, *For the children of the wife forlorn shall outnumber those of the espoused—said the Lord* (Isa 54:1) [and this is why she cele-brates]. What then is [the meaning of] *Celebrate, O barren one?* Let the Congregation of Israel celebrate, for they resemble a barren woman who bore no children for Gehenom [Hell] as you have."

PART VI:

ROMANS, GENTILES AND OTHERS

Chapter 24

ALEXANDER MACEDON
AND THE WORLD COURT
(BAVLI SANHEDRIN 91 a)

Legends about Alexander the Great circulated among many nations throughout the Greco-Roman world and beyond. A number of these legends appear in rabbinic literature, refracted through rabbinic lenses and transformed to serve the interests of the storytellers. Many of the Alexander traditions involve cultural conflicts or comparisons, a reflex of the popular conception of Alexander as the synthesizer of cultures.

The following story has many of the typical marks of a folktale: the tripartite structure with verbatim repetition (A-C), the challenges to outsmart the other side, the commoner succeeding where the wise men cannot, and the reversals: Geviha b. Pesisa turns the tables on his foes by using their own methods, luring them to admit that they base their case on the Torah and then providing an irrefutable argument from another verse.[1]

At a deeper level the story is an apologetic for issues that troubled the rabbis themselves. To place charges in the mouths of adversaries is a way of raising problematic subjects in a less threatening way.[2] The accusation that the Israelites unjustly stole "the promised land" from the native Canaanite inhabitants (A) and the Ishmaelite [= Arab] claims to the land have provoked controversies throughout history and to the present day. Similarly, the Bible's unabashed admission that the Israelites "stripped" or "despoiled" the Egyptians has long been a point of indictment and apology (C). Refuting the charges so completely through other biblical verses sends a loud message: to attack us on the basis of our own scriptures is futile, for those same scriptures demonstrate not only that your charges are false, but that you treated us unjustly.[3]

[A1] Our sages have taught: When the Africans came to dispute with Israel before Alexander Macedon,[4] they said to them, "The Land of Canaan belongs to us, as it says, *This is the land that shall fall to you as your portion, the land of Canaan with its various boundaries* (Num 34:2). And Canaan was our ancestor."

[A2] Geviha b. Pesisa said to the sages, "Give me permission to go and dispute with them before Alexander Macedon. If they defeat me you will say to them, 'You defeated a commoner from among us.' But if I defeat them, say 'The Torah of Moses our Rabbi defeated you.'" They gave him permission and he went to dispute with them before Alexander.

[A3] He said to them, "From where do you bring proof?" They said to him, "From the Torah." He said to them, "I too will bring you proof exclusively from the Torah, as it says, *Cursed be Canaan, the lowest of slaves shall he be to his brothers* (Gen 9:25). If a slave acquires property, to whom does the slave belong? To whom does the property belong? Moreover, you have not been serving us now for some years."

[A4] Alexander Macedon said to them, "Answer them back." They said to him, "Give us some time." He gave them three days' time. They searched but could not come up with an answer.

[A5] Immediately they fled and left behind their sown fields and planted vineyards. And that year was the Sabbatical.[5]

[B1] The Egyptians came to dispute with Israel before Alexander Macedon. They said to them, "Behold, it says, *And the Lord disposed the Egyptians favorably toward the people, and they let them have their request; thus they stripped the Egyptians* (Exod 12:36). Give us the silver and gold which you took from us."

[B2] Geviha b. Pesisa said to the sages, "Give me permission to go and dispute with them." If they defeat me you will say, "You defeated a commoner from among us." But if I defeat them, you will say, "The Torah of Moses defeated you." They gave him permission and he went to dispute with them.

[B3] He said to them, "From where do you bring proof?" They said to him, "From the Torah." He said to them, "I too will bring you proof exclusively from the Torah, as it says, *The length of time that the Israelites lived in Egypt was four hundred and thirty years* (Exod 12:40). Give us the wages for the work of the six hundred thousand [people] you enslaved in Egypt for four hundred and thirty years."

[B4] Alexander Macedon said to them, "Answer them back." They said to him, "Give us some time." He gave them three days. They searched but could not come up with an answer.

[B5] Immediately they left behind their sown fields and planted vineyards and fled.

[C1] The Ishmaelites and Qeturites came to dispute with Israel before Alexander Macedon. They said to him, "The Land of Canaan is both ours and yours, as it is written, *This is the line of Ishmael, Abraham's son* (Gen 25:12), and it is written, *This is the line of Isaac, son of Abraham* (Gen 25:19)."

[C2] Geviha b. Pesisa said to the sages, "Give me permission to go and dispute with them before Alexander Macedon. If they defeat me you will say, 'You defeated a commoner from among us.' But if I defeat them, say to them, 'The Torah of Moses [our master] defeated you.'" They gave him permission and he went to dispute with them.

[C3] He said to them, "From where do you bring proof?" They said to him, "From the Torah." He said to them, "I too will bring you proof exclusively from the Torah. It is written, *Abraham willed all that he owned to Isaac; but to Abraham's sons by concubines Abraham gave gifts* (Gen 25:6). If a father gives a legacy to his sons during his lifetime and sends away the one from before the other, can one claim anything from the other?"

Chapter 25

ALEXANDER MACEDON AND THE FARAWAY KING (YERUSHALMI BAVA METSIA 2:5, 8c)

The story of "Alexander and the Faraway King" contrasts the base motives of Alexander with the wisdom of an ideal king who lives in a distant land. Alexander portrays himself as a seeker of knowledge, claiming that he travels to remote places in order to learn of justice and good government (A). His true objectives become clear when he confesses that in his culture the king would commit an unjust murder so as to maximize his own gain, a sharp contrast to the Faraway King's wise decision (B1–B2). The story thus parodies the image of Alexander as the integrator of the cultures of East and West. His travels and conquests—and by extension those of all conquerors—are motivated by greed.

The lesson that the Faraway King attempts to teach Alexander by serving him golden food is a familiar folkloristic trope (C).[1] But the concluding theological observation and scriptural exegesis puts a Jewish stamp on the tale. God tolerates evil human societies because of his provident care for all of his creatures. Were it not for the innocent animals, God would remove the blessings of nature from unjust human societies.

Jonah Fraenkel suggests that the story contrasts two rabbinic images of Gentiles. The Faraway King represents the ideal Gentile, who acts justly and wisely despite his lack of Torah. Alexander represents the stereotypical Gentile, who violates law and justice in a relentless pursuit of wealth.[2]

[A] Alexander Macedon traveled to the Faraway King.³ He [the king] showed him much gold. He showed him much silver. He [Alexander] said, "I do not need your gold or your silver. Rather, I have come to observe your ways: how you do business; how you judge."

[B1] While he was occupied with him, a certain man approached disputing with his fellow. He had bought a field, and while he was digging it up he found a treasure of golden coins. The one who bought it said, "I bought a mound. I did not buy a treasure." The one who sold it said, "I sold you a mound and everything in it." While they were arguing with one another, the king said to one of them, "Do you have a male child?" He said, "Yes." He said to the other, "Do you have a female child?" He said, "Yes." He said, "Marry them one to the other, and the treasure will go to both of them."

[B2] He [Alexander] began to laugh. He [the king] said to him, "Why do you laugh? Did I not judge well?" [Then] he [the king] said, "If this case had come before you, how would you have judged?" He said, "We would kill both the one and the other, and the treasure would fall to the king."

[C] He [the king] said to him, "Then you love gold so much?" He made him a meal. He brought before him meat [made out] of gold [and] fowl [made out] of gold. He [Alexander] said to him, "Do I eat gold?" He said to him, "Blast your bones!⁴ If you don't eat gold, then why do you love it so much?"

[D] He [the king] said to him, "Does the sun shine for you?" He said to him, "Yes." "Does the rain fall for you?" He said to him, "Yes." He said to him, "Perhaps there is small cattle among you?" He said to him, "Yes." [He said,] "Blast your bones. You continue to live solely on account of the small cattle, as it says, *You save man and beast, O Lord* (Ps 36:7)."⁵

Chapter 26

ANTONINUS AND RABBI

Numerous rabbinic stories describe friendly encounters between a Roman emperor named Antoninus or Antolinus and Rabbi, the sobriquet of Rabbi Yehuda HaNasi (=the patriarch).[1] For many years historians attempted to identify the intended emperor, since seven emperors of the second and third centuries bore the surname Antoninus, while still other emperors seemed to be likely candidates on the basis of their character.[2] These stories, however, are fictions. Their historical kernel perhaps is to be found in that R. Yehuda HaNasi may have received some sort of official recognition from Rome, the title patriarch and limited authority over portions of Palestine.[3] During part of the late second and early third centuries CE, relations between rabbis and Roman governors—or at least between some rabbis and Roman governors—were amicable. Stories of the friendship between the Jewish patriarch and Roman emperor illustrate this period of cordial relations. They probably suggested to rabbis of succeeding centuries, especially during times of increased tension, that the two nations could coexist in peace.

Several stories report discussions between Rabbi and Antoninus regarding a variety of theological and philosophical topics. Rabbi is generally portrayed as the teacher; he instructs Antoninus based on his religious expertise and knowledge of scripture. In story A, for example, Rabbi answers Antoninus's question concerning the relationship of soul and body. These encounters resemble a well-known genre of Hellenistic literature in which a king asks questions of a foreign wise man and is impressed by his wisdom.[4] However, in story B Antoninus has the upper hand. The Roman convinces

Rabbi of the accuracy of his opinion, and Rabbi concedes after realizing that the Bible supports Antoninus's claims.

In a number of stories Antoninus appeals to Rabbi for political advice and Rabbi invariably solves the emperor's problems (story C). These anecdotes demonstrate the superior wisdom of the Jews, who surpass the Romans in their own game. The rabbis always celebrated their excellence in knowledge of Torah and of God's ways. That their political expertise outstripped that of the Romans, despite both the august Roman political tradition and the power of the Roman Empire, created an additional reason for national pride.

The Bavli, as in so many cases, provides exaggerated expressions of the relationship between the two leaders (story D). Antoninus consults Rabbi daily, traveling from Rome to Palestine through a subterranean tunnel and killing his attendants lest they report his visits (a). The emperor serves Rabbi food and drink and even beckons Rabbi to use him as a footstool when ascending to bed (e). No longer are Rabbi and Antoninus friends or teacher and student, as in the Palestinian sources, but master and servant. Antoninus seems to be motivated by concern for a share in the world to come, a legitimate worry given rabbinic Judaism's general belief that the Romans will be punished posthumously for their abuses in this world (e-f). In this respect the story foreshadows the situation that the rabbis expected to prevail in the next world, that the Gentiles, though dominant in this world, would be subservient to the Jews. The story also exhibits the common Bavli theme that powerful Gentiles, including those who attacked the Jews, eventually recognize the truth of Judaism and renounce their ways[5] (see chapter 4, story A, sections C and Q).[6]

A. The Body and the Soul (Bavli Sanhedrin 91a)

[A] Antoninus said to Rabbi: The body and the soul can exempt themselves from judgment [after death]. How so? The body can say, "The soul sinned! For as soon as she departed from me I have remained in my grave, as lifeless as a stone." The soul can say, "The body sinned! For as soon as I departed from it I have flown in the air like a bird."

[B] He said to him: I will tell you a parable. To what is this similar? To a king of flesh and blood who had a beautiful orchard, and he had excellent figs there. He appointed two watchmen, one lame and the other blind. The lame man said to the blind man: I see fine figs in the orchard. Come and hoist me up and we will get them and eat them. The lame man stood upon the blind man, and they got them and ate them. After a little while the owner of the orchard came. He said, "Where are those fine figs?" The lame man said, "Do I have legs to walk upon?" The blind man said, "Do I have eyes to see?" What did he do? He stood the lame man upon the blind man and judged them together.

[C] So too the Holy One, blessed be He, will bring the soul and cast it into the body and judge them together, as it is written, *He summoned the heavens above, and the earth, for the judgment of his people* (Ps 50:4): "He summoned the heavens above"—this refers to the soul [which comes from the heavens]. "And to the earth, for the judgment of his people"—this refers to the body [which comes from the dust of the earth].[7]

B. The Evil Inclination (Genesis Rabbah 34:10)[8]

[A] Antoninus asked our Rabbi [Yehuda HaNasi]. He said to him: "When is the evil inclination put into a human being? When it comes out of its mother's womb or before it comes out of its mother's womb?" He said to him, "Before it comes out of its mother's womb." He said to him, "No. For if the soul were put into it while still in its mother's womb, it would dig at the chamber in her womb [trying] to get out. Rather, from the time it comes out." And Rabbi conceded to him, since [his opinion] conformed to that of scripture: *For the inclination of man's mind is evil from youth* (Gen 8:21). R. Yudan said, "It is written, 'From youth *[mi-ne'urav]*'—from the time it wakes up *[ne'or]* to go forth into the world.'"[9]

[B] Antoninus also asked him, "When is the soul put into a human being? When it comes out of its mother's womb or before it comes out of its mother's womb?" He [Rabbi] said to him, "When it comes out of its mother's womb." He [Antoninus] said to him, "If one leaves meat for three days without salt, will it not rot? It rots immediately![10] Rather, from the time of visitation *[peqida]*."[11] And our Rabbi conceded to him, since [his opinion] conformed with that of scripture: *You bestowed on me life and care; Your providence* (pequdatkha) *watched over my spirit* (Job 10:12). When did you put the soul in me? When you visited me.[12]

C. Political Consultation (Genesis Rabbah 67:5)

[A] Antoninus sent [a letter] to Rabbi. He said to him, "The treasuries are wanting. What can we do to fill them?"

[B] He [Rabbi] took the messenger and brought him into an orchard. He began to uproot large radishes and plant small ones. He [the messenger] said to him, "Give me a written response." He said to him, "You don't need one."

[C] He [the messenger] went back to him [Antoninus].

(1) He said to him, "Where is the written response?" He said to him, "He did not give me anything."

(2) He said to him, "What did he say to you?" He said to him, "He did not say anything to me."

(3) He said to him, "Did he not do anything in your presence?" He said to him, "He took me and brought me into an orchard, and he began to uproot large radishes and plant small ones."

[D] The emperor began to exile nobles[13] [and confiscate their money] and promote [other] nobles until the treasuries were filled.[14]

D. Antoninus, Servant of Rabbi (Bavli Avodah Zarah 10b)

[a] There was a tunnel through which he [Antoninus] traveled each day from his house to Rabbi's house.[15] Each day he brought with him two servants. He slew one at the entrance of Rabbi's house and he slew the other at the entrance of his own house.[16] He said to him [Rabbi], "Let no one be present with you at the time of my visit."

[b] One day he found R. Hanina b. Hamma sitting there. He said to him [Rabbi], "Did I not already tell you, 'Let no one be present with you at the time of my visits'?" He said to him, "This one is no human."[17] He [Antoninus] said to him [R. Hanina b. Hamma], "Let him tell that slave who lies at the door to get up and come in."

[c] R. Hanina b. Hamma went. He found him slain. He said, "What should I do? Should I go and tell him that he is slain? One does not bring sad tidings. Should I leave him and depart? That would be demeaning to the king." He prayed for him and resurrected him and sent him [to Antoninus].

[d] He [Antoninus] said, "I know that even the least important among you can resurrect the dead. Nevertheless, let no one be present with you at the time of my visit."

[e] Every day he served Rabbi. He fed him. He brought him drink. When Rabbi wished to ascend upon his bed, he [Antoninus] would crouch before the bed. He said to him, "Ascend upon me to your bed." He said to him, "It is not proper to demean the king so much." He said to him, "Would that I should be a mattress beneath you in the world to come!"

[f] He [Antoninus] said to him, "Will I enter the world to come?" He said to him, "Yes." He said to him, "Is it not written, *No survivor shall be left of the House of Esau* (Obad 1:18)?"[18] [He said to him,] "This refers only to those who act as Esau acted."[19]

Chapter 27

JESUS AND HIS DISCIPLES

Few classical rabbinic traditions mention Jesus and Christianity explicitly. The Babylonian rabbinic community was somewhat removed from the Roman-Christian Empire, while the Palestinian Talmud and midrashic collections antedate the emergence of Christianity as the dominant religion it was to become in the Middle Ages.[1] These compilations were redacted in the fourth and fifth centuries but primarily contain traditions from earlier times.[2] From a legal point of view, the rabbis seem to have considered Christianity as another type of idolatry *(avodah zarah)* that merited no particular discussion of its own. The conception of Christianity (and subsequently Islam) as a monotheistic religion occurred in post-talmudic times.

Isolated rabbinic passages that explicitly mention Jesus and Christianity do not appear in the standard printed editions of the texts, although they are generally found in the manuscripts. These passages were removed by Christian censors or by the Jewish printers for fear of Christian censors. Generally rabbinic traditions classify Jesus under the rabbinic category of heresy *(minut)* or under the biblical rubric of the "enticer" *(meisit)* mentioned in Deuteronomy 13:7–12, one who "entices" Israel to worship foreign gods.

The source translated below from the Tosefta (A) is set in the second century CE, before the clear separation of the two religions, when debates between Jewish-Christians and Jews probably were common. It refers to Jesus as Yeshua (=Joshua), "son of Pantera." While the name literally means "panther," a typical name for a Roman soldier, it is perhaps a play on the Greek *parthenos* (=virgin), although there is no scholarly consensus on this issue (A). A later source found in the Bavli identifies "Pandira" as the paramour

169

of Jesus' mother, inverting the image of Mary as virgin into Mary as adulteress.[3] The identity of Jesus' disciple Yaakov [=Jacob] of Kefar Samma or Kefar Sakhnia (A, H) is unknown.

The first Toseftan anecdote takes the extreme position that it is better to die than to solicit medical help from a Christian (A-C).[4] R. Ishmael's midrash on Qoheleth 10:8 interprets "fence-breakers" in terms of those who violate rabbinic "fences," that is, rabbinic edicts designed to remove Jews from situations where they may sin unwittingly (C). In this case the rabbinic edict to which he alludes apparently prohibited any interaction with heretics, including the solicitation of medical assistance, since such encounters might turn to theological discussions and eventually lead to heresy or apostasy. While preservation of life generally takes precedence over all the commandments—one must violate the Sabbath, for example, to save a life—this source suggests that the danger to Judaism from Christian contact overrides the loss of life.[5]

R. Ishmael describes the dying R. Eleazar b. Damma as "fortunate" and implies that had he consulted the Christian disciple he would have been "bitten by a snake" (=experience sufferings). Ironically, R. Eleazar b. Damma finds himself on death's door precisely because a (real) snake bit him. The storyteller probably hints that R. Eleazar b. Damma consulted Christians in the past, as indicated by his readiness to prove that their medical advice is permitted, and for that reason suffered the snakebite. R. Ishmael accordingly means that his colleague will avoid posthumous suffering and enjoy otherworldly happiness by forgoing further contact. This irony combined with the literal and midrashic understandings of the snakebite enhances the story's narrative quality. There may also be resonances of the biblical snake, the seduction of Adam and Eve with the promise of knowledge (parallel to medical knowledge), the tree of life, and the punishment (or lack thereof) of death for violating God's commandment not to eat from the forbidden fruit.

The Tosefta's second story takes place during the Roman persecutions of Christianity (D-H). Jews who associated with Christians not only risked divine punishment, as in the previous story, but torture and death at the hands of the Romans. While R. Eliezer knows that he is innocent of heretical leanings, and while he manages to escape punishment by a crafty ambiguous statement, he interprets his arrest and close call with death as divine punishment. He therefore refuses to be consoled until he understands what caused the terrifying experience (G). Again we learn that just about any interaction with heretics counts as a serious sin: simply to have taken pleasure at a heretical teaching heard in the market explains why he almost lost his life. Lest a rabbi think himself in no danger from the Romans because he never engaged in actual Christian practice, our storyteller warns that God may nonetheless exact punishment for minor contact by causing the rabbi to be arrested.

The tradition R. Eliezer attributes to Yaakov and Yeshu (=Jesus) is a parody of a midrashic exegesis (H). The form is typical of rabbinic and early Christian biblical interpretation: a question concerning the scope of a biblical law solved by adducing biblical prooftexts. However, the content—whether a prostitute's earnings can be used to pay for the high priest's toilet—parodies Christian teaching. Rabbis should not bother speaking with Christians as they will find neither serious biblical learning nor sophisticated theology but only vulgar answers to silly questions. R. Eliezer's final teaching concerning the importance of distancing oneself from heresy appropriately cites Proverbs 5:8. In context the verse refers to a foreign woman who seduces the aspiring student from attaining wisdom. So too the rabbis had to guard themselves from the seductive attraction of Christian tradition.[6]

Two legendary traditions from the Bavli (stories B and C) deal with the origins and demise of Jesus. A fascinating passage depicts Jesus as a disciple of a prominent rabbi; Jesus abandoned Judaism after a falling out with his master (a–h). Here Jesus' turn to heresy results from a tragedy of misunderstanding. Jesus first misconstrues his teacher's comment and receives a rebuke, and then he misinterprets a gesture of reconciliation, leaves his master and introduces heretical practices. The founding of Christianity is portrayed as the unfortunate outcome of the deterioration of a relationship between a master and student, and there is as much criticism of the rabbinic sage as of his disciple. Indeed, the purpose of the story, indicated by the opening comment, warns rabbinic masters not to berate their students too harshly lest they drive the pupils away. Yet one also detects a more hostile attitude to Jesus in a brief tradition introduced as a type of appendix to the story (h).

The account of Jesus' death emphasizes that he received a very fair trial and thoroughly deserved his punishment (i-k). Although God commands that no compassion be extended to "enticers" who lead Jews to heretical worship, the Jewish court, wary that Jesus "was close" to the Roman authorities, nevertheless granted forty days to find some evidence in his favor. Since none was found, we can conclude that his guilt was absolute. Moreover, since Jesus' friends in high places failed to intervene, it appears that they too recognized his guilt. Here we have a rather different perspective on the trial of Jesus than that found in the gospel accounts. Where the gospels blame the Jews or Jewish authorities ("his blood be on our hands") and emphasize the innocence of Jesus, the Bavli relates that the Jewish courts gave Jesus more than he deserved.[7]

A. Rabbis and Christians (Tosefta Hullin 2:22-24)

[A] Once R. Eleazar b. Damma was bitten by a snake. Yaakov of Kefar Samma came to heal him in the name of Yeshua b. Pantera [=Jesus], but R. Ishmael would not let him.[8]

[B] He [R. Ishmael] said, "You are not permitted, Son of Damma." He [R. Eleazar b. Damma] said to him, "I will bring proof that he is permitted to heal me." But he did not manage to bring proof before he died.

[C] R. Ishmael said, "Fortunate are you, Son of Damma, that you departed in peace, and you did not break the decree (gezeira) of the sages. For whoever breaks the fence of the sages will eventually experience sufferings, as it says, He who breaks a fence (gader) will be bitten by a snake (Qoh 10:8)."[9]

[D] Our rabbis taught: Once R. Eliezer was arrested on a charge of heresy, and they brought him up to the tribunal for punishment. The [Roman] governor said to him, "An elder such as you involves himself with these vain matters?!" He said to him, "I trust the judge."

[E] That governor thought that he [R. Eliezer] was speaking about him. But he [R. Eliezer] spoke exclusively of his Father in Heaven.

[F] He [the governor] said to him, "Since you accepted me—*dimos*,[10] you are free."

[G] When he returned to his house, all of his disciples came to comfort him, but he would not accept their comforting. R. Akiba said to him, "My master! Will you permit me to say one teaching of that which you have taught me?" He said to him, "Speak." He said to him, "My master. Perhaps you came upon a heretical teaching and found it pleasing, and for that reason you were arrested."

[H] He said to him, "Yes, by Heaven, you have reminded me: Once I was walking in the upper market in Sepphoris when one of the disciples of Yeshu the Notsri [Christian][11] came upon me, and his name was Yaakov of Kefar Sakhnia. He said to me, 'It is written in your Torah, *You shall not bring the fee of a whore or the price of a dog into the house of the Lord your God in fulfillment of any vow* (Deut 23:19). Is it lawful to [use the money] to build a toilet for the high priest?' I gave no response. He said to me that his master Yeshu taught him thus: '*For they were amassed from whores' fees and they shall become whores' fees again* (Mic 1:7). It [the money] came from a filthy place; it may be used for a filthy place.' This teaching pleased me, and for that reason I was arrested [on a charge of] heresy. For I transgressed that which is written in the Torah, *Keep yourself far away from her* (Prov 5:8)—this refers to heresy. *Do not come near the doorway of her house* (Prov 5:8)—this refers to the government."[12]

🔥

B. Jesus the Wayward Disciple (Bavli Sanhedrin 107b)

[a] Always let the left hand rebuff while the right hand encourages—not like Elisha, who rebuffed Gehazi with both hands, and not like Yehoshua b. Perahia, who rebuffed Yeshu the Notsri [Christian] with both hands....[13]

[b] "Yehoshua b. Perahia"—what is the reference?

[c] When Yannai the King was killing our rabbis, Yehoshua b. Perahia and Yeshu went to Alexandria in Egypt.[14] When there was peace, Shimon b. Shetah sent to him [Yehoshua], "From me, Jerusalem the Holy city, to you, Alexandria in Egypt, my sister! My husband lies in your midst, while I sit deserted."[15]

[d] He [Yehoshua] rose, set out and arrived at a certain lodging. They treated him with great honor. He said, "How beautiful is this *aksania* [inn]!" He [Yeshu] said to him, "But master, her [the innkeeper's] eyes are slanted." He said to him, "Wicked one! Are you occupied with that?"[16] He sounded 400 shofar [blasts] and banned him.[17]

[e] He [Yeshu] came before him [Yehoshua] several times. He said to him, "Take me back." He [Yehoshua] paid him no attention.

[f] One day he [Yehoshua] was reciting the *Shema*.[18] He [Yeshu] came before him. He intended to take him back. He gestured with his hand [to wait until he could finish the prayer]. He [Yeshu] thought that he was rejecting him. He set up a brick and worshiped it.

[g] He [Yehoshua] said to him, "Repent." He [Yeshu] said to him, "Thus I have received a tradition from you: 'He who sins and leads others to sin is not given the opportunity to repent.'"

[h] And there is a tradition:[19] "Yeshu the Notsri engaged in sorcery and enticed and turned Israel to idolatry."

C. The Trial and Death of Jesus (Bavli Sanhedrin 43a)

[i] On the eve of Passover they hanged Yeshu the Notsri.[20] The herald went forth for forty days [saying], "Yeshu the Notsri is going out to be stoned for he engaged in sorcery, enticed and turned Israel to idolatry. Whoever knows anything relating to his innocence, let him come and testify for him." And they found no grounds for innocence. They hanged him on the eve of Passover.

[j] Ulla said, "Is this plausible? Could there be grounds for innocence for Yeshu the Notsri? He was an enticer, and the Merciful One said, *Show him no pity or compassion* (Deut 13:9)."

[k] Yeshu the Notsri was different, for he was close to the [Roman] authorities.[21]

Chapter 28

ONQELOS THE CONVERT (BAVLI AVODAH ZARAH 11a)

Rabbinic tradition attributed the Aramaic translation of the Pentateuch to "Onqelos the Convert."[1] (The name seems to be related to "Aqilas the Convert," to whom the Church Fathers attribute a Greek translation of the Pentateuch.[2]) The following story recounts the futile efforts of the emperor to arrest Onqelos and return him to Rome. Why the emperor should concern himself with Onqelos is not stated—apparently Onqelos was a high-ranking Roman or member of the emperor's household, and his conversion to Judaism was an embarrassment. The imperial attention, at all events, suggests that a Roman of significant status, and not a mere commoner, found Judaism of such value as to renounce his prominent station. Onqelos's exchanges with the three companies of Romans sent by the emperor point to the attractions Judaism held for pagans in the rabbinic imagination. The beauty of scripture and the Jewish conception of a God who cares for the people of his covenant impress the Roman soldiers to the point that they too convert.[3]

[A] Onqelos b. Qaloniqos converted [to Judaism].[4]

[B1] The emperor sent a company of Roman [soldiers] after him. He interested them in lengthy discussions of scripture, and they converted.

[B2] He [the emperor] then sent another company of Roman [soldiers] after him. He said to them, "Don't speak to him at all." When they arrested him and started out, he said to them, "May I tell you something? A torch-bearer carries the torch for the over-seer, the overseer [carries the torch] for the commander, the commander for the general, the general for the magistrate—but does the magistrate carry a torch for the people?"[5] They said to him, "No." He said to them, "The Holy One, blessed be He, car-ries a torch before Israel, as it says, *The Lord went before them in a pillar of cloud by day, to guide them along the way, and in a pillar of cloud by night* (Exod 13:21)." They all converted.

[B3] He [the emperor] then sent another company after him. He said to them, "Don't discuss anything at all with him." While they were taking him out, he saw a *mezuza*.[6] He placed his hand upon it and said to them, "What is this?" They said, "You tell us." He said to them, "It is the way of the world that a human king sits inside and his servants guard him outside. But the Holy One, blessed be He, guards Israel from outside, as it says, *The Lord is your guardian, the Lord is your protection at your right hand* (Ps 121:5)." They all converted.

[C] He [the emperor] did not send [soldiers] after him again.

PART VII:

THE LIFE OF PIETY: CHARITY, COMMANDMENTS, VIRTUES

Chapter 29

HILLEL, SHAMMAI AND CONVERTS: VIRTUES AND THEOLOGICAL BASICS (BAVLI SHABBAT 31a)

Rabbinic storytellers used the early rabbinic hero Hillel and his counterpart Shammai to model values. This narrative, appearing only in the Bavli, teaches the importance of *anvetanut*, meaning gentleness, humility, modesty and patience. Such a disposition was crucial not only for rabbinic interactions with outsiders, but also within the rabbinic academy. Passionate arguments and the heat of legal debate often provoked anger, insults and recriminations (see Part III). When sages conducted themselves with humility, they created a healthy and productive environment for discussion.

The storytellers probably combined several sources to create the text below. A tightly crafted structure is particularly clear. The opening and ending mention gentleness and impatience, associating the former with Hillel and the latter with Shammai (A, H). This frame brackets two main units, each introduced by "Our sages taught" (1, 2). The first establishes the patience of Hillel; the second contrasts Hillel's gentleness with Shammai's impatience. Three times a man approaches Hillel with annoying questions in the first unit (C1–C3); three times prospective converts approach Shammai and Hillel in the second (E1–E2, F1–F2, G1–G2).

Rabbinic attitudes to converts are diverse. The Bavli, for example, contains traditions such as "God dispersed Israel among the nations solely in order that converts join them" (Pesahim 87b), at the same time lamenting that "converts are as difficult to Israel as a scab" (Yevamot 47a). The purpose of the three dialogues placed in the mouths of converts may be more to answer basic questions about rabbinic theology than to teach a specific attitude to conversion (other than the value of patience). The first grapples with the authority of the Oral Torah. How do we know that Moses received it on Mount Sinai and that the sages passed it down from generation to generation?[1] Answer: we rely on the sages to know that the Written Torah too came from God, to know how to read it, and to be certain that scribes copied it accurately over the centuries. The same authority in fact grounds both Torahs. The second addresses the core value of the Torah. If one fundamental principle must be singled out, it is the proper treatment of fellow human beings. The rest of the Torah, however, is also important and must be studied ("Go and learn it"). The third teaches that God loves all Jews equally, notwithstanding the higher lineage of priests and the (now defunct) privileges of the high priest. Even the convert enters beneath the Divine Presence and essentially possesses the same status as David, King of Israel.[2]

[1][A] Our sages taught: One should always be a gentle man *[anvetan]* like Hillel and never be an impatient man like Shammai.

[B] Once two men made a wager between them. They said, "Whoever goes and angers Hillel will get 400 *zuz*." One of them said, "I will anger him."

[C1] That day was the Sabbath eve, and Hillel was washing his head. He [that man] went and passed by the entrance to his house and said, "Who here is Hillel? Who here is Hillel?" He [Hillel] covered himself and went out to greet him. He said to him, "My son, what do you want?" He said, "I have a question to ask." He said, "Ask, my son, ask." He said to him, "Why are the heads of Babylonians round?" He said to him, "My son. You ask an important question. Because they have no skilled midwives."

[C2] He went and waited one hour. He returned and said, "Who here is Hillel? Who here is Hillel?" He covered himself and went out to greet him. He said to him, "My son, what do you want?"

He said, "I have a question to ask." He said, "Ask, my son, ask." He said to him, "Why are the eyes of the Tadmorians slanted?"[3] He said to him, "My son. You ask an important question. Because they dwell among the deserts."

[C3] He went and waited one hour. He returned and said, "Who here is Hillel? Who here is Hillel?" He covered himself and went out to greet him. He said to him, "My son, what do you want?" He said, "I have a question to ask." He said, "Ask, my son, ask." He said to him, "Why are the feet of Africans wide?" He said to him, "My son. You ask an important question. Because they dwell among ponds of water."

[D] He said to him, "I have many questions to ask, but I am afraid lest you get mad at me." He [Hillel] covered himself and sat before him. He said to him, "Ask all the questions that you want to ask." He said to him, "Are you Hillel who is called the patriarch (nasi) of Israel?" He said to him, "Yes." He said to him, "If it is you, may there not be many like you in Israel." He said to him, "Why, my son?" He said, "Because I lost 400 zuz on your account." He said to him, "Be careful about your disposition. It is worth your losing four hundred zuz on Hillel's account, and yet another 400 zuz, and Hillel not become angry."

[2][E1] Our sages taught: Once a Gentile came before Shammai. He said to him, "How many Torahs do you have?" He said to him, "Two, the Written Torah and the Oral Torah." He said to him, "I believe you about the Written but not about the Oral. I will convert on the condition that you teach me the Written Torah [alone]."[4] He rebuked him and dismissed him with a reproach.

[E2] He [the Gentile] came before Hillel. The first day he [Hillel] said to him, "Aleph, beit, gimmel, dalet." The next day he reversed it.[5] He [the Gentile] said to him, "Yesterday, you did not tell it to me this way." He said to him, "Did you not rely on me [for that]?[6] As regards the Oral [Torah], you should rely on me too!"

[F1] Another time a Gentile came before Shammai. He said to him, "I will convert on the condition that you teach me the entire Torah while I stand on one leg." He drove him away with the builder's cubit that was in his hand.[7]

[F2] He came before Hillel. He converted him. He said to him, "That which is hateful to you, do not do to your fellow. That is the entire Torah. The rest is its commentary. Go and learn it."[8]

[G1] Another time a Gentile was passing behind the academy, and he heard the scribe's voice saying, "*These are the vestments they are to make: a breastpiece, an ephod, a robe, a fringed tunic, a headdress, and a sash* (Exod 28:4)." He said, "Whom are these for?" They said to him, "For the high priest." That Gentile said to himself, "I will go and convert so that they can make me the high priest." He came before Shammai. He said, "I will convert on the condition that you make me the high priest." He drove him away with the builder's cubit that was in his hand.

[G2] He came before Hillel. He converted him. He said to him, "They only appoint as royalty one who knows the protocol of royalty. Go and learn the protocol of royalty."

[G3] He went and read [scripture.] When he came to *Any outsider who encroaches [near the Tabernacle] will be put to death* (Num 1:51), he said to him [Hillel], "To whom does this verse apply?" He said to him, "Even to David, King of Israel."

[G4] That Gentile made a *qal va-homer*[9] inference about himself: "Israel are called the sons of the Omnipresent, and he loved them so much that he called them *Israel, my firstborn son* (Exod 4:22). If it is written about them, *Any outsider who encroaches will be put to death* (Num 1:51), then how much the more so [does this apply to] the lowly (*qal*) convert, who comes with [only] a staff and bag!"[10]

[G5] He came before Shammai. He said to him, "I am certainly not worthy to be the high priest. Is it not written in the Torah,

Any outsider who encroaches will be put to death (Num 1:51)." He came before Hillel. He said to him, "Hillel, may your gentleness bring you blessings, for you brought me under the wings of the Divine Presence."

[H] Later the three [Gentiles] chanced to be in one place. They said, "The impatience of Shammai almost drove us from the world. The gentleness *[anvetanut]* of Hillel brought us under the wings of the Divine Presence."

Chapter 30

THE COMMANDMENT OF THE FRINGES AND ITS REWARD (SIFRE NUMBERS § 115)

Rabbinic sources offer two perspectives on the reward for per-forming the commandments. Some claim that God provides the reward both in this world, usually in the form of long life and numer-ous children, as well as in the world to come. Others suggest that God always defers the reward until the world to come, or even that God punishes the righteous in this world for their few sins so that they will merit a greater reward in the next (see chapter 37 herein). The following story, which has many characteristics of a folktale, makes a strong argument for reward both in this world and in the world to come based on the commandment of the fringes.[1] The protagonist ultimately receives a tangible and very earthly reward, the hand in marriage of the most beautiful woman, and the narrator anticipates greater things in the hereafter (H-I).

To fully appreciate the story one must realize that it is simulta-neously an exegesis of the scriptural passage describing the fringes *(tsitsit)*, Numbers 15:37–41. The Torah explains that one should look at the fringes to recall and observe the commandments, in order "that you do not go seeking about after your heart and eyes, after which you go a whoring *(zonim)*." A narrative created from this figure of speech generates the core of the story: the man indeed "goes seeking about after" his heart by seeking out a prostitute in a distant place and traveling there. He also "goes a whoring" *(zonim)* by visiting a whore *(zonah)*.[2] His personified fringes then remind him of the reward for keeping the commandments by appearing as witnesses and even compel him to refrain from sin by physically intervening (E-F). That the fringes prevent both his "going a whoring" and ultimately move the prostitute to cease whoring with others is an enchanting literal interpretation of the biblical metaphor.

A number of literary and structural features contribute to the story's dramatic effect. The story divides into two halves: in the first, the man pursues the woman for sin; in the second, the woman pursues the man for a virtuous purpose. The man must first wait for an appointment and then travel both far horizontally, to the cities by the sea, and vertically, to the top of the stack of couches, in order to gratify his lust (B, D). These efforts enhance the woman's eroticism and desirability, as do the silver couches crowned by the golden couch. The deflation of his passion correspondingly is marked by his descending to the ground and return home (E, H). The prostitute first swears by a pagan deity, but after she hears the Jew make a similar oath "by the temple service" she too swears in this way, imitating his expression and subsequently his religion (F, G). Ironically, the man in the end will "enjoy" this most beautiful woman as a reward for observing the commandment of the fringes, although he initially resists her for the same reason, his allegiance to his fringes. He abstains from illicit pleasure in this world because he worries about his reward and punishment in the world to come, and thereby merits those this-worldly pleasures. A play on "wages/reward" (*sekhar*) helps emphasize the moral: the prostitute gives up the tremendous *sekhar* she earns each day, and the man the high *sekhar* he paid, for the *sekhar* of the commandments (A, F, I). Those who observe the commandments, we are assured, enjoy true reward in this world and in the next.

[A] R. Natan says: There is not a single commandment (*mitzvah*) in the Torah, the promise of reward (*sekhara*) for which is not [written] together with it.[3] Go and learn from the commandment of the fringes.

[B] There once was a certain man who was punctilious with the commandment of the fringes. He heard that there was a prostitute in the cities by the sea[4] who received 400 gold coins as her wage (*sekhara*). He sent her 400 gold coins, and she set a time for him.

[C] When his time arrived he went and sat at the entrance of her house. Her servant-girl entered and said to her, "That man for whom you set a time—behold, he is sitting at the entrance of the house." She said to her, "Let him come in."

[D1] When he entered she prepared for him seven couches of silver and the top one was of gold.

[D2] There were benches of silver between them all, and the top one was of gold.

[D3] There were steps of silver between them all, and the top one was of gold.[5]

[E] When they came around to "that act" his four fringes came and appeared to him as four witnesses and they beat him on the face. Immediately he withdrew and sat on the ground. She too withdrew and sat on the ground.

[F] She said to him, "By the Love-[Goddess] of Rome,[6] I won't leave you be until you tell me what blemish you saw in me." He said to her, "By the [temple] service, I saw no blemish in you, for there is no beauty equal to yours in the whole world. But the Lord our God commanded us a minor commandment called 'fringes,' and he wrote about it '*I am the Lord your God....I am the Lord your God* (Num 15:41)' two times.[7] 'I am the Lord your God'—I will provide a reward (*sekhar*) in the future [world]. 'I am the Lord'—I am the judge who will exact punishment [for violating the commandments]."

[G] She said to him, "By the [temple] service, I will not leave you be until you write down for me your name and the name of your city and the name of your school in which you study Torah." And he wrote down for her his name and the name of his city and the name of his school in which he studied Torah.

[H] She went forth and distributed all of her money, one-third to the monarchy, and one-third to the poor and one-third she took with her, and she came and she stood in the study-house of R. Hiyya. She said to him, "My master, convert me." He said to her, "Perhaps you have set your eyes on one of the disciples." She held out to him the text in her hand.[8] He [R. Hiyya] said to him [the man], "Come forth and enjoy your acquisition."

[I] Those beds which she prepared for him unlawfully, she prepared for him lawfully. This is the giving of its reward *(sekhara)* in this world. And in the world to come—I don't know how much!

Chapter 31

THE POWER OF RIGHTEOUSNESS (BAVLI SHABBAT 156b)

Biblical and rabbinic theologies maintain the principle of free will: human beings freely choose good or evil and God rewards or punishes them on that basis. While the Bible and rabbis generally believed in divine omniscience as well, they saw no conflict between these two doctrines. As a famous rabbinic maxim puts it, "Everything is foreseen, yet free will is given" (Mishna Avot 3:15).

To reject predestination or determinism, however, was not always easy, particularly when Jews lived in surrounding cultures that held to such beliefs. The encounter with forms of astrology in late antiquity made the clash of worldviews particularly acute, for astrology in antiquity was tantamount to what we call science. The distinction between astrology and astronomy—the former the stuff of fortunetellers, the latter objective scientific truth—would not be made for at least another millennium. The late antique astrologer who predicted the fate of individuals by reading the constellations can be compared to a doctor who diagnoses an illness today. The rabbis accordingly struggled to reconcile their belief in free will with the deterministic orientation of the science of their times.

The two stories below express an ambivalent attitude toward astrology with the principle "Israel has no constellation"; that is, the stars do not determine the fates of Jews. Gentile astrologers turn out to be partially right in predicting the death of the Jewish protagonists: they would have died were it not for the deeds of righteousness *(tsedaqa)* that they performed. Thus the constellations do in fact reveal something of the fate of Jews. Yet despite the recognition of astrological claims there persists the fundamental belief that performing good deeds and observing the commandments *(mitzvot)* can change one's fate. Against this background the rabbinic faith in free will takes on greater significance. Righteousness not only benefits the lives of its recipients, but its reward may deliver the doers from predestined suffering and death.

[A1] From the case of Shmuel too [we learn that] "Israel has no constellation."[1]

[B1] For Shmuel and Ablet[2] were sitting, and certain men passed by [on the way to] the fields. Ablet said to Shmuel, "That man is going but will not return, for a snake will bite him and he will die." Shmuel said to him, "He will go and return."

[C1] They were still sitting while he went and returned. Ablet stood up and cast off his [the man's] bag. He found there a snake sliced apart and cut into two pieces.[3]

[D1] Shmuel said to him [the man], "What have you done?" He said to him, "Every day we toss all our bread together [into a basket] and we eat. Today there was one among us who had no bread, and he felt ashamed.[4] I said to them, 'I will get up and toss [the bread in the basket].' When I got to him I pretended as if I took from him in order that he not be ashamed." He [Shmuel] said to him, "You did a righteous deed *(tsedaqa)!*"

[E1] Shmuel went forth and expounded, "Righteousness *(tsedaqa)* saves from death, not only from an unusual death, but from death itself."[5]

[A2] And from the words of R. Akiba too [we learn that] "Israel has no constellation."

[B2] For R. Akiba had a daughter. The Chaldeans [astrologers] said to him, "On the day that she enters the bridal chamber, a snake will bite her and she will die." He worried a great deal about this matter.

[C2] On the day that she was to be married she took a brooch and stuck it into [a fissure in] the wall.[6] It so happened that it went into the eye of a snake. The next morning when she removed it, a snake clung to it and came out after it.

[D2] Her father said to her, "What have you done?" She said to him, "At dusk a poor man came and called at the door.[7] Everyone else was busy preparing the meal and no one heard him. I got up and took the portion that was given to me, and I gave it to him." He said to her, "You did a *mitzvah!*"

[E2] R. Akiba went forth and expounded, "A *mitzvah* saves from death, not only from an unusual death, but from death itself."

Chapter 32

THE HONOR OF PARENTS

"You shall honor your father and mother," one of the Ten Commandments (Exod 20:12), was a cornerstone of rabbinic ethics. Numerous anecdotes illustrate the extreme lengths to which the rabbis went in order to fulfill the commandment (story A, sections A-B; story B, sections a-b). These *exempla* (example stories) hold up the rabbis as models of filial piety for future generations to emulate. At the same time, rabbinic sources grapple with the difficulty of fulfilling a potentially unlimited commandment. Thus R. Zeira, an orphan, lamented that he had no opportunity to honor parents until he saw the demands placed upon his colleagues (story A, section F).[1] His ironic comment thanking God that he never saw his parents recognizes the challenge involved in living up to the precept. In a story that resonates even today, R. Asi's aging mother made numerous and unreasonable requests until he fled to the Land of Israel (story B, sections d-h). He wished to avoid the possibility of dishonoring her by refusing or becoming angry. Even this drastic course did not totally free R. Asi from his obligation, for he soon learned that his mother followed after him!

An interesting series of rabbinic traditions lauds the filial piety of a Gentile named Damma b. Netina (stories C-E). Honor of parents is a value found in most cultures, and the rabbis seem to have relished this opportunity to make a Gentile into a role model. If a Gentile showed such respect to his father and received divine reward, how much the more so should Jews honor their parents and expect reward.

The different versions of these traditions found in the two Talmuds provide good evidence of the malleability of the rabbinic

193

story. Compare the stories of R. Tarfon honoring his mother (story A, sections A-B *vs.* story B, section a). In the Yerushalmi, R. Tarfon allows his mother to tread on his hands on one occasion, a Sabbath on which her sandal happened to break. In the Bavli this has become a routine occurrence: she steps upon him every time she wishes to alight to or descend from her bed. Second, the Yerushalmi's tradition of the orphan R. Ami is applied to R. Yohanan in the Bavli (A, G *vs.* b, c). The traditions of Damma b. Netina are also related in significantly different forms in the two Talmuds (C *vs.* D). Both of these accounts seem to be expansions of a brief report of the Tosefta that the rabbis once bought a red cow, which they required for a certain purification ritual, from a Gentile (E). In the Tosefta, however, the cow is named Duma, probably a play on the Hebrew word for red, *aduma.* In the talmudic stories the Gentile, not his cow, is named Damma. Here we have a nice example of how traditions change as they are reworked in later times.[2]

A.
(Yerushalmi Qiddushin 1:6, 61b)

[A]   R. Tarfon's mother went out for a stroll in her courtyard one Sabbath day and her shoe split apart. R. Tarfon went forth and placed his two hands under the soles of her feet, and she walked upon them until she reached her couch.[3]

[B]   Once he fell ill and the sages went to visit him. She said to them, "Pray for my son Tarfon, for he treats me with excessive honor." They said to her, "What has he done for you?" She told them of his deed. They said, "Even if he should do that a thousand thousand times, he would not have attained even half the honor that the Torah requires."

[C]   R. Ishmael's mother came and complained to the sages about him. She said, "Rebuke my son Ishmael, for he does not treat me with honor."

[D] At that moment the faces of the sages turned pale. They thought, "Is it possible that R. Ishmael does not observe [the commandment of] honoring parents?" They said to her, "What did he do to you?" She said, "When he leaves the assembly house, I wish to wash his feet and to drink of the water, but he does not permit me."

[E] They said, "Since that is her wish, that is her honor."[4]

[F] ...R. Zeira was distressed. He said, "Would that I had a father and mother, for I would honor them and inherit [a place in] the Garden of Eden."[5] When he heard those two accounts, he said, "Thank the Merciful One that I have neither father nor mother. I could not act as R. Tarfon nor take upon myself [such a thing] as R. Ishmael."

[G] R. Ami said, "I am exempt from [the commandment] of honoring one's father and mother." They said that his father died while his mother was pregnant with him, and she died while giving birth.

B.
(Bavli Qiddushin 31b)

[a] Whenever R. Tarfon's mother wished to ascend to her couch, he would bend down and lift her up. Whenever she wished to step down, she would step down upon him. He came and praised himself in the academy. They [the sages] said to him, "You have not even reached half the [required] honor. Did she ever throw a moneybag into the ocean before your eyes, and yet you did not reproach her?"

[b] Whenever Rav Yosef heard the sound of the footsteps of his mother he would say, "Let me stand before the Presence [of God] that approaches."

[c] R. Yohanan said, "Happy is he who never saw them [his parents]." R. Yohanan's father died while his mother was pregnant, and his mother died when she gave birth to him....

[d] R. Asi had an elderly mother. She said to him, "I want jewelry." He procured it for her. [She said,] "I want a husband." [He said,] "I will search for you." [She said,] "I want a husband who is as handsome as you." He left her and went to the Land of Israel.

[e] He heard that she was following after him. He came before R. Yohanan and said to him, "Is it permitted to leave the Land of Israel [to settle in] the diaspora?"⁶ He said to him, "It is forbidden." He said to him, "Is it permitted [to leave Israel] to greet one's mother?" He said to him, "I do not know."

[f] He [Asi] waited a little. Again he went and asked him [R. Yohanan]. He [R. Yohanan] said, "Asi. You have resolved to go. May God bring you back in peace."

[g] He [R. Asi] went before R. Eleazer. He [R. Asi] said, "Heaven forbid that he [R. Yohanan] was angry with me?" He [R. Eleazer] said, "What did he say to you?" He said to him, "May God bring you back in peace." He said to him, "Had he been angry with you, he would not have blessed you."

[h] Meanwhile he [R. Asi] heard that her [his mother's] coffin was coming. He said, "Had I known [that she had died] I would not have [considered] leaving [the Land of Israel]."

C.
(Yerushalmi Qiddushin 1:6, 61b)

[A] They asked R. Eleazer, "What is the limit of [the commandment] of honoring parents?" He said to them: "Why do you ask me? Go ask Damma b. Netina."

[B] "Damma b. Netina was the head of the city council. Once his mother slapped him in front of his council, and the slipper [with which she was slapping him] fell from her hand. He held it out for her so that she would not become upset."

[C] R. Hizqia said, "He [Damma b. Netina] was a Gentile from Ashqelon, and he was head of the city council. His whole life he never sat on a stone upon which his father had sat. And when he [the father] died, he made it [the stone] into an idol."

[D] Once the jasper for Benjamin was lost [from the high priest's breastplate].[7] They [the sages] said, "Who has [a jewel] as beautiful as that one?" They said that Damma b. Netina had one. They [the sages] went to him and settled with him on a price of one hundred dinars. He went up to get it and found that his father was sleeping [on the jewel]. And some say that the key to the box [containing the jewel] was on his father's finger. And some say his [father's] leg was resting on the box.

[E] He came down to them. He said to them, "I can't bring it to you." They [the sages] thought, "Perhaps he wants more money." They raised [the price] to two hundred. They raised [the price] to one thousand.

[F] When his father awoke from his sleep, he [Damma] went up and brought it to them. They wanted to give him the price they had offered in the end, but he would not accept it. He said, "Do you think I would put a price on my father's honor? I will not benefit from the honor of my forefathers at all."

[G] How did the Holy One, blessed be He, reward him? R. Yose b. R. Bun said, "That night his cow gave birth to a red cow, and Israel weighed out for him its weight in gold and took it."[8]

[H] R. Shabtai said, "*Justice and abundant righteousness He will not withhold* (Job 37:23). The Holy One, blessed be He, does not delay giving a reward to Gentiles who perform the commandments."[9]

D.
(Bavli Qiddushin 31a)

[a] They asked Rav Ula, "What is the limit of [the commandment] of honoring parents?"

[b] He said to them, "Go and see what a certain Gentile of Ashkelon, by the name of Damma b. Netina, did.

[c] "Once the sages offered him a business deal at a 600,000 profit, but the key was under the head of his father, and he would not disturb him [and thus lost the opportunity]."

[d] Rav Yehuda said that Shmuel said: They asked R. Eliezer, "What is the limit of [the commandment] of honoring parents?"

[e] He said to them, "Go and see what a certain Gentile of Ashkelon, by the name Damma b. Netina, did for his father. The sages requested from him jewels for the [high priest's] breastplate at a 600,000 profit—Rav Kahana taught an 800,000 profit—but the key was under the head of his father, and he [Damma] would not disturb him.

[f] "The next year the Holy One, blessed be he, gave him his reward, for a red cow was born in his flock. The sages of Israel approached [to buy it]. He said to them, 'I know that should I demand of you all the money in the world, you would give it to me.[10] But I will ask you only for that money that I lost on account of honoring my father.'"

[g] R. Hanina said, "If someone who is not commanded [to honor parents] but does so [receives such a reward], how much the more so one who is commanded and does so [will be rewarded]."[11]

[h] …When Rav Dimi came [from Palestine], he said, "Once he [Damma] sat among the notables of Rome wearing silk [embroidered] with gold. His mother came and tore it off of him and beat him on the head and spit in his face, but he did not scold her."

❦

E.
(Tosefta Para 2:1)

R. Eliezer said, "It [the red cow] may not be bought from the Gentiles." They said to him, "Once they bought it from one of the Gentiles in Sidon, and Duma was its [the cow's] name."

Chapter 33

THE PURSUIT OF TORAH

"Torah is only established for those who kill themselves over it"—so runs a telling rabbinic proverb.[1] Many narratives, presumably intended for disciples and aspiring rabbis, offer examples of sages who made tremendous sacrifices in order to pursue their studies. The first passage below contends that no excuses will be tolerated in the next world when the heavenly court sits in judgment of human beings. Neither the pressures of abject poverty, nor the distraction of tremendous wealth, nor the hunger of carnal desire prevented dedicated sages from studying Torah.

In the second narrative Samuel the Little appears uninvited at the meeting of elite sages who gather to discuss the intercalation of the calendar.[2] His unabashed explanation that he comes to learn the law illustrates his zeal to master all aspects of Torah. Torah, then, must be actively pursued, not passively absorbed.

The third brief anecdote pertains less to the sacrifices necessary to master the Torah than to Torah's vast scope. A disciple had to be resourceful in order to learn the myriad ways to apply the Torah to every aspect of behavior. To hide under one's master's bed and observe his lovemaking technique was apparently as inappropriate in talmudic times as it is today. Of course the greater the impropriety, the more emphatic the point of the story: no part of life is beyond the realm of Torah.

A.
(Bavli Yoma 35b)

[1] Our rabbis taught: The poor man, the rich man and the wicked man will come for judgment [in the next world].

[A1] To the poor man they [the heavenly court] will say, "Why did you not busy yourself with Torah?" If he should say, "I was poor and was preoccupied with my sustenance," they will say to him, "Were you poorer than Hillel?"

[A2] It was said of Hillel the Elder that every single day he would work and earn one *tropik*. He would give half to the guard of the academy, and he would use half to support himself and the members of his household. Once he was not able to earn [the money] and the guard of the academy would not allow him to enter. He climbed up and sat upon the aperture [in the roof] so that he could hear the words of the living God from the mouths of Shemaya and Avtalion. It was said that that day was the eve of the Sabbath, and it was the winter season,³ and snow fell upon him. When dawn broke Shemaya said to Avtalion, "Avtalion, my brother. Each day this building is light, and today it is dark!" They looked about and saw the figure of a man in the aperture. They went up and found him covered with three cubits of snow. They extracted him and washed him and rubbed him with oil and sat him next to the fire. They said, "This one is worthy of having the Sabbath desecrated on his behalf."⁴

[B1] To the rich man they will say, "Why did you not busy yourself with Torah?" If he should say, "I was rich and was preoccupied with my possessions," they will say to him, "Were you richer than R. Eleazar?"

[B2] It was said of R. Eleazar b. Harsom that his father left him 1,000 cities on land and 1,000 ships in the sea. But he never went to see them. Rather, the whole day and the whole night he would sit and busy himself with Torah. Each day he would put his daily bread upon his shoulder,[5] and he would go from city to city and from region to region to learn Torah. Once his servants came upon him and imposed forced service upon him.[6] He said to them, "Please leave me be." They said to him, "By the life of Eleazar b. Harsom we will not leave you be." And he did not wish to reveal to them that he was their master.[7]

[C1] To the wicked[8] man they will say, "Why did you not busy yourself with Torah?" If he should say, "I was handsome and was preoccupied with my [evil] inclination," they will say to him, "Were you more handsome than Joseph?"

[C2] It was said of Joseph the Righteous that every day the wife of Potiphar would try to seduce him. The clothes she wore during the day—she did not wear them at night. The clothes she wore at night—she did not wear them during the day. She said to him, "Listen to me!" He said to her, "No." She said to him, "I will throw you in prison." He said to her, *"The Lord sets prisoners free* (Ps 146:7)." She said to him, "I will break your back." He said to her, *"The Lord makes those who are bent stand straight* (Ps 146:8)." [She said,] "I will put out your eye." [He said,] *"The Lord restores sight to the blind* (Ps 146:8)." She gave him 1,000 talents of gold, but he would not consent.

[1'] Thus [the example of] Hillel condemns the poor. R. Eleazar b. Harsom condemns the rich. Joseph condemns the wicked.[9]

❦

B.
(Bavli Sanhedrin 10a)

[A] Once Rabban Gamaliel said, "Summon seven [sages] to my upper-story tomorrow morning [in order to intercalate the calendar]."

[B] When he arrived there he found eight. He said, "He who came up here without permission—let him descend." Samuel the Little stood up and said, "It was I who came up here without permission. I did not come here to intercalate the year, but I needed to learn the practical law [of how intercalation is done]." He [Gamaliel] said to him, "Sit down, my son, sit down. It is fitting that all years be intercalated with your [participation]. However, the sages have said, 'The intercalation of the year may be done only by those who were invited.'"

[C] And it was not Samuel the Little [who had not been invited] but another man. But he [Samuel] acted this way [to avoid] shaming [his colleague].[10]

C.
(Bavli Berakhot 62a)

Rav Kahana went in and lay down under the bed of Rav Shemaya, who was conversing and laughing and doing his business [with his wife]. He said, "It seems that my master's mouth has never tasted the dish!" He said to him, "Kahana! Get out. This is not proper." He said to him, "This is [a matter of] Torah, and I need to learn it."

PART VIII

SUFFERING, MARTYRDOM AND THEODICY

Chapter 34

Nahum of Gamzu: Happy that You See Me Suffer

The story of Nahum of Gamzu, for which we again have a version in each Talmud, offers different perspectives on suffering. Both versions relate that Nahum invites the sufferings upon himself as punishment for not immediately assisting a poor and hungry man. In the Yerushalmi R. Akiba bemoans Nahum's condition and describes his suffering as a curse. Whatever the didactic function of suffering, he wants no part of it. Nahum surprisingly laments that R. Akiba does *not* suffer. He presumably considers sufferings a salutary means for expiating sin, teaching sympathy for others and spurring atonement.

The Bavli also expresses a difference of opinion, this time between Nahum and his students, over whether sufferings are to be seen as desirable or lamentable. Here the reason for Nahum's contentment with suffering is less clear. It may be that, as in the Yerushalmi, he considers suffering a way to atone for his sin. However, the addition of a miracle-story suggests that sufferings are useful in that they bestow upon the victim supernatural powers: because of his suffering Nahum protects his students from harm (b). Suffering—at least self-inflicted suffering—is an extremely righteous act that gives the victim the status of a holy man and the accompanying abilities.[1]

A. To Suffer or Not to Suffer
(Yerushalmi Peah 8:9, 21b)

[A] Nahum of Gamzu was taking a gift to his father-in-law's house. A certain man afflicted with boils came upon him. He said to him, "Give me something of that which you have with you." He said to him, "When I return."

[B] When he returned, he found him dead. Right there he said, "Eyes that saw you but did not give you, let them be blind! Hands that did not reach out to give you, let them be cut off! Feet that did not run to give you, let them be broken"! And so it happened.

[C] R. Akiba went to him. He said, "Woe am I that I see you so." He said to him, "Woe am I that I do *not* see *you* so."

[D] He [Akiba] said to him, "Why do you curse me?" He [Nahum] said to him, "Why do you disdain sufferings?"

※

B. The Rewards for Suffering
(Bavli Taanit 21a)

[a] They said about Nahum of Gamzu that he was blind in both eyes, stumped in both hands, amputated in both legs, that his whole body was covered with boils, and that his bed rested on saucers of water so that ants would not climb upon him [by crawling up the legs of the bed].

[b] Once his bed had been left in a rickety house and his students wished to remove it. He said to them, "First remove the utensils and then remove my bed. For as long as my bed is within the house, you can be assured that the house will not collapse." They removed the utensils and then they removed the bed. The house immediately collapsed.

[c] His students said to him, "Our Master. Since you are a completely righteous man, why did this come upon you?" He said to them, "I did it to myself—

> Once I was walking to the house of my father-in-law, and I had with me a load [carried by] three asses. One of food, one of drink and one of types of precious goods. I came upon a certain man. He said to me, 'My master, sustain me.' I said to him, 'Wait until I unload the ass.' After I unloaded the ass I turned around and found him dead. I fell upon him and said, 'My eye which had no pity on your eyes—let it be blind! My hands that had no pity on your hands—let them be stumped! My feet that had no pity on you feet—let them be amputated.'

And my mind was not set at ease until I said, 'Let all my body be covered with boils.'"

[d] They said to him, "Woe are we that we see you so!" He said to them, "Woe am I if you did *not* see me so!"

Chapter 35

SUFFERING: NOT THEM
AND NOT THEIR REWARD

The following stories of rabbis and their afflictions, like the stories of Nahum of Gamzu (chapter 34), offer a variety of perspectives on suffering. The Palestinian version from *Song of Songs Rabbah* portrays suffering as a test of faith. Three parables teach that God specifically imposes suffering on the righteous, who can be expected to pass the test because of their resolute faith and piety (C1–C3). Because the wicked will surely lose faith and fail the test, there is no point in causing them to suffer. Thus R. Hanina instructs R. Yohanan that he should not reject the sufferings he experiences but continue to profess his faith in God (A1). When R. Hanina in turn becomes sick, R. Yohanan consoles him with the message that God only sends suffering upon those who can tolerate it, those who are as "soft" as the lily, who will not break and lose their faith or lash out at God (B3). What the righteous gain by passing the test is explicitly stated by R. Yohanan—"how great is their reward" (B3). By suffering peacefully and faithfully the righteous earn tremendous reward in the world to come. According to this explanation, the suffering of the righteous (and the prospering of the wicked) should not occasion a theological crisis; paradoxically, this is the situation to be expected.

Yet these stories contain seeds of protest against such benign views of suffering. R. Hanina heals R. Yohanan's sufferings when he realizes that they have become too painful to tolerate (A3). Beyond a certain point, then, suffering is neither beneficial nor desirable. Ironically, the same R. Hanina who chastised R. Yohanan for complaining

210

about infirmity declares of his own suffering that he wants "neither them nor their reward" (B1). We begin to sense that it is much easier to explain the utility of suffering in the abstract, or at least while of sound mind and body. As soon as one starts to suffer, the prospect of the reward loses its appeal.

The story in Bavli Berakhot 5a seizes on these hints of protest against suffering and makes them the center of its version. All three rabbis want no part of suffering. They allude to the belief that suffering brings reward only to reject it, stating that they desire "not them and not their reward" (a, b, c4). In the Bavli, R. Hanina quickly heals R. Yohanan, whereas in the Palestinian version R. Hanina defers healing him until his pains increase.

This story follows a lengthy Bavli passage that provides numerous explanations for suffering: punishment for sin or for neglect of Torah study, warning to repent, means to reward, even a sign of God's love. These claims are backed up by the citation and exegesis of biblical prooftexts. In this context the story amounts to a strong protest against such views. Traditional wisdom and biblical teachings tell you one thing—but no one, not even the holiest rabbis, relishes real suffering.[1]

A. Test of the Righteous (Song of Songs Rabbah 2:16)

[A1] R. Yohanan became afflicted and endured fevers for three and one-half years. R. Hanina went up to visit him. He said to him, "What has come upon you?" He said to him, "My burden is too great to bear."[2] He said to him, "You should not say that. Rather you should say, 'The faithful God.'"

[A2] When his [R. Yohanan's] suffering increased he would say, "The faithful God."

[A3] And when his suffering became too difficult for him to stand, R. Hanina would go up [to him] and say a word and heal him.[3]

[B1] After some time R. Hanina became sick. R. Yohanan went up to visit him. He said to him, "What has come upon you?" He said to him, "How difficult are sufferings!" He said to him, "But how great is their reward!" He said to him, "I want neither them nor their reward."

[B2] He [R. Yohanan] said to him, "Why don't you say that word that you said for me and heal yourself?" He said to him, "When I was outside, I could serve as a guarantor for others. Now that I am inside, do I not need others to be guarantors for me?"[4]

[B3] He [R. Yohanan] said to him, "It is written, *[My beloved is mine and I am his], who browses among the lilies* (Song 2:16). The rod of the Holy One, blessed be He, only searches about among those whose hearts are as soft as lilies."[5]

[C1] R. Eleazar said, "[This can be compared] to the owner of two cows, one strong and one weak. Upon which one does he impose? Is it not upon the strong one? So too God does not test the wicked. Why? Because they cannot take it, as is written, *But the wicked are like the troubled sea* (Isa 57:20). Whom does he test? The righteous, as it says, *The Lord tests the righteous man* (Ps 11:5); *some time afterward God put Abraham to the test* (Gen 22:1); *after a time, his master's wife cast her eyes upon Joseph* (Gen 39:7)."[6]

[C2] R. Yose b. R. Hanina said, "The flax-maker—when his flax hardens he does not beat it too much. Why? Because it would break. But when his flax is good, however much he beats it, the more he improves its quality. So too God does not test the wicked, for they cannot bear it. But he tests the righteous, as it says, *God tests the righteous man* (Ps 11:5)."

[C3] R. Yohanan said, "The potter—when he checks his kiln, he does not check it with fragile vessels. Why? Because when he strikes them they break. With what does he check [his kiln]? With good vessels, because even though he strikes them several times, they do not break. So too God does not test the wicked.

But whom does he test? The righteous, as it says, *God tests the righteous man* (Ps 11:5)."

B. Not Them and Not Their Reward (Bavli Berakhot 5b)

[a] R. Hiyya bar Abba became ill. R. Yohanan visited him. He [R. Yohanan] said to him, "Do you cherish sufferings?" He said to him, "Not them and not their reward." He said to him, "Give me your hand." He gave him his hand and he healed him.

[b] R. Yohanan became ill. R. Hanina visited him. He [R. Hanina] said to him, "Do you cherish sufferings?" He said to him, "Not them and not their reward." He said to him, "Give me your hand." He gave him his hand and he healed him. (Why did R. Yohanan not heal himself [since he was able to heal R. Hiyya bar Abba]? A prisoner cannot deliver himself from jail.)[7]

[c1] R. Eleazar became ill. R. Yohanan visited him. He [R. Yohanan] saw that he was lying in a dark room. He uncovered his arm and light shone.[8]

[c2] He saw that R. Eleazar was weeping. He said to him, "Why do you weep?
    (i) "[Do you weep] because of Torah, that you did not proliferate it? Have we not learned, *All the same is a large measure and a small measure, as long as his intention is for the sake of Heaven* (Mishna Menahot 13:11)?[9]
    (ii) "[Do you weep] because of [your lack of] sustenance? Every man does not merit two tables.[10]
    (iii) "[Do you weep] because of your children [who died]? This here is the bone of my tenth child [who died, yet I do not weep]."[11]

[c3] He [R. Eleazar] said to him, "I weep for that beauty [of yours], which will wither." He said to him, "For that you may justly weep," and the two of them wept together.

[c4] Meantime, he [R. Yohanan] said to him, "Do you cherish sufferings?" He said to him, "Not them and not their reward." He said to him, "Give me your hand." He gave him his hand and he healed him.

Chapter 36

THEODICY AND TORAH
(BAVLI MENAHOT 29b)

This account of Moses traveling through time to visit the academy of R. Akiba is a most unusual rabbinic story. The juxtaposition of these two characters violates the typically strict separation between the biblical world and post-biblical times. The story also juxtaposes two critically important theological questions: the expansion of Torah and the problem of theodicy.

The first half of the story addresses the tension created by the theological dogma that God revealed both the Written and Oral Torahs to Moses on Sinai over against the reality that each generation of rabbis added its traditions to the "Torah" of its predecessors. Statements of the form "Rabbi So-and-so said..." make up the bulk of the Mishna and other rabbinic works. But if the tradition was formulated by Rabbi So-and-so, how can it be part of the Torah of Moses? In what sense does it constitute the revelation on Mt. Sinai? The story exhibits a remarkable self-consciousness about this difficulty. Moses cannot follow the discussions in the academy of R. Akiba because Torah has expanded and developed to a great extent in the intervening centuries. In some ways the later Torah of talmudic times is light years beyond the Torah given at Sinai. Yet when pressed for the source of his ruling, Akiba attributes the tradition to Moses. Later traditions, paradoxically, ultimately derive from Moses. The paradox is compounded by God's explanation that God makes crowns on letters because Akiba will derive heaps of laws from them. While Akiba did not receive these laws from his teachers but rather expounded them himself, they somehow inhere in the original Torah. The point of the story is to recognize the paradox, not to resolve it completely. Like Moses, later rabbis must have "peace of mind" that their Torah is part of revelation.

The crux of the story, however, is to be found in the contrast between Moses's two visions of R. Akiba (C1–C3 *vs.* D1–D3) and God's two responses to Moses's questions, "Silence! Thus have I decided" (C3, D3). Here the message of the story is less clear. Is the point to contrast the nature of Torah as presented in the first half of the story with the nature of "reward" presented in the second half? While humans can apprehend the paradoxical nature of Torah, they cannot hope to understand the reasons for the happy destinies of some and cruel suffering of others. Or is the story a failed theodicy, or a protest against the unjust suffering of the righteous? The greatest Torah scholar ever, perhaps greater even than Moses, suffers the cruelest death, and yet God gives no explanation. God takes great care for his Torah, meticulously adding crowns to each individual letter, but apparently cares less about those who dedicate their lives to it. Does the story teach that one should not complain against undeserved suffering because there is unmerited reward as well? God simply "decided" that Moses would enjoy the great honor of receiving the Torah just as God decided that Akiba would be tortured to death. Or is the story a daring statement that there is not necessarily a reward for Torah?

Moses cannot understand the discourses in the academy of R. Akiba but takes comfort at the discussion's end. Nor can he understand the martyrdom of R. Akiba. But there is no comfort, either for Moses or for the reader, at Akiba's end. These multiple and mixed messages give the story its enduring power.[1]

[A] Rav Yehuda said that Rav said: At the time when Moses ascended on high [to receive the Torah] he found God sitting and attaching crowns to the letters.[2] He said before Him, "Master of the Universe! Who stays your hand?"[3]

[B] He said to him, "There is a certain man who will live a few generations into the future, and Akiba b. Yosef is his name. He will derive heaps and heaps of laws from all the tips [of the crowns of the letters]."

[C1] He said to him, "Master of the Universe! Show him to me." He said to him, "Turn around."[4]

[C2] He [Moses] went and sat at the back of eighteen rows of students,[5] but he did not understand what they were saying. His strength failed him. When they came to a certain matter, his [Akiba's] students said to him, "Master, how do you know this?" He said to them, "It is a law [given] to Moses at Sinai." His [Moses'] [peace of] mind was restored.

[C3] He returned and came before the Holy One, blessed be He. He said to him, "Master of the Universe! You have such a one in your world and you give the Torah through me?" He said to him, "Silence! Thus I have decided."[6]

[D1] He said before him, "Master of the Universe! You showed me his Torah. Show me his reward." He said to him, "Turn around."

[D2] He turned around. He saw them weighing his flesh in the meat market.[7]

[D3] He said to him, "Master of the Universe! This is Torah and this is the reward?" He said to him, "Silence! Thus I have decided."

Chapter 37

STORIES OF MARTYRDOM

The concept of martyrdom or *qiddush hashem*, the "sanctification of [God's] name," rose to prominence in the Second Temple Period as a response to the persecutions imposed by Antiochus Epiphanes and his associates (168–64 BCE). This was the first significant attempt to force Jews to forsake Judaism and to adopt another religion, and some Jews submitted to torture and death rather than violate the commandments. Their consummate faith demonstrated to both their co-religionists and oppressors the power, greatness and holiness with which they honored their God. Halakhic literature discusses at length the precise circumstances in which a Jew must submit to martyrdom rather than comply. Narrative sources, by contrast, present models of those who sanctified God's name and address theological questions: Why does God allow his chosen people to suffer? How can the death of the martyrs be justified and explained? What is the ultimate fate of both martyrs and persecutors?

"The Woman and Her Seven Sons" (A) is one of the most famous Jewish martyrologies.[1] It first appears in 2 Maccabees in the accounts of the persecutions that preceded the Hasmonean rebellion.[2] The rabbinic version found in Bavli Gittin 57b, however, locates the martyrdom after the first revolt against Rome in 70 CE—a nice illustration of the "transportability" of ancient tradition. Comparing these two versions would provide the interested reader with a striking example of the differences between written and oral narrative. The Book of 2 Maccabees, written in Greek and influenced by Hellenistic literature, offers a lengthy and dramatic account with rich description, extended dialogue and impressive speeches placed in the mouths of the martyrs. The rabbinic tradition, originally formulated and transmitted orally, is terse and repetitive, and lacks all but the most essential details. We should assume, however, that when rabbinic storytellers or homilists actually related the tale to a live audience, they expanded the skeletal core and fashioned a detailed and dramatic narrative.[3]

The stories of rabbinic martyrs are set primarily in the early second century, presumably during the persecutions allegedly imposed by the emperor Hadrian after the Bar Kokhba revolt (see chapter 5 herein). The first story (B) explains the suffering of two great sages in two ways. Their cruel fate is punishment for extremely minor transgressions, for times when they caused a slight amount of pain to other human beings (B). While God's standards might seem excessively harsh to us, the martyrs in the story find comfort: at least there is a reason for their suffering. The second half of the story takes a different tack. R. Akiba explains that the entire generation will soon experience great suffering (E). God wished to spare those two martyrs that pain, so he removed them prematurely from the world. The scriptures cited at the end of his speech assure us that the martyrs will enjoy a blissful repose in the next world while the evil perpetrators will face God's wrath.

The stories of Akiba's death introduce a new understanding of martyrdom.[4] Akiba "smiles" at his death because he finally fulfills the biblical passage recited as the *Shema*, one of the most important prayers in the liturgy (F-G). As he explains, "*You shall love the Lord your God with all your soul* (Deut 5:6)—even if He takes your soul" (G, I, O). Thus Akiba construes martyrdom as the fulfillment of a biblical commandment, as a *mitzvah*. It is an expression of one's love of God, not only a testimony to faith and awe. This stance transforms martyrdom from a tragic, unfortunate experience into a positive value of sorts.

The Bavli's expanded version of Akiba's martyrdom (D) broaches several related issues. Should one refrain from the study of Torah when threatened by death? Akiba argues that Jews should never desist because Torah lies at the center of Jewish life (L). The whims of persecutors are such that they are liable to kill Jews for trivial reasons or for no reason at all. Better to die a death for the sake of Torah than to die for a meaningless offense. Second, the angels protest the cruel fate of Akiba with the same words that Moses speaks upon seeing Akiba's end in chapter 36: "This is Torah and this is its reward?" (Q). Here, however, a heavenly voice responds by assuring that Akiba will enter the world to come. While the conviction that the martyrs receive their reward in the next world is presupposed by all rabbinic sources, God's direct testimony provides an inspiring expression of the principle.[5]

A. The Mother and Her Seven Sons (Bavli Gittin 57b)

[a] *It is for Your sake that we are slain all day long, that we are regarded as sheep to be slaughtered* (Ps 44:23). Rav Yehuda said, "This [verse] refers to the woman and her seven sons."

[b1] They brought the first one before the emperor. They said to him, "Bow down to the idol." He said to them, "It is written in the Torah, *I am the Lord your God* (Exod 20:1)." They took him out and killed him.

[b2] They brought out the next one before the emperor. They said to him, "Bow down to the idol." He said to them, "It is written in the Torah, *You shall have no other gods besides me* (Exod 20:2)." They took him out and killed him.

[b3] They brought out the next one. They said to him, "Bow down to the idol." He said to them, "It is written in the Torah, *Whoever sacrifices to a god other than the Lord alone shall be proscribed* (Exod 22:19)." They took him out and killed him.

[b4] They brought out the next one. They said to him, "Bow down to the idol." He said to them, "It is written in the Torah, *You must not worship any other god besides the Lord* (Exod 34:14)." They took him out and killed him.

[b5] They brought out the next one. They said to him, "Bow down to the idol." He said to them, "It is written in the Torah,

Hear O Israel! The Lord our God, the Lord is one (Deut 6:4)." They took him out and killed him.

[b6] They brought the next one. They said to him, "Bow down to the idol." He said to them, "*Know therefore this day and keep in mind that the Lord alone is God in Heaven above and on earth below; there is no other* (Deut 4:39)." They took him out and killed him.

[b7] They brought the next one. They said to him, "Bow down to the idol." He said to them, "It is written in the Torah, *You have affirmed this day that the Lord is your God, that you will observe his laws and commandments and rules, and that you will obey him. And the Lord has affirmed this day that you are, as He promised you, His treasured people* (Deut 26:16–18). We have sworn to the Holy One, blessed be He, that we will not exchange him for another god. And He has sworn to us that He will not exchange us for another people."

[c] The emperor said to him, "Let me throw my seal before you. Bend down and pick it up such that they will say that you accepted the authority of the king."

[d] He said to him, "Shame on you, O emperor. Shame on you, O emperor. If [you have] such [concern] for your own honor, for the honor of God—how much the more so!"[6] They took him out to kill him.

[e] His mother said to them, "Give him to me that I might kiss him." She said to him, "My sons. Go and tell Abraham our Father: You bound [a sacrifice] on one altar. I bound [sacrifices] on seven altars." She then went up to the roof and cast herself off and died. A heavenly voice went forth and said, *[He sets the childless woman among her household as] a happy mother of children* (Ps 113:9).[7]

❦

B. The Martyrdom of R. Ishmael and R. Shimon (Mekhilta d'Rabbi Ishmael, Neziqin, §18)

[A] When R. Ishmael and R. Shimon were taken out to be killed, R. Shimon said to R. Ishmael, "Master, my heart goes out, for I do not know why I am being killed."

[B] R. Ishmael said to R. Shimon, "In all your days did no man come before you for judgment or with a question and you made him wait until you sipped your drink or tied your sandals or put on your cloak? The Torah says, *[You shall not mistreat any widow or orphan.] If you do mistreat them [...My anger shall blaze forth and I will put you to the sword]* (Exod 22:21–23). All the same is serious mistreatment and slight mistreatment."

[C] At this word he said to him, "My master, you have comforted me."

[D] When R. Shimon and R. Ishmael were being killed, R. Akiba said to his students, "Prepare yourselves for suffering. For if good were in store for our generation, none other than R. Shimon and R. Ishmael would be the first to receive it.

[E] "As it is, these men were removed from among us because it is revealed and known before Him-who-spoke-and-the-world-was that great suffering will soon afflict our generation. And this fulfills what is said, *The righteous man perishes and no one considers; pious men are taken away and no one gives thought* (Isa 57:1). And it says, *Yet he shall come to peace, they shall have rest on their couches, who walked straightforward* (Isa 57:2). And in the end, *But as for you, come closer, you sons of a sorceress, you offspring of an adulterer and a harlot* (Isa 57:3)."[8]

❦

C. The Martyrdom of R. Akiba (1) (Yerushalmi Berakhot 9:5, 14b)

[F] R. Akiba was being tortured before Turnusrufus the Wicked.[9] The time came for reciting the *Shema*. As he began to recite [the *Shema*], he smiled.[10]

[G] He said to him, "Old man, Old man. You are either an imbecile or you are contemptuous of suffering." He said to him, "Blast your bones![11] I am neither an imbecile nor am I contemptuous of suffering. But all my life I read this verse and was distressed thinking, When will I fulfill the three of them?: *You shall love the Lord your God with all your heart, with all your soul, with all your muchness* (Deut 6:5). I loved him with all my heart. I loved him with all my money.[12] But I was never tested by 'with all your soul.' But now that [the opportunity for] 'with all your soul' has come and the time for reciting the *Shema* has arrived, my mind has not wavered. Because of this I recite and smile."

[H] He hardly finished saying it when his soul ascended [he died].[13]

❦

D. The Martyrdom of R. Akiba (II) (Bavli Berakhot 61b)

[I] R. Akiba says, *"With all your soul* (Deut 6:5)—even if He takes your soul."

[J] Our sages taught: Once the Evil Empire [Rome] decreed that they may not busy themselves with Torah. Pappos b. Yehuda came and found R. Akiba assembling a congregation in public and busying himself with Torah. He said to him, "Akiba! Do you not fear the empire?"

[K] He said to him, "Let me tell you a parable. To what is this matter similar? To a fox who was walking beside the river when he saw fish gathering together [and moving] from place to place. He said to them, 'From what are you fleeing?' They said to him, 'From the nets that men cast upon us.' He said to them, 'Why don't you come up to the land and you and I will dwell together, just as my ancestors dwelt with your ancestors?' They said to him, 'Are you the one whom they call the wisest of animals? You are not wise but stupid. If we fear in the place that gives us life, in the place that kills us—how much the more so?'

[L] "So too with us. If it is so now that we are sitting and busying ourselves with Torah, about which it is written, *It is your life and length of days* (Deut 30:20), then if we go and avoid *(mevatlin)* it—how much the more so?"

[M] They said: Not a few days passed before they arrested R. Akiba and imprisoned him in jail, and they arrested Pappos b. Yehuda and imprisoned him with him [Akiba]. He said to him, "Pappos, what brought you here?" He said to him, "Happy are you, Akiba, for you were arrested on account of Torah. Woe to you, Pappos, for you were arrested on account of void *(beteilin)* matters."[14]

[N] When they took R. Akiba out to die it was the time for reciting the *Shema*. While they combed his flesh with iron combs, he accepted upon himself the yoke of the kingdom of Heaven [by reciting the *Shema*].

[O] His students said to him, "This far?"[15] He said to them, "All my life I was distressed about this verse, *With all your soul* (Deut 6:5)—even if He takes your soul. I thought, 'When will the opportunity come that I might fulfill it.' Now that the opportunity is here, shall I not fulfill it?"

[P] He drew out [the word] *One*[16] until his soul departed. A heavenly voice went forth and said, "Happy are you, R. Akiba, for your soul departed with *One*."

[Q] The angels of the Presence said before the Holy One, blessed be He, "This is Torah and this is its reward? [He deserved to be] *Among those who die by your hand, O Lord* (Ps 17:14)." He [God] said to them, *"Their portion is life* (Ps 17:14)." A heavenly voice went forth and said, "Happy are you, R. Akiba, for you are destined for the world to come."[17]

PART IX:

SIN
AND
REPENTANCE

Chapter 38

STORIES OF ELISHA b. ABUYA

The famous stories of Elisha b. Abuya, the sage whose sins so outraged his colleagues that they called him *Aher*, "the Other," must be counted among the most colorful rabbinic biographical traditions. Historians have offered a great many conjectures to account for his banishment, variously portraying him as a mystic, gnostic, heretic, Christian, philosopher or atheist. Such speculations, however, distract attention from the interests of the talmudic storytellers. They construct the figure of Elisha as a sinning sage, a master of Torah who went astray. With this figure they ponder an important question in rabbinic theology: is the merit accrued from study of Torah inviolable or can it be annulled by sin? Does Elisha lose his share in the world to come because of his sins? Or does the Torah he once mastered earn him a place in the next world despite his sins?

Both the Bavli and Yerushalmi contain a lengthy story about Elisha, together with other brief traditions. Several of the traditions are based on a cryptic source found in the Tosefta, the account of the four sages who "entered the *pardes* (orchard)," which probably refers to the study of esoteric aspects of Torah.[1] The Tosefta states:

[A] Four sages entered the *pardes* (orchard). One [sage] gazed and perished, one gazed and was smitten, one gazed and cut the shoots, and one went up whole and came down whole....

[B] Aher gazed and cut the shoots. Concerning him scripture says, *Let not your mouth lead you into sin [and do not say before the malakh (angel/messenger) that it was an error, else God may be angered by your talk and destroy the work of your hands]* (Qoh 5:5).

The meaning of the phrase "cut the shoots" and the sense of the biblical verse in this context are unclear, and were apparently unclear to the talmudic storytellers as well.[2] Later sources interpret the phrase and verse in very different ways to generate elements of the stories about Elisha. This is an important feature of many rabbinic stories: they are products of exegesis, of the interpretation of earlier sources, not oral traditions that derive from actual historical events. The particular interpretations are explained in the introductions and notes to the stories.

The main stories of the Bavli and Yerushalmi about Elisha b. Abuya are presented first, followed by a secondary story from the Yerushalmi.

A. Elisha as Sinning Sage: The Inviolability of Torah (I) (Bavli Hagiga 15a-b)

The first two sections of the Bavli story are generated largely through an interpretation of the Toseftan tradition. Following the description of the Tosefta, "Aher gazed," the story begins, "What did he see?," and describes an angelic vision. Elisha's mouth led him to sin, as the verse states, because he said, "Perhaps there are two divine powers?!" God's anger at Elisha's talk is the punishment of Metatron. The phrase "destroy the work of your hands" is interpreted as Metatron erasing Elisha's merits, his "good works." Section B then accounts for the name Aher, "Other," with the prostitute's remark and understands "cut the shoots" as his uprooting the radish. The rabbis often construct stories about biblical characters through exegeses of the biblical text. We see a similar process here with the exegesis of an earlier rabbinic source.[3]

Many scholars connect Elisha's supernatural vision to Hekhalot mysticism, the leading form of ancient Jewish mysticism before the advent of Kabbala in the twelfth and thirteenth centuries. The mystics aspired to ascend through numerous levels of heavens and their palaces *(hekhalot)* to attain a vision of the enthroned God surrounded by millions of angels. At each level hostile angels attempt to prevent the mystic from progressing or to kill him. Some Hekhalot texts mention Metatron as one of the archangels and even call him the "Lesser God." Yet the relationship between the talmudic story and Metatron's vision is debated. Metatron appears already in talmudic sources among the named angels (Gabriel, Uriel, Raphael), so it is possible that the mystical texts were inspired by the talmudic account.

Within this story the Metatron episode functions to construct the figure of the sinning sage. Because Metatron erases Elisha's merits and the heavenly voice precludes repentance, Elisha can have no share in the world to come and, with nothing more to lose, goes forth to sin (B). But he retains his superb knowledge of Torah, as the dialogues with R. Meir demonstrate (C). In this way Torah and sin stably coexist until death, when rewards and punishments materialize. By these maneuvers the story poses a fundamental question concerning the merit of Torah: Can it be completely annulled, as the heavenly voice asserts and as the oracular study-verses of children confirm (D)? Or is the merit of Torah, the highest value in the rabbinic worldview, inviolable? Eventually Elisha is saved, thanks in part to the efforts of the disciples who have learned Torah from him and remain loyal (E). God initially rejects the sage despite his Torah because of his sin (or his error in identifying Metatron), whereas his students remain faithful despite his sin because of his Torah.

Section D' rehearses the lesson of the story by taking us to the next generation and describing the rehabilitation of Elisha's daughters. R. Yehuda HaNasi first spurns them because of their father's sins but then provides for them because of the merit of Elisha's Torah. Torah brings both salvation to Elisha in the world to come and life to his daughters in this world.

The concluding sections of the story take up two related issues, the propriety of a disciple learning Torah from a sinful master such as Elisha and the question of whether the Torah itself can be tainted by sin. We encounter a rehearsal of the basic trajectory of the plot in section A'. God rejects Meir's Torah by not repeating traditions in his name because he studied with a sinful master. When another sage insists that Meir succeeded in separating the corrupt teachings from the true Torah, God relents and restores Meir's name. Sections C' and B' provide further support for Meir's policy through statements attributed to later sages. One senses the preciousness of Torah to the sages: proximity to sin proves no deterrence when Torah can be acquired.

The length of the story should not obscure its coherence and narrative sophistication. Elisha's interpretations of biblical verses in his discussions with Meir relate to the concerns of the story (C1–C2). There is wordplay involving "turn back"/"repent" *(hazor)* in C3 and again when a stuttering child mispronounces the name *ule'elisha*, "to Elisha," as *ulerasha*, "to the wicked one" (D).[4] A series of vegetable images and metaphors appears, from Elisha uprooting the radish and going out to "evil growth" (B), to the date, nut and pomegranate in C', B' and A'. Above all, the entire story is unified by a chiastic structure:

[A] Aher rejected by God and God's servant (Metatron)
  [B] Sins of Aher
    [C] Meir learns Torah from Aher
    (1), (2), (3)
      [D] God again rejects Aher; Aher brings death to the child
        [E] Death, Punishment and Redemption of Aher
        (1), (2), (3)
        [D'] God accepts Torah of Aher; Aher's Torah brings life to the child
      [C'] Defense of Meir learning Torah from Aher
      (1), (2), (3)
  [B'] Defense of Torah of Aher
[A'] Torah of Meir who learned Torah from Aher accepted by God and God's servant (Elijah).

The chiastic structure focuses attention on the center (E), the death and redemption of Elisha. Torah always bestows merit and salvation.

   [A] *Aher gazed and cut the shoots. About him scripture says, "Let not your mouth lead you into sin, [and do not say before the malakh (angel/messenger) that it was an error, else God may be angered by your talk and destroy the work of your hands]* (Qoh 5:5)." (=Tosefta Hagiga 2:3)

What did he see? He saw Metatron, to whom was given permission one hour each day to sit and write the merits of Israel. He said, "It is taught that 'On high there is no sitting and no jealousy and no rivalry and no back and no weariness.' Perhaps—Heaven forbid—there are two divine powers?!"[5] Immediately they brought out Metatron and struck him with sixty lashes of fire.[6] He was given permission to burn the merits of Aher.[7] A heavenly voice went out and said to him, *"Return, rebellious children* (Jer 3:22)—except Aher."

[B] He said, "Since that man [=since I] has been banished from that world [=the next world], I will go and enjoy myself in this world."[8] Aher went out to evil ways [literally, "evil growth"]. He found a certain prostitute. He propositioned her. She said to him, "Are you not Elisha ben Abuya, whose name went out throughout the world?" He uprooted a radish on the Sabbath and gave it to her. She said, "It is another *(aher)."*[9]

[C](1) After he went out into evil ways, Aher asked R. Meir, "What is written, *The one no less than the other is God's doing* (Qoh 7:14)?" He (Meir) said, "Everything that God made, he made its counterpart. He made mountains, he made hills. He made seas, he made rivers." He (Aher) said to him, "Akiba, your master, did not say this. [Rather], He made righteous, he made wicked. He made the Garden of Eden, he made Gehenom. Each and every person has two portions, one in the Garden of Eden and one in Gehenom. The righteous man, having earned merit, takes his portion and the portion of his fellow in the Garden of Eden. The wicked man, having been found guilty, takes his portion and the portion of his fellow in Gehenom."[10]

Rav Mesharshia said, "What is the verse [that supports this idea]? *They shall have a double share in their land* (Isa 61:7). And it is written, *Shatter them with double destruction* (Jer 17:18)."[11]

233

(2) After he went out into evil ways Aher asked R. Meir, "What is written, *Gold or glass cannot match its [wisdom's] value, nor vessels of fine gold be exchanged for it* (Job 28:17)?" He [Meir] said, "This refers to matters of Torah that are difficult to acquire, like vessels of gold and vessels of fine gold, and easy to lose, like vessels of glass." He [Aher] said to him, "By God! Are they even like clay vessels that have no value?"[12] He [Aher] said to him, "Akiba, your master, did not say thus. Rather, just as vessels of gold and vessels of glass, even if they are broken, can be restored, so a sage, even though he sins, can be restored." He said to him, "Then you too should repent."[13] He said to him, "No, I have already heard from behind the curtain, *Return, rebellious children* (Jer 3:22)— except Aher."

(3) Our sages taught: It once happened that Aher was riding his horse on the Sabbath going on his way and R. Meir was walking after him to learn Torah from his mouth.[14] He said to him, "Meir, return *(hazor)* back, since I have already measured by the footsteps of my horse that the Sabbath boundary is here."[15] He said to him, "Then you too should repent *(hazor)*." He said to him, "No, I have already heard from behind the curtain, *Return, rebellious children* (Jer 3:22)—except Aher."

[D] He [Meir] took hold of him [Aher] and
(1) He brought him to the study-house. He said to a child, "Tell me your study-verse." He said to him, "*There is no peace— said the Lord—for the wicked* (Isa 48:22)."[16]
(2) He brought him to another study-house. He [the child] said to him, "*Though you wash with natron and use much lye, [your guilt is ingrained before me—declares the Lord God]* (Jer 2:22)."
(3) He brought him to another study-house. He [the child] said to him, "*And you, who are doomed to ruin* (Jer 4:30)."
(4) He brought him to thirteen study-houses. They recited for him in similar ways. The child in the thirteenth said, "*And to the wicked* [ulerasha] *God said: Who are you to recite my laws [and mouth the terms of my covenant, seeing that you spurn my discipline, and brush my words aside?]* (Ps 50:16)." That child stuttered so it

sounded as if he said, "And to Elisha [*ule'elisha*] God said...."
Some say he [Aher] took a knife and cut him up and sent him to
thirteen study-houses. And some say, he [Aher] said to him, "If I
had a knife with me I would cut you up."[17]

[5] (1) When Aher died, they [the angels?] said, "Let him
not be punished and let him not enter the world to come. Let
him not be punished because he studied Torah regularly. Let him
not enter the world to come because he sinned."
(2) R. Meir said, "When I die I shall cause smoke to rise
from his grave."[18] When R. Meir died, smoke rose up from Aher's
grave.
(3) R. Yohanan said, "Is it a mighty deed to burn one's master with fire? One was among us and yet we cannot save him? If I
were to take him by the hand, who would tear him away from me?
When I die I will extinguish the smoke from his grave." When R.
Yohanan died, the smoke ceased from the grave of Aher. (The
eulogizer said of him [Yohanan], "Even the guard of the gate [of
Gehenom] could not stand before you, our master.")[19]

[D'] The daughter of Aher came before Rabbi [Yehuda
HaNasi]. She said to him, "My master, support me." He said to
her, "My daughter, whose daughter are you?" She said to him,
"The daughter of Aher." He said, "Is there still his seed in the
world? *He has no offspring or descendant among his people, no survivor where he once lived* (Job 18:19)."[20] She said to him, "My master. Remember his Torah and do not remember his deeds." Fire
came down from Heaven and tried to burn Rabbi.[21] Rabbi wept
and said, "If this [happens] for those who dishonor her [Torah],
how much the more so for those who respect her?"

[C'] How did R. Meir learn Torah from Aher? Did not
Rabba bar bar Hanna say that R. Yohanan said, "What is the
meaning of *For the lips of a priest guard knowledge, and men seek rulings from his mouth; for he is a malakh* (messenger/angel) *of the
Lord of hosts* (Mal 2:7)? If the master is similar to the *'malakh* of

235

the Lord of hosts,' then they should seek Torah from his mouth, and if not, do not seek Torah from his mouth."

(1) Resh Laqish said, "R. Meir found a verse and expounded it: *Incline your ear and listen to the words of the sages; pay attention to my wisdom* (Prov 22:17). It does not say 'to their wisdom' but 'to my wisdom.'"[22]

(2) R. Hanina said, "From here: *Take heed, daughter, and note, incline your ear; forget your people and your father's house* (Ps 45:11)."[23] (The verses contradict each other! There is no difficulty. One is about an adult, one a child).[24]

(3) When Rav Dimi came up [from Israel] he said, "They say in the West [Israel]: Eat the date and throw the peel away."

[B'] Rava expounded: "What is written, *I went down to the nut grove to see the budding of the vale* (Song 6:11)? Why are words of Torah compared to a nut? To tell you that just as a nut, even though it is dirtied with mud and filth, its inside is not soiled, so too a sage, even though he sins, his Torah is not soiled."[25]

[A'] Rabba bar Rav Sheila came upon Elijah. He said to him, "What is the Holy One, blessed be He, doing?"[26] He said to him, "He recites traditions from the mouths of all the sages, but he does not recite from the mouth of R. Meir." He said to him, "Why?" He said to him, "Because he learned traditions from the mouth of Aher." He said to him, "So what? R. Meir found a pomegranate. He ate the inside and threw away the peel." He said to him, "Now He (God) says: 'Meir, my son, says, "*When a human being suffers, the Shekhina—what expression does it say? 'I am light (=pained) in my head. I am light in my hand.' If it says 'I am saddened' on account of the blood of the wicked who are killed, how much the more so for the blood of the righteous that is spilled?*" (=Mishna Sanhedrin 6:5).'"[27]

॥

B. Elisha as Sinning Sage: The Inviolability of Torah (II) (Yerushalmi Hagiga 2:2, 77b-c)

The Yerushalmi's version of the saga of Elisha shares much in common with the Bavli, although there are significant differences as well. Here too Elisha appears as a type of tragic figure, a former master of Torah who went astray and sinned. The fundamental question again is the inviolability of Torah. This version plays out the tension between Torah and sin by focusing on the relationship between R. Meir and Elisha. Meir was (and is) Elisha's student, and because he learned Torah from Elisha, he remains loyal to him throughout his life. While God rejects Elisha, Meir seeks his master's welfare, even confronting God and somehow forcing the Almighty to change his mind and allow Elisha to enter the world to come (C2). Meir succinctly captures the moral of the story in an explanation to his students, "They save Elisha-Aher for the merit of his Torah" (C3). The study of Torah bestows inviolable merit, if not directly, then at least through the efforts of disciples.

The major difference is that the Yerushalmi lacks the Metatron incident. Elisha rebels against God for several reasons, partly a result of causes beyond his control, such as the sins of his father and mother, and partly from his loss of faith (A2, A3, B3). In response to his rebellion God precludes Elisha from repenting. Thus in the Yerushalmi the divine voice rejecting Elisha is a *response* to his sins; in the Bavli the divine voice rejects Elisha because of the Metatron affair and *precipitates* his sin. Furthermore, in the Yerushalmi the voice comes from the Holy of Holies in the earthly temple. In the Bavli a heavenly voice comes from the heavenly temple that Elisha experiences in his vision. Thus the Talmuds construct the figure of a master of Torah who cannot repent in different ways in order to grapple with the same basic question.

The Yerushalmi story, like the Bavli, has been crafted with great skill. Each of the four parts has a tripartite structure. Sections A2–A3 and C1–C3 contain wordplay. Numerous phrases are repeated in order to link the units together.[28] A2, A3 and B present flashbacks to earlier points in Elisha's life. These stories-within-a-story gradually reveal to the audience why Elisha went astray. Moreover, Elisha's account in A3 of riding his horse on the Day of Atonement and Sabbath mirrors the current situation of Elisha riding his horse on the Sabbath. Similarly, the burning fire produced by the rabbis studying Torah that impresses Elisha's father foreshadows the burning fire that consumes Elisha's grave (A2, C2). The interpretation of verses in the dialogues between Meir and Elisha are strikingly self-referential and relate to the content (A1–A3). As in the Bavli, the story rehearses its lesson by taking us to the next generation and describing the rehabilitation of Elisha's daughters (D). Torah again contains the enduring power to save in both worlds.

[A] R. Meir was sitting and expounding in the academy in Tiberias. His master Elisha passed by riding on a horse on the Sabbath. They came and said to R. Meir, "Behold your master is outside." He ceased his homily and went out to him.

(1) He [Elisha] said to him, "What were you expounding today?" He said, "*The Lord blessed the latter days of Job's life more than the beginning* (Job 42:12)." He said to him, "And how did you begin it?" He said to him, "*The Lord gave Job twice what he had before* (Job 42:10)—that he doubled his money." He said, "Alas for things lost and not found. Akiba your master did not expound it like that. Rather, *The Lord blessed the latter days of Job's life more than the beginning* (Job 42:12)—on account of the commandments and good deeds that he had done from the beginning."[29]

(2) He [Elisha] said to him, "What else were you expounding?" He (Meir) said to him, "*The end of a thing is better than its beginning* (Qoh 7:8)." He said to him, "And how did you begin it?"

(a) He said to him, "[By comparing it] to a man who had children in his youth who died, and in his old age who lived. Behold, 'The end of a thing is better than its beginning.'

(b) "[By comparing it] to a man who did business in his youth and lost money, and in his old age and earned. Behold, 'The end of a thing is better than its beginning.'

(c) "[By comparing it] to a man who learned Torah in his youth and forgot it, and in his old age and fulfilled it. Behold, 'The end of a thing is better than its beginning.'"

He [Elisha] said, "Alas for things lost and not found. Akiba your master did not expound it like that. Rather, *The end of a thing is better than its beginning* (Qoh 7:8)—when it is good from its beginning.[30] And this very matter happened to me: Abuya my father was one of the notables of Jerusalem. On the day he was to circumcise me he invited all the notables of Jerusalem and seated them in one room. [He invited] R. Eliezer and R. Yehoshua [and seated them] in a separate room. When they were eating and drinking and singing and clapping and dancing, R. Eliezer said to R. Yehoshua, 'As long as they are busying themselves with their own [business], let us busy ourselves with ours.' They sat and busied themselves with words of Torah. From the Torah to the Prophets and from the Prophets to the Writings, and fire came down from the heavens and encircled them. Abuya said to them, 'My masters! Have you come to burn down my house upon me?' They said to him, 'God forbid. But we were sitting and turning *(hozrin)* words of Torah. From the Torah to the Prophets and from the Prophets to the Writings. And the words rejoiced as when they were given at Sinai, and fire enveloped them as the fire enveloped them at Sinai. At Sinai they were given primarily in fire, *And the mountain was ablaze with flames to the very skies* (Deut 4:11).' Abuya my father said to them, 'My masters: If that is the power of Torah, if this son of mine prospers, I will dedicate him to Torah.' Since his intention was not for the sake of Heaven, therefore it did not prosper for that man [= for me]."

(3) He [Elisha] said to him, "What else were you expounding?" He [Meir] said to him, "*Gold or glass cannot match its value* (Job 28:17)." He said to him, "And how did you begin it?" He

said, "The words of Torah are as difficult to acquire as vessels of gold and as easy to lose as vessels of glass. But just as if vessels of gold and vessels of glass are broken one can return *(lahazor)* and make the vessels as they were, so a sage who forgets his Torah can return *(lahazor)* and learn it as at the beginning." He said to him, "Enough, Meir, the Sabbath limit is up to this point." He said to him, "How do you know this?" He said to him, "From the steps of my horse, which I have been counting. And he has walked 2,000 cubits."[31] He said to him, "You have all this wisdom yet you will not repent *(hazar)?*"[32] He said to him, "I cannot." He said to him, "Why?" He said to him, "Once I was passing by the Holy of Holies, riding my horse on Yom Kippur that fell on a Sabbath. I heard a heavenly voice come out of the Holy of Holies and say, *'Return, rebellious children* (Jer 3:22)—except Elisha ben Abuya, for he knew my power and rebelled against me.'"[33]

[B] And why did all this happen to him?

(1) Once he was sitting and learning in the plain of Genesaret[34] and he saw a man ascend to the top of a palm and take the mother bird together with her young and descend safely from there. The next day he saw a man ascend to the top of the palm and take the young after shooing away the mother. He descended from there, and a snake bit him and he died. He said, "It is written, *[Do not take the mother together with her young.] Let the mother go, and take only the young, in order that you may live well and have a long life* (Deut 22:6). Where is the welfare of this man? Where is the long life of this man?"

He did not know that R. Yaakov had previously expounded it: "*In order that you may live well*—in the world to come that is all good. *And have a long life*—in the future that is all long."

(2) Some say [it happened to him] because he saw the tongue of R. Yehuda the Baker dripping blood in the mouth of a dog. He said, "This is Torah and this is its reward? This is the tongue that used to bring forth fitting words of Torah? This is the tongue that labored in Torah all its days? It seems that there is no giving of reward and there is no resurrection of the dead."

(3) And some say that when his mother was pregnant with him she would pass by houses of idol worship and smell that stuff. The aroma seeped into his body like the venom of a snake.

[C] (1) Years later Elisha became sick. They came and said to R. Meir, "Behold your master is sick." He went desiring to visit him *(mivqarteih)* and found him sick. He said to him, "Will you not repent?" He said to him, "If one repents, is it accepted?" He said, "Is it not written, *You return man to dust* (dakka), *[You decreed, Return you mortals]* (Ps 90:3)? Until life is crushed *(dikhdukha)* it is accepted." At that point Elisha wept and passed away and died. R. Meir rejoiced in his heart thinking, "It seems that my master died repenting."[35]

(2) After they buried him *(qivruneih)* fire came down from Heaven and burned his grave *(qivro)*. They came and said to R. Meir, "Behold, your master's grave is burning."[36] He left desiring to visit it *(mivqarteih)* and found it burning. What did he do? He took his cloak and spread it upon him.

He said, "*Stay the night, [then in the morning if he will redeem you, good. But if he does not want to redeem you, I will redeem you myself, as God lives]* (Ruth 3:13).

"*Stay the night* (Ruth 3:13)—in this world that is similar to night.

"*Then in the morning* (Ruth 3:13)—this is the world to come that is completely morning *(boqer)*.

"*If he will redeem you, good* (Ruth 3:13)—this refers to the Holy One, blessed be He, who is good, as it says, *He is good to all, and his mercy is upon all his creatures* (Ps 145:9).

"*But if He does not want to redeem you, I will redeem you myself, as God lives!* (Ruth 3:13)."

And it was extinguished.

(3) They said to R. Meir, "If they say to you in that world, 'Whom do you desire to visit?,' [will you say] your father or your master?" He said to them, "I will first approach *(miqrav)* my master and then my father."[37] They said to him, "Will they listen to you?" He said to them, "Did we not learn, *They save the casing of the scroll with the scroll, the casing of the phylacteries with the*

phylacteries (=Mishna Shabbat 16:1)? They save Elisha-Aher for the merit of his Torah."[38]

[D] Years later his daughters went to ask for alms from Rabbi [Yehuda HaNasi].
(1) Rabbi decreed and said, "*May no one show him mercy, may none pity his orphans* (Ps 109:12)."[39] They said to Rabbi, "Do not look at his deeds. Look at his Torah."
(2) At that point Rabbi wept and decreed that they be supported.
(3) He said, "If this one, who labored in Torah not for the sake of Heaven—see what [children] he raised, then one who labored in Torah for its own sake, how much the more so!"

C. Elisha the Heinous Sinner (Yerushalmi Hagiga 2:1, 77b)

This brief story appears in the same section of the Yerushalmi as the previous story. However, it derives from a different source and portrays Elisha in a strikingly different way. The story is generated almost exclusively from interpretations of the tradition of the four who "entered the *pardes*" from Tosefta Hagiga 2:3 (see above). Whereas the Bavli incorporated its interpretation of the Tosefta (the Metatron encounter and aftermath) into the lengthy story above, the Yerushalmi provides this independent story. The two narrative interpretations of the same source offer a fine example of how many rabbinic stories result from creative readings of earlier traditions.

The story consists of descriptions of three sins that devolve from three different interpretations of the Tosefta. The first interprets "cut" as "kill" (cut down) and "shoots" (=young plants) as young students of Torah (A). Because the Tosefta states that "Aher gazed," the story adds that Elisha "saw" the student distinguish himself.

Section B interprets "cut" as "cut off from": Elisha cut the students off from Torah by sending them to other professions. "Shoots" again is interpreted as young students. This scenario begins to interpret the verse as well, which begins, "Let not your mouth lead you into sin." Elisha's mouth led him into sin by telling the students to abandon the Torah. The phrase at the end of the verse, "work of your hands," is interpreted as the commandments and their merits in many rabbinic sources. Actually the story fleshes out the phrase in multiple ways, for Elisha destroys not just the "work of the hands" of the students (by disengaging them from Torah), but his own former merits, "the work of his hands," through such sins. Yet other rabbinic traditions interpret "work of your hands" as children.[40] Elisha also "destroys" the "work of your hands" by disengaging children from their studies.

C's strange scenario is based primarily on the verse. Again Elisha's mouth causes the sin by advising the persecutors how to force the Jews to violate the Sabbath. The Jews are doing work with their hands by carrying loads and then flasks. If they put down the flasks they will break and thereby "destroy the work of [their] hands." Once more Elisha "destroys the work of [his] hands," his merits, by his sins. In addition, he forces the Jews to violate (=destroy) the commandments (=the work of their hands).[41]

Aher gazed and cut the shoots (=Tosefta Hagiga 2:3).

[A] Who is Aher? Elisha ben Abuya, who would kill the young students of Torah. They said: He would kill every student whom he saw distinguish himself in Torah.

[B] Not only that, but he would go to the meeting-place and see children in front of their teacher, and he would say, "What are these sitting and doing here? This one's profession is a builder. That one's profession is a carpenter. This one's profession is a hunter. That one's profession is a tailor." When they heard this they would leave him and go away.

About him scripture says, "Let not your mouth lead you into sin, [and do not say before the messenger that it was an error, else God may be angered by your talk and destroy the work of your hands] (Qoh 5:5)." (=Tosefta Hagiga 2:3) For he destroyed the works of that man [= himself].

[C] Also, when there was a persecution, they made them [Jews] carry burdens, but they [Jews] arranged to have two carry one burden, on account of [the rule that] two who perform one labor [on the Sabbath are not culpable]. He [Elisha] said, "Make them carry individually." They went and made them carry individually, but they arranged to set [the burdens] down in a *karmelit* in order that they not carry out from a private domain to a public domain.[42] He said, "Make them carry flasks." They went and carried flasks [which could not be set down, for they would break].

Chapter 39

THE POWER OF REPENTANCE
(BAVLI AVODAH ZARAH 17a)

The doctrine of repentance or "return" *(teshuva)* is central to both biblical and rabbinic theology. In his great mercy God forgives all human beings who sincerely regret their sins and turn from their evil ways. But is repentance always possible? Can even the most relentless sinners repent? If so, is there no accountability for sin?

As with all theological issues, rabbinic sources are not monolithic. The following story is among those that grant tremendous power to repentance. An inveterate sinner repents and then dies before he can demonstrate his changed ways by living a life of virtue. Nevertheless, a heavenly voice informs us that he "is destined for the world to come." A comment attributed to Rabbi Yehuda HaNasi, however, may exhibit a bittersweet attitude to this idea (F). Rabbi "wept" at the realization that some may earn a share in the world to come after one brief moment of repentance. The virtuous struggle their entire lives to study Torah, perform the commandments and conquer their evil inclinations. Yet the wicked earn the same reward if their deaths are preceded by an instant of honest repentance. Is this remark resentful, a sardonic observation at yet another injustice by which the wicked profit? Or is it said with reverence and wonder at the immeasurable scope of God's mercy?

[A] It was said of Eleazar b. Dordia that there was not one prostitute in the world with whom he had not had sex.

[B] One day he heard that there was a certain prostitute in the cities by the sea who took a purse [full of] *denars* for her wages.

He took a purse [full of] *denars* and went and crossed seven rivers on her account.

[C] When they began the [sex] act, she farted. He thought, "Just as this fart will never return to its place, so Eleazar b. Dordia's repentance will never be accepted."[1]

[D1] He went and sat between mountains and hills. He said, "Mountains and hills! Pray for me." They said to him, "Before we pray for you, we should pray for ourselves, since it says, *For the mountains may move and the hills be shaken* (Isa 54:10)."[2]

[D2] He said, "Heaven and earth! Pray for me." They said to him, "Before we pray for you, we should pray for ourselves, since it says, *Though the heavens should melt away like smoke, and the earth wear out like a garment* (Isa 51:6)."

[D3] He said, "Sun and moon! Pray for me." They said to him, "Before we pray for you, we should pray for ourselves, since it says, *Then the moon shall be ashamed, and the sun shall be abashed* (Isa 24:23)."

[D4] He said, "Stars and constellations! Pray for me." They said to him, "Before we pray for you, we should pray for ourselves, since it says, *All the hosts of Heaven shall wither* (Isa 34:4)."

[E] He said, "Then the matter depends exclusively on me." He put his head between his knees and broke out in sobs until his soul departed. A heavenly voice went forth and said, "Rabbi Eleazar b. Dordia is destined for life in the world to come."

[F] ...Rabbi [Yehuda HaNasi] wept and said, "Some acquire their [share in] the world [to come] in many years. And some acquire their [share in] the world [to come] in one moment."

[G] And Rabbi [Yehuda HaNasi] said, "Not only are penitents accepted, but they even call them 'Rabbi'!"[3]

Chapter 40

A Sinner's Good Deed
(Yerushalmi Taanit 1:4, 64b)

The ability to bring rain in times of drought was the mark of holy men and the most pious rabbis (see chapter 18 herein). Yet in the following brief story a rabbi learns that a certain chronic sinner has this power because he once performed an extremely compassionate act. In the optimistic rabbinic worldview, even the most abject sinner has the potential to do good deeds and to have his prayers answered in the same manner as the most righteous of the sages.

[A] It appeared to R. Abbahu [in a dream] that Pantokakos [=Mr. Completely Evil][1] should pray so that rain would come down.

[B] R. Abbahu sent and had him brought before him. He said, "What is your profession?" He said, "I commit five sins every day. I sweep the theater. I hire out prostitutes. I carry their [the prostitutes'] garments to the baths. I clap and dance before them. And I clash the cymbals before them."

[C] He said to him, "What good deed have you done?" He said to him, "One day when I was sweeping the theater a certain woman entered. She stood behind a column [posing as a prostitute] and wept. I said to her, 'What is the matter?' She said, 'My husband is incarcerated and I want to see what I can do to free him."² I sold my bed and bedding and gave her its cost, and I said to her, 'This is for you. Free your husband and do not sin.'"³

[D] He [R. Abbahu] said to him, "You are worthy to pray and to be answered."

Notes

INTRODUCTION

1. Yerushalmi Peah 2:4, 17a.

2. While the initial redaction or editing—the organization of discrete traditions into a fixed form—may have been accomplished by aid of the technology of writing, the texts were then memorized and transmitted orally. See Martin Jaffee, "Writing and Rabbinic Oral Tradition: On Mishnaic Narrative, Lists and Mnemonics," *The Journal of Jewish Thought and Philosophy* 4 (1994), 123–46, and "How Much 'Orality' in Oral Torah? New Perspectives on the Composition and Transmission of Early Rabbinic Traditions," *Shofar* 10 (1992), 212–33.

3. *HaNasi* is a title generally translated as "the patriarch." See the introduction and notes to chapter 26.

4. For a fine study of how stories are generated from close reading and interpretation of details of the biblical text, see James Kugel, *In Potiphar's House* (San Francisco: Harper, 1990).

5. Some stories are introduced by technical terms such as *maaseh* and *uvada*, both of which mean "event," "case," "deed," and can be translated idiomatically as "Once...." However, these terms are not specific to a particular type of story.

6. For a sophisticated taxonomy of types of rabbinic stories, see Catherine Hezser, *Form, Function and Historical Significance of the Rabbinic Story in Yerushalmi Neziqin* (Tübingen: J.C.B. Mohr, 1993), 283–320.

7. Mishna Berakhot 1:1.

8. Bavli Ketubot 67b.

9. In the rabbinic worldview, malevolent angels have the ability to harm humans who put themselves in a dangerous situation: in our idiom, "to tempt fate." The angel presumably could not have harmed the rabbis were it not that they sat beneath an unstable wall.

10. "Eternal life" is the study of Torah, which earns eternal reward in the world to come. "Temporal life" refers to business, which provides material riches in the here and now. The rabbis abandoned their studies in order to make money, thus trading enduring merit for this-worldly prosperity.

11. Bavli Taanit 21a.

12. A folktale is generally defined as a story passed down by word of mouth and therefore subject to change in each retelling. Folktales

include legends, fables and tall stories, and often involve magic and mythical creatures.

13. See chapters 24–25 herein.

14. Josephus, *The Jewish War* 3:392–408. While Josephus ostensibly wrote history, many of the stories he included originated as folktales. His accounts of the course of the revolt and his own exploits probably circulated more by word of mouth than by the reading of his work, as books were hard to come by in antiquity. The rabbis—a century or two later—most likely picked up folkloristic versions of a few of his stories and modified those versions for their own purposes.

15. *Antiquities* 14:22.

16. See Marjorie Lehman, "The *'Ein Ya'aqov:* A Collection of Aggadah in Transition," *Prooftexts* 19 (1999), 21–40, and "The *'Ein ya'aqov:* A Talmudic Anthology of Aggadah" (Ph.D. dissertation, Columbia University, 1993).

17. Lehman, *"The 'Ein Ya'aqov:* A Collection of Aggadah in Transition," 31.

18. The same is true to some extent of pre-modern historiography. I focus on biography because even those rabbinic stories that concentrate on historical events such as the destruction of the temple recall the event through the exploits of the leading characters. Hence rabbinic historiography is essentially a type of biography.

19. See Arnaldo Momigliano, *The Development of Greek Biography* (Cambridge, Mass.: Harvard University Press, 1971); Patricia Cox, *Biography in Late Antiquity* (Berkeley and Los Angeles: University of California Press, 1983); *Latin Biography*, ed. T. A. Dorey (London: Routledge & Kegan Paul, 1967).

20. The citation is found in *Alexander* 1.2.

21. In principle, oral literature can be as fixed as written texts. Stories, however, tend to be particularly subject to modification. Stories transmitted orally will tend to change more than laws transmitted orally.

22. See Bavli Bava Metsia 86a.

23. On the literary characteristics of rabbinic stories, see the many works of Jonah Fraenkel, especially, *Darkhei ha'aggada vehamidrash* (The Methods of the Aggada) (Masada: Yad Letalmud, 1991), 260–73; "Paronomasia in Aggadic Narratives," *Scripta Hierosolymitana* 27 (1978), 27–51; "Bible Verses Quoted in Tales of the Sages," *Scripta Hierosolymitana* 22 (1971), 80–99; "The Structure of Talmudic Legends," *Folklore Research Center Studies* 7 (1983), 45–97 (Hebrew).

NOTES

24. See Robert Alter, *The Art of Biblical Narrative* (New York: Basic Books, 1981), 63–87.

25. See Moshe Garsiel, *Biblical Names: A Literary Study of Midrashic Derivations and Puns*, trans. Phyllis Hackett (Ramat Gan: Bar-Ilan University Press, 1987).

26. The terms *chiasm* and *chiastic* come from the Greek letter *chi* (xi), which looks like our X. The letter gives a graphic representation of a chiastic structure.

PART I
CHAPTER 1. HASMONEAN MEMORIES

1. 2 Macc 1:18, 10:5–8. The connection to Sukkot also appears in 2 Macc 1:9, a quotation from an earlier source.

2. 1 Macc 4:36–59.

3. *Antiquities* 12:324–26. Josephus conjectures that the name derives "from the fact that the right to worship appeared to us at a time when we hardly dared hoped for it." That is, the victory was like a light that suddenly pierced their darkness.

4. 1 Macc 7:26–38; 2 Macc 14:30—15:37. The rabbinic tradition is an almost verbatim citation from 1 Maccabees 7:34 and 47: "He sneered at them [the priests], and jeered at them and polluted them, and spoke disdainfully. He swore with rage, saying, 'Unless Judah and his army are delivered into my hands right now, it shall come to pass when I return in peace, that I will burn down this house.'…They took the spoil and plunder, and cut off Nikanor's head and right hand, which he had stretched forth so arrogantly, and brought them and hanged them near Jerusalem." (Translation from *The First Book of Maccabees*, ed. S. Zeitlin, trans. S. Tedesche [New York: Harper & Brothers, 1950], 143.)

5. *Antiquities* 14:25–28.

6. Additional literature: Zeitlin, *The First Book of Maccabees*, 1–63; Lawrence H. Schiffman, *From Text to Tradition: A History of Second Temple and Rabbinic Judaism* (Hoboken, N.J.: Ktav, 1991), 72–78, 98–102; E. Schürer, *The History of the Jewish People in the Age of Jesus Christ*, rev. G. Vermes, F. Millar, et al. (Edinburgh: T. & T. Clark, 1973–87), 1:125–233; O. S. Rankin, *The Origins of the Festival of Hanukkah* (Edinburgh: T. & T. Clark, 1930). On Josephus, see H. W. Attridge, "Josephus and His Works," *Jewish Writings of the Second Temple Period*, ed. Michael Stone (Philadelphia: Fortress; Assen: Van Gorcum, 1984), 185–232.

7. This line refers to the next, the citation from *Megilat Taanit:* what happened on Hanukka that fasting and eulogies should be prohibited?

8. The Hallel ("Praise") is a liturgy comprised of Psalms 113–18 recited on festivals and joyous occasions.

9. Cf. Judg 1:6–7: Adoni-bezek fled, but they pursued him and captured him; and they cut off his thumbs and his big toes. And Adoni-bezek said, "Seventy kings, with thumbs and big toes cut off, used to pick scraps under my table; as I have done, so God has requited me."

10. The theme of measure-for-measure punishment is clear. Yerushalmi Taanit 2:12, 66a preserves a similar version of this tradition, which begins by citing *Megilat Taanit:* "The thirteenth [of Adar] is the Day of Nikanor." The Talmud then comments: "What is the 'Day of Nikanor'? A governor of the Greek Empire was passing [through Judea] toward Alexandria and he saw Jerusalem. He sneered, reviled and insulted saying, 'When I return in peace I will destroy this fortress.' A member of the Hasmonean dynasty set forth against him. He slaughtered his soldiers until he reached his retinue. When he reached his retinue he sliced off his [Nikanor's] hand and cut off his head. He stuck them on a stake and wrote beneath them, '[This is] the mouth that spoke contemptuously and the hand spread forth arrogantly.' He hung them on a post facing Jerusalem."

11. Dan 3:19–37. King Nevuchadnezzar threw them into a fiery furnace, but God sent an angel to protect them and they emerged unscathed.

12. That is, we are not pure righteous ones and have committed various sins in our lives, and so deserve divine punishment.

13. A parallel to the martyrdom of Lulianus and Pappus appears in *Sifra Emor* 9:5.

14. The "regular sacrifice" *(tamid)* was offered each morning and twilight as prescribed by Numbers 28:3–8.

15. "Greek wisdom" refers to Hellenistic culture, including what we would call secular knowledge.

16. A parasang is a unit of measure, a "Persian mile."

17. Parallels: Bavli Bava Qamma 82b, Menahot 64b. On the different versions, see Jonah Fraenkel, *Darkhei ha'aggada vehamidrash* (The Methods of the Aggada) (Masada: Yad Letalmud, 1991), 236–38.

18. On the regular sacrifice, see note 14 of this chapter.

19. About 10:00 A.M. It was usually offered at dawn (=the first hour).

NOTES

CHAPTER 2. THE SAGES AND KING YANNAI

1. Josephus reports that Janneus frequently came into conflict with the people in general and the Pharisees in particular (*Antiquities* 13:372–83, 398–404.) At one point he even killed 6,000 people who objected to his acting as high priest. Memories of those conflicts, perhaps deriving from oral traditions ultimately based on Josephus, may form the background of the rabbinic stories.

2. Josephus relates a similar story in which the members of the Sanhedrin refrained from speaking against Herod, who was summoned to trial by John Hyrcanus II (67–63 BCE; *Antiquities* 14:168–84). A man named Samaias then rebuked the sages of the Sanhedrin for their timidity.

3. While other talmudic sources generally do not require defendants to stand throughout the trial (except when testifying or being sentenced; see Bavli Shevuot 30a), this story seems to assume that they must stand or at least obey the judges.

4. Additional literature: Tsvia Kephir, "King Yannai and Shimon b. Shetah: Sanhedrin 19a–b," *Tura* 1 (1989), 85–96 (Hebrew); Schürer, *The History of the Jewish People in the Age of Jesus Christ*, 219–28.

5. The full verse is: *If that ox had been in the habit of goring, and its masters have been warned, and it kills a man or a woman—the ox shall be stoned and its master, too, shall be put to death* (Exod 21:29). A common rabbinic midrash interprets the phrase "its masters have been warned" to teach that the master stands in judgment with the ox. Shimon b. Shetah applies the same principle to a slave: the master is responsible for the damage his slave causes and must stand trial.

6. The verse mandates that the parties "stand" to show respect to God, or at least to God's agents, whereas Yannai sat down. Shimon b. Shetah clearly considered the rabbis to be "the magistrates in authority," an equation that creates a powerful argument for rabbinic authority. At issue here and in many other sources is the respect due to sages from kings, high priests and other high offices.

7. Literally, "they pressed their faces to the ground."

8. The story does not make clear who turned to the sages, Shimon b. Shetah or King Yannai. The ambiguity is effective, for we picture both the king peering imperiously at the sages, who turn away in fear, and Shimon looking to the sages for support, as they avoid his eyes in shame. Note that Shimon exhorts his colleagues to "set their eyes" upon the king, that is, to attend to his case (B). They "set their eyes" upon him idiomatically,

by summoning him to court, but not literally, for they look down to the ground.

9.   Printings of the Talmud and some manuscripts add "and they died." Note the intimations of measure-for-measure punishment. The sages were "preoccupied with thoughts" and the "master of thoughts" punished them. The sages command Yannai, "Let the master of the ox come…," and Shimon calls for retribution, "Let the master of thoughts come…." The sages turned their eyes to the ground, so Gabriel strikes them to the ground.

CHAPTER 3. HEROD AND BAVA B. BUTA

1.   Josephus reports that Antigonus asked the Romans not to appoint Herod king on the grounds that he was "a commoner and Idumean, that is, a half-Jew" (*Antiquities* 14:403). This is upper-class snobbery, not an official determination of religious or national status. See Shaye Cohen, *The Beginnings of Jewishness: Boundaries, Varieties, Uncertainties* (Berkeley and Los Angeles: University of California Press, 1999).

2.   Josephus reports that Herod later executed Mariamme on the mistaken belief that she had been unfaithful to him.

3.   Additional literature: Meir Ben-Dov, "Herod's Mighty Temple Mount," *Biblical Archaeology Review* 12/6 (1986), 40–49; Solomon Zeitlin, *The Rise and Fall of the Judaean State* (Philadelphia: Jewish Publication Society, 1967), 2:3–99.

4.   The verse begins "In the days to come the Mount of the Lord's house shall stand firm above the mountains." In context the verse means, "All the nations shall gaze on it with joy." The story connects *naharu* (gaze) with the Aramaic *naher* (shine).

5.   Such is a literal rendering of the verse.

6.   *Reikha*, probably an Aramaicized transliteration of *rex*, king.

7.   Note the irony: Herod eliminates the sages because they know the scriptural prohibition against foreign kings and will expose him, and he keeps alive Bava b. Buta alone for advice. Bava's advice on how to atone for eliminating the sages leads to the Romans threatening to expose Herod's true origins.

NOTES

CHAPTER 4. STORIES OF DESTRUCTION

1. Josephus, *The Jewish War* 2:293–411. For a convenient summary of the course of the revolt see Schürer, *The History of the Jewish People in the Age of Jesus Christ*, 1:485–508.

2. Even the names appear to be related: Josephus writes of Zacharias b. Amphicalleus (*The Jewish War* 4:225) and Compsus the son of Compsus (*Life* 33). However, in Josephus the former is among the leaders of the rebels in Jerusalem, not a sage, and the latter leads one faction in Tiberias and encourages fidelity to Rome. These names seem to have been transformed into R. Zecharia b. Avqulos and Qamza b. Qamza in the rabbinic retelling (A, B). The relationship of rabbinic stories to Josephus's accounts is a vexing historical question. See Shaye J. D. Cohen, "Parallel Historical Tradition in Josephus and Rabbinic Literature," *Proceedings of the Ninth World Congress of Jewish Studies—1985* (Jerusalem, 1986), 7–14.

3. The episode of Marta and her inept servant rehearses this moral (E). The servant is also extremely meek, afraid to deviate from Marta's precise orders despite seeing the looming food shortage. His lack of initiative and unwillingness to act cause Marta to starve to death.

4. Versions of parts of the story appear in *Lamentations Rabbah* 1:5, 1:16 and 4:2, and in *Avot d'Rabbi Natan*, text A, §4 (see below, story B of this chapter) and text B, §6. Portions of the Titus traditions appear in *Sifre Deuteronomy* §328, *Leviticus Rabbah* 22:3, *Genesis Rabbah* 10:7, *Qohelet Rabbah* 5:8, *Avot d'Rabbi Natan*, text B, §7.

5. Additional literature: Jacob Neusner, "Story and Tradition in Judaism," *Judaism: The Evidence of the Mishna* (Chicago: University of Chicago Press, 1981), 307–28; idem, *A Life of Yohanan ben Zakkai* (Leiden: Brill, 1970); Jonah Fraenkel, "Bible Verses in Tales of the Sages," *Scripta Hierosolymitana* 22 (1971), 80–87; Anthony Saldarini, "Johanan ben Zakkai's Escape from Jerusalem: Origin and Development of a Rabbinic Story," *Journal for the Study of Judaism* 6 (1975), 189–220; Jeffrey L. Rubenstein, "Bavli Gittin 55b–56b: An Aggada and its Halakhic Context," *Hebrew Studies* 38 (1997), 21–45; Pinhas Mandel, "'Aggadot hahurban: bein bavel le'erets yisra'el," *Israel-Diaspora Relations in the Second Temple and Talmudic Periods*, ed. I. Gafni et al. (Jerusalem: Zalman Shazar Center, forthcoming).

6. This gloss links the story to two other stories that appear later in the unit. See story C of this chapter, sections A and J.

7. Printings of the Talmud add "this implies that they approved" to clarify Bar Qamza's motives.

8. That is, they considered compromising the law to keep peace with the Romans.

9. People might mistakenly conclude from the fact that the sages sacrificed this blemished animal that blemished animals in general may be sacrificed.

10. R. Yohanan identifies the ultimate cause of the disaster as Zecharia b. Avqulos's meekness. The story now proceeds to relate the course of events that resulted in the destruction. The opening verse, Proverb 28:14, should be understood in relation to this statement as well. R. Zecharia "hardened his heart" and stubbornly refused to act, and therefore he "fell into misfortune."

11. Both the arrows and the study-verse of a child are types of omens, ways of ascertaining God's will. See Ezekiel 21:26–27 (arrows) and Saul Lieberman, *Hellenism in Jewish Palestine* (New York: Jewish Theological Seminary, 1950), 194–99 (study-verses).

12. The sages interpreted Edom as Rome. The verse accordingly means that God and Israel will destroy Edom (=Rome). Yet the arrows indicate that God wants Nero to destroy Jerusalem. Nero realizes that God is using him to punish the Jews, but his victory will be short-lived, and the Jews will triumph in the end.

13. The thugs intended to force the people to fight by creating a desperate situation.

14. Apparently she was disgusted to death. Some commentaries suggest that her bare foot became infected and she soon died.

15. R. Yohanan b. Zakkai realizes that this biblical prophecy is materializing (Deut 28:15–68). The lengthy passage warns that starvation and degradation will be accompanied by defeat and exile (Deut 28:36–37, 43–48). This explains why R. Yohanan decides to leave the city and how he knows that Vespasian will become king (G, H).

16. The digression to the story of R. Zadoq creates interesting contrasts with the main story. He fasted; the rabbis ate at the banquet. He voluntarily starved himself; Marta and the people of Jerusalem involuntarily starved. Ironically, while R. Zadoq sucked the juice of figs to heal himself, Marta became sick after eating from those figs in a futile attempt to avoid starvation. He threw away the figs and lived; Marta throws away her treasures and dies.

17. *Abba Siqra* means "Father Murderer" or "Chief Assassin" (from the Latin *sicarius*, "assassin," or *sica*, "dagger"). The name is ironic, for Abba Siqra is no chief, having lost control of his own followers.

18. Familial relationships among characters, and especially sages, is a common motif in the Bavli. See section Q below, chapter 9, and Shmuel Safrai, "Tales of the Sages in the Palestinian Tradition and the Babylonian Talmud," *Scripta Hierosolymitana* 22 (1971), 229–32.

19. If the thugs carry the coffin they will realize that R. Yohanan b. Zakkai is alive. The belief that a living person weighs less than his corpse was common in antiquity.

20. They intend either to push the body to make sure he is dead, or to push the coffin over the wall. Their concern with the reaction of the Romans is not completely clear. They may be worried about "the desecration of God's name": desecrating the body of a holy man is an offense to God. Or they may worry that the Romans will take heart and feel more confident if they see the Jews desecrating the body of a rabbinic master.

21. To call someone king (or to be called king) is tantamount to treason against the current emperor.

22. The following clause refers to the ruler, understood as the king.

23. The verse comes from Moses's plea to God to enter the Land of Israel. On the tradition that Lebanon refers to the temple, see Geza Vermes, "Lebanon: The Historical Development of an Exegetical Tradition," *Scripture and Tradition in Judaism* (Leiden: Brill, 1961), 26–39.

24. Jerusalem (the jar) was encircled by a snake (the thugs). The rabbis should have broken the jar (turned over the city to the Romans or breached its walls) to remove the danger of the snake. At least the honey (the people), or some honey, could be recovered.

25. Yavneh (Jamnia) was the town in which the sages gathered following the destruction of the temple. Rabban Gamaliel, according to rabbinic tradition, held the office of patriarch, and R. Zadoq, as we know from his fasting, was an extremely holy man. Thus R. Yohanan b. Zakkai assures the survival of Judaism after the destruction by securing the sages, patriarch, R. Zadoq and a place to study Torah.

26. They gave him water in which bran (then coarse flour, then flour) had been soaked.

27. The story interprets the verse as expressing what the enemies of God will say. The full verse reads: "*He will say:* Where is their God, the rock in whom they sought refuge, who ate the fat of their offerings...." The story claims that the words "He will say" refer to Titus, who spoke (or would speak) them when he destroyed the temple. On this understanding of the verse, see the biblical commentaries of R. Shmuel b. Meir (Rashbam) and Nahmanides (Ramban).

28. See Exodus 26:31–35 and Leviticus 16. A curtain separated the outer chamber, which contained the lampstand, incense altar and table, from the inner sanctum, which contained the Ark of the Covenant adorned by cherubs. The inner sanctum was entered only by the high priest on Yom Kippur.

29. Literally, "he killed himself." This is a common euphemism.

30. The exegesis is as follows: "I saw wicked men (=Titus) coming from the Holy Site (=returning from the temple) and gathering (=gathering up the temple vessels), and those who acted thusly were celebrated in the city (=he intended to celebrate a triumph in Rome.)" The verse means something different in context.

31. In this reading the exegesis is: "I saw wicked men (Titus) coming from the Holy Site (having destroyed the temple) and [carrying things that] were buried (the hidden treasures of the temple)."

32. Exod 13:26–31; Jgs 4:12–21, 5:20–21.

33. Esau was the ancestor of Edom, which the rabbis associated with Rome.

34. The regular beating of the hammer soothed the gnat so that it stopped boring.

35. The Tannaim are the sages mentioned in the Mishna and Tosefta; they flourished prior to 200 CE.

36. Some scholars see a historical kernel of this episode in the affair of Flavius Clemens, a relation of Titus, whom the emperor Domitian killed on the grounds of atheism. See Menahem Stern, *Greek and Latin Authors on Jews and Judaism* (Jerusalem: Israel Academy of Sciences and Humanities, 1980), 2:379–84.

37. The context of the verse is significant: *"No Ammonite or Moabite shall be admitted into the congregation of the Lord...because they did not meet you with food and water on your journey after you left Egypt, and because they hired Bilaam son of Beor, from Pethor of Aram-naharaim to curse you....You shall never concern yourself with their welfare"* (Deut 23:4–7). The story playfully puts the verse in Bilaam's mouth.

38. Literally, the pupil of his eye. See Deuteronomy 32:10.

39. Jesus mocked the words of the sages by engaging in heresy and not obeying them.

40. Jesus is a "sinner of Israel" (a Jew) and advises Onqelos to seek the welfare of the Jews. Bilaam, the Gentile prophet, advises that Onqelos not seek their welfare.

41. As punishment for the shaming of Bar Qamza. On the severity of shame in Bavli stories see chapter 9 herein.

42. This is the version of *Avot d'Rabbi Natan*, text A, §4 (11b–12b). A slightly different version appears in *Avot d'Rabbi Natan*, text B, §6 (10a–b). Still another version appears in *Lamentations Rabbah* 1:5, ed. Salomon Buber (Vilna, 1899; reprint, Hildesheim: Georg Olms, 1967), 33a–34b.

43. The Bavli has Abba Siqra devise the plan and deceive the guards (F). He therefore deserves some credit for the escape. Abba Siqra does not appear in *Avot d'Rabbi Natan*. R. Yohanan designs the plan himself and deserves all of the credit.

44. In the preceding story R. Yehoshua expresses extreme distress at the destruction of the temple, lamenting that Israel will no longer be able to atone for sin. R. Yohanan b. Zakkai responds that the third pillar, acts of piety, serves as a replacement for the atonement sacrifices.

45. He asks for a symbolic token to indicate that they submit to him in principle.

46. The story does not identity the "two predecessors." The point is that the warmongers in Jerusalem had a false sense of confidence based on earlier victories.

47. See note 23 of this chapter.

48. The text is difficult here. I follow Judah Goldin, *The Fathers According to Rabbi Nathan* (New Haven, Conn.: Yale University Press, 1955), 37.

49. Clearly this account differs from the Bavli (story A of this chapter, sections J-L) in attributing the victory to Vespasian and saying nothing of Titus's role in the destruction.

50. Eli, the high priest, awaited news of the fate of the Ark of the Covenant, which the Israelites had taken into battle. The Philistines defeated them and captured the Ark.

51. Thus the story of Betar suffices with the report that the emperor "came against them" (M). We know that he destroyed the city only from the exposition (J). Additional literature: Richard Marks, *The Image of Bar Kokhba in Traditional Jewish Literature: False Messiah and National Hero* (University Park, Pa.: Pennsylvania State University Press, 1994), 13–56; Gedaliah Alon, *The Jews in Their Land in the Talmudic Age (70–640 C.E.)*, trans. Gershon Levi (Jerusalem: Magnes Press, 1980), 2:592–640.

52. Note the parallel structure of A-D and J-M. This suggests that the talmudic redactors inserted the story of Bar Daroma, E-I, which they borrowed from another source.

53. Bar Daroma therefore attributed his success to his own power. The emperor, by contrast, realized that God determined the course of the war and prayed that he not be defeated.

54. The objection is that David, the original author of Psalms (according to the rabbis), was not punished. The answer is that David said it in wonder: "Have you rejected us...?," whereas Bar Daroma stated it affirmatively, "You have rejected us."

55. The meaning may be that he died of prolapse. This is a literary and theological motif: the man who denies God with his words (mouth) is smitten in his anus (other mouth). Cf. Judas's death in Acts 1:18. (I am indebted to Willis Johnson for this insight.)

CHAPTER 5. BAR KOKHBA: HUBRIS AND DEFEAT

1. Casius Dio (160–230 CE) writes: "Very few of them (the Jews) in fact survived. Fifty of their most important outposts and nine hundred and eighty-five of their most famous villages were razed to the ground. Five hundred and eighty thousand men were slain in numerous raids and battles, and the number of those that perished by famine, disease and fire was past finding out. Thus nearly the whole of Judaea was made desolate, a result of which the people had had forewarning before the war....Many Romans, moreover, perished in this war. Therefore Hadrian in writing to the senate did not employ the opening phrase commonly used by the Emperors, 'If you and your children are in health, it is well; I and the legions are in health...'" (*Historia Romana*, LXIX, 14:1–3). See also Eusebius, *Ecclesiastica Historia*, 4, 6, 3.

2. A brief tradition found in Bavli Sanhedrin 93b also reports Bar Kokhba's messianic pretensions: "Bar Koziba ruled for two and one-half years. He said to the rabbis, 'I am the Messiah.' They said to him, 'It is written concerning the Messiah that he smells and judges. Let us see. If he smells and judges, that is well. If he does not smell and judge, we will kill him.' When they saw that he did not smell and judge, they killed him." Of course there is no historical basis to the tradition. It expresses the attitude of Babylonian sages to (pseudo-)Messiahs and serves as a warning to messianic pretenders.

3. This parallels the Bavli traditions about Bar Daroma. See chapter 4, story C, section E.

4. A similar version of this text appears in *Lamentations Rabba* 2:2 (50b–52b). For additional literature, see Schürer, *The History of the Jewish*

People in the Age of Jesus Christ, 1:514–57; Peter Schäfer, "The Causes of the Bar Kokhba Revolt," *Studies in Aggadah, Targum and Jewish Liturgy in Memory of Joseph Heinemann,* ed. J. Petuchowski and E. Fleischer (Jerusalem: Magnes Press, 1981), 74–94; E. Mary Smallwood, *The Jews Under Roman Rule* (Leiden: Brill, 1981), 428–66.

5. Mishna Taanit 4:6 lists "the capture of Betar" among the five disasters that occurred on the ninth day of the month of Av. The following block of Talmud comments on this Mishnaic quotation by describing the fall of Betar. See too the traditions in Bavli Gittin 57a (chapter 4C).

6. Rabbi Yehuda HaNasi died in c. 220 CE, R. Yohanan in c. 279 CE.

7. They had to cut off their fingers to prove their courage and worthiness to fight in his army.

8. This translation reflects the exegesis. In context the verse translates, "But you have rejected us, O God; God you do not march with our armies (Ps 60:12)."

9. "Three and one-half years" probably derives from Daniel 7:25 and 12:7.

10. This is the fourth blessing of the grace after meals. The tradition thus offers an etiology for the institution of this blessing.

11. To celebrate the destruction of Jerusalem, as explained by the following story.

CHAPTER 6. REBUILDING THE TEMPLE

1. Some scholars suggest that the background to the story is to be found in the Roman emperor Hadrian's putative grant of permission to rebuild the temple, and its repeal was the cause of the Bar Kokhba revolt of 132–35 CE. (The hero of the story, R. Yehoshua b. Hananiah, lived during the time of Hadrian's reign.) There is no evidence, however, that Hadrian granted permission to rebuild the temple. See Schürer, *The History of the Jewish People in the Age of Jesus Christ,* 1:535–36.

2. The Samaritans lived to the north of Judea. They regarded themselves as descendants of the Northern Israelites and for many years worshiped at a temple located on Mt. Grizim. Samaritan scriptures included the Pentateuch (in a slightly different version), but not the Prophets or the Writings, and certainly not any works of rabbinic literature. The rabbis therefore considered the Samaritans to be quasi-Jews or heretics. See chapter 5 herein for another example of Samaritan treachery.

3. Additional literature: G. W. Bowersock, *Julian the Apostate* (Cambridge, Mass.: Harvard University Press, 1978), 88–90, 120–22; Schürer, *The History of the Jewish People in the Age of Jesus Christ*, 1:535–36.

4. Acco (also known as Ptolemais) was located in Phoenicia and Antioch was located in Syria. Hearing the news, the Jews started returning from the communities in the diaspora to help rebuild the temple.

5. The terms *minda*, *belo* and *halakh* are terms for Persian taxes, usually translated "tribute," "poll-tax" and "land-tax." The story coordinates the obscure Persian terms with the more familiar Roman taxes.

6. And cannot rescind it. The assumption that a royal decree, once issued, cannot be repealed, seems to derive from Esth 8:8.

7. Jewish law defines the location and dimension of the temple precisely. The people would not build the temple if they were required to violate these laws.

8. Marcus Jastrow, *A Dictionary of the Targumim, the Talmud Babli and Yerushalmi and the Midrashic Literature* (reprint, New York: Jastrow Publishers, 1967), 56.

9. That is, the Romans destroyed the temple and crushed the Bar Kokhba revolt of 132–35 CE (see chapter 5 herein). This time they simply frustrated the building of the temple. The outcome could have been a great deal worse.

PART II
CHAPTER 7. THE BANNING OF AKAVIA B. MEHALALEL

1. A sage who refused to accept the decision of the Sanhedrin, the High Court, was considered a "rebellious elder" and could be put to death. See Mishna Sanhedrin 11:2, based on Deuteronomy 17:8–13. The Sanhedrin ceased to function with the destruction of the temple in 70 CE. At issue here is the authority of the sages in the rabbinic academy. (The offer that Akavia be "head of the court" either applies to the rabbinic court or assumes that the conflict took place during temple times.)

2. Tractate Eduyyot, meaning "testimonies," is an unusual tractate of Mishna. It is not organized topically but collects the "testimonies" of sages about traditions they received concerning assorted issues.

3. Upon reading the line, "*At the time of his [Akavia's] death*, he said to his son, 'My son, retract the four issues that I stated,'" we may think that he submits only because he is about to die under the ban and wishes to spare his son the same fate. The next line removes the ambiguity and

informs us that he remained true to his tradition. Moreover, Akavia instructs his son to accept the sages' position despite their banning him— evidence again of his character.

4. See, for example, chapter 9 herein. Additional literature: Anthony Saldarini, "The Adoption of a Dissident: Akabya ben Mahalaleel in Rabbinic Tradition," *Journal of Jewish Studies* 33 (1982), 547–57; Haim Licht, *Tradition and Innovation* (Israel: Givat-Haviva, 1989), 47–62 (Hebrew); Hugo Mantel, *Studies in the History of the Sanhedrin* (Cambridge, Mass.: Harvard University Press, 1961), 114–18.

5. For the law of the residual hair see Leviticus 13:1–8 and Mishna Negaim 5:3. If a discoloration appears on the skin and then the hair turns white, it is a sign of leprous affection and the person is impure. If the hair turns white prior to the appearance of the discoloration, it is not considered a leprous affection (Mishna Negaim 4:11). The question concerns the case when the discoloration disappears but a "residual hair" remains, and then the discoloration returns. Is the discoloration new, in which case the hair preceded the discoloration and the person is pure? Or is it the same discoloration, in which case it preceded the hair and the person is impure? The dispute over the law of greenish blood appears in Mishna Niddah 2:6. Menstrual blood renders a woman impure. The question is whether a discharge of greenish blood is menstrual blood or some other secretion.

6. This dispute is found in Mishna Bekhorot 3:4. One may not shear or derive benefit from the hair of a firstling (Deut 15:19). However, if a firstling suffers a blemish it may not be sacrificed and may be slaughtered and consumed by a priest. What is the status of the hair that fell out prior to the slaughter? Is it now, like the animal itself, permitted? Or does it retain its forbidden status?

7. This dispute appears in *Sifre* Numbers §7. The "waters of bitterness" established the guilt or innocence of a suspected adulteress (Num 5:11–31). The issue seems to be whether this law, which is directed to "the Israelite People" (Num 5:12), includes converts and emancipated (Gentile) bondmaidens or only native-born Jews.

8. Perhaps to frighten her into confessing or as a deterrent to others. Shemaya and Avtalion were two of the early rabbinic masters (c. 60 BCE), the teachers of Hillel and Shammai.

9. The image is that of the Temple Court during the pilgrimage festivals. Among the throngs of worshipers in the Temple Court none could be found as wise and sin-fearing as Akavia.

10. The laws of the purity of hands differ from those governing the rest of the body. See Mishna Yadaim 3:1–2.

11. The precise meaning of this phrase is unclear. Apparently the son wants his father to attest to his character so that he will be accepted or favorably received by the sages.

CHAPTER 8. HILLEL AND THE PASSOVER

1. For additional literature, see Henry Fischel, "Story and History: Observations on Greco-Roman Rhetoric and Pharisaism," *Essays in Greco-Roman and Related Talmudic Literature*, ed. H. Fischel (New York: Ktav, 1977), 67–70; Yizhak Buxbaum, *The Life and Teachings of Hillel* (Northvale, N.J.: Jason Aronson, 1994), 22–32; Jacob Neusner, *The Rabbinic Traditions About the Pharisees Before 70* (Leiden: Brill, 1971), 1:231–35, 246–48, 254–57; Aaron Blumenthal, *If I Am Only for Myself: The Story of Hillel* (n.p: United Synagogue Commission on Jewish Education, 1973), 29–38.

2. Throughout this text *Passover* refers to the Passover sacrifice, not the entire festival.

3. Does the obligation to offer the Passover sacrifice supersede the prohibition of labor on the Sabbath, which includes slaughter?

4. Hillel refers to the "regular sacrifice" (see section D) and means that there are about 300 cases similar to the Passover sacrifice that supersede the Sabbath.

5. The regular sacrifice (the *tamid*) is prescribed in Numbers 28:3–8. It was the first and last sacrifice brought every day, including the Sabbath.

6. A logical inference *a minori ad maius*, from the lighter (less significant) to the weighty (more significant).

7. "Excision" *(karet)* is a biblical punishment interpreted by the sages as premature death or childlessness. Numbers 9:13 warns that one who fails to offer the Passover sacrifice will be "cut off" *(nikhrat)* from his people.

8. The Second Passover takes place one month later, on the fourteenth of Iyyar. Those who are impure or on a journey during the First Passover must bring the sacrifice at this time. See Numbers 9:6–14. When the majority of the community is impure and cannot offer the sacrifice, those individuals who remain pure celebrate an individual Passover at the proper time.

9. To carry anything within a public domain is forbidden on the Sabbath. Had the people known the law, they would have prepared by

bringing their animals and knives to the temple on Friday. The story assumes that while slaughtering on the Passover supersedes the Sabbath, other violations must be avoided by taking the appropriate measures on Friday.

10. So they will intuitively act according to the law.

11. They carry neither their animals nor their knives and therefore do not violate the Sabbath. These methods of bringing knives and leading animals apparently are permitted.

12. Consistent with the theme of forgetting, the question concerns one who forgot to bring the slaughtering knife on Friday. Compare again the Tosefta's version.

13. Note the tripartite structure and the numerous repeated words and phrases.

14. That is, they forgot the law. The identity of the Bnei Betera is shrouded in mystery. The story presents them as the leaders of the Jewish community at this time.

15. See note 6 of this chapter.

16. See note 11 of this chapter.

17. Note that the Bavli does not mention tradition at all. In the Tosefta it is Hillel's fourth and final argument but does not seem to be superior to the other three.

18. The term *tanna* here refers to "repeaters" of traditions in the Amoraic period, those who committed traditions to memory and could be called upon to repeat them for the sages. This is a different usage than "Tanna" for a sage who lived in the Tannaitic period, from 70–200 CE.

19. This paragraph appears in Aramaic and comprises a commentary to the story. It explains what Hillel means by the "many Passovers" that supersede the Sabbath throughout the year and how many of them there are. According to different *tannaim* (see the previous note), Hillel stated either one hundred, two hundred or three hundred sacrifices.

20. On these terms, see the introduction to chapter 8, story A.

21. See note 6 of this chapter.

22. See note 7 of this chapter.

23. See the similar phrases in sections B and E. A subtheme in this version is the tension between the Palestinian and Babylonian sages. The Palestinian Talmud naturally plays down the superiority of Babylonian tradition. Also see note 27 of this chapter.

24. Therefore the sacrifices are of two different classes, and no analogy based on the rules of one need necessarily apply to the other.

25. Therefore the Passover is not, as Hillel argued, a weightier case, despite the punishment of excision. The regular sacrifice actually is in a "weightier" category of sacrifices with more stringent laws than those that govern the Passover. The laws of the Most Holy and Lesser Holy sacrifices appear predominantly in Tractate Zevahim.

26. There follows an interpolation, an Amoraic discussion of the details of this rule against creating a new *gezeira shava*.

27. As opposed to me, Hillel, who came from distant Babylonia, and yet carefully preserved the traditions I received from them.

28. Note the parallel to the opening (A) and the measure-for-measure theme. Hillel rebukes the Elders of Betera for not knowing the law and immediately he does not know a law.

CHAPTER 9. THE "OVEN OF AKHNAI"

1. See Daniel Boyarin, *Intertextuality and the Reading of Midrash* (Bloomington, Ind.: Indiana University Press, 1990), 35–36. In context Deuteronomy 30:11–12 reads: "Surely the instruction that I enjoin upon you this day is not too baffling for you, nor is it beyond reach. It is not in heaven, that you should say, 'Who among us can go up to heaven and get it for us and impart it to us, that we may observe it?'" Exodus 23:2 reads, "You shall neither side with the multitude to do wrong—you shall not give perverse testimony in a dispute so as to pervert it in favor of the majority."

2. For another expression of the significance of shame, see chapter 4, story A, section S.

3. There is so much literature on this story that only a few studies can be listed here: Daniel Gordis, *God Was Not in the Fire: The Search for a Spiritual Judaism* (New York: Scribners, 1995), 157–59, 198–202; Alexander Guttman, "The Significance of Miracles for Talmudic Judaism," *HUCA* 20 (1947), 363–81; David Weiss Halivni, *Peshat and Derash* (New York: Oxford University Press, 1991), 107–8; David Hartman, *A Living Covenant* (New York: The Free Press, 1985), 32–33, 46–48; Rubenstein, *Talmudic Stories: Narrative Art, Composition, and Culture* (Baltimore, Md.: Johns Hopkins University Press, 1999), 34–63; Izhaq Englard, "Majority Decision vs. Individual Truth: The Interpretations of the 'Oven of Achnai' Aggadah," *Tradition* 15 (1975), 137–52; Suzanne Last Stone, "In Pursuit of the Counter-Text: The Turn to the Jewish Legal Model in Contemporary American Legal Theory," *Harvard Law Review* 106 (1993), 813–94. For references to additional literature, see Rubenstein, *Talmudic Stories*,

nn. 1–4; Stone, "In Pursuit of the Counter-Text," 855–57; and Englard's discussion.

4. According to rabbinic law it is not possible to purify clay vessels that have become impure. But once a vessel is broken and no longer a vessel, it becomes pure. In this case the owner cuts his oven into sections, thus breaking it, but he puts sand between the sections so that it can be used. The dispute is whether this loophole gives the oven the status of a broken vessel and thus renders it pure or whether the segments of sand effectively reconstitute the oven.

5. The story symbolically interprets the proper name Akhnai as "snake," *akhna*. On one level the segments of alternating sand and oven resemble the coils of a snake. But the story also explains that the rabbis "surrounded" R. Eliezer "with words like this snake." This metaphor has an ominous ring, suggesting that the sages acted with cunning.

6. For another example of the motif of a sage asking Elijah about God's reaction, see chapter 38, story A, section A'.

7. Akiba realizes that the sages have perpetrated an outrage and that word of the ban will cause great pain to R. Eliezer. He tries to inform R. Eliezer in the most sensitive manner possible so as to minimize his pain and consequently to minimize God's punishment.

8. Black dress and the removal of shoes are signs of mourning. The story seems to assume that one must remain four cubits distant from a person under a ban.

9. R. Eliezer accepts the ban by following the rituals of mourning incumbent upon one under a ban. Yet the posture of sitting in mourning has additional significance in that the motif of postures recurs throughout the story. The opponents of R. Eliezer "stand on their feet" in E and K. The walls "incline" in C3, neither "standing" in honor of R. Yehoshua nor "falling" in honor of R. Eliezer. When R. Eliezer shifts from sitting on the ground to "falling on his face," a full expression of his anguish, Rabban Gamaliel dies (L). Imma Shalom then tells him to "stand up." The cycle of postures has been brought to completion with his prostration.

10. It is crucial to realize that the destruction occurs only after R. Eliezer reacts to the news of the ban. It is not the mere fact of the ban that angers God, but the pain that a human being suffers at being informed of that fact.

11. It failed to rise normally, as if made without a leavening agent.

12. Another example of the destructive gaze of a sage appears in chapter 17, story B, sections B2 and C3.

13. Although R. Yehoshua opposed R. Eliezer at the outset, God directs his wrath at Rabban Gamaliel. As patriarch and leader of the sages he apparently bears primary responsibility for the ban. For detailed discussion of this question see Rubenstein, *Talmudic Stories*, 44, 55.

14. The three destructions, J1–J3, balance R. Eliezer's three supernatural proofs, C1–C3, and the destructive wave, K, balances the proof from the heavenly voice, D. Moreover, there appears to be an intrinsic connection that creates a measure-for-measure theme: the sages reject R. Eliezer's backward-flowing water and Rabban Gamaliel is threatened by water rising up against him. The sages reject the miracle of a disruption in the course of nature, the uprooting of a carob tree, and the world experiences a corresponding disruption in the vegetable realm, the ruination of crops. The sages burned R. Eliezer's purities (H), so the world burns from his gaze. The sages filled his eyes with tears (K); now his eyes blaze with fire. God stated that the law follows Eliezer "in every place," and destruction consequently occurs "in every place" he gazes (D, G3). Gamaliel's death eventually avenges the social death of the ban.

15. Just as R. Yehoshua rejected the heavenly voice by adducing a principle about the integrity of the law (E), so Rabban Gamaliel temporarily wards off heavenly punishment by citing a principle regarding the integrity of the law.

16. On the motif of kinship relations among the sages, see chapter 4, story A, sections F and Q.

17. To "fall on the face" is to lie prostrate in private prayer. Like Akiba (I), she realizes that God intends to punish the sages for the pain they caused R. Eliezer. She too tries to prevent or restrain his expression of pain.

CHAPTER 10.
THE NEW MONTH AND THE AUTHORITY
OF THE PATRIARCH

1. Additional literature on the calendar: Arnold Lasker and Daniel Lasker, "Behold, a Moon Is Born! How the Jewish Calendar Works," *Conservative Judaism* 41/4 (1989), 5–19; M. D. Herr, "The Calendar," *The Jewish People in the First Century*, vol. 2, eds. S. Safrai and M. Stern (Philadelphia: Fortress, 1992), 834–64.

2. Apparently Rabban Gamaliel thought that one sighting was the new moon and the other simply a mistake.

3. That is, "I accept your position." Because the moon could not be seen, Dosa and Yehoshua believe that the first sighting was mistaken. So the second day of the month according to Gamaliel's calculation was the first for them. Gamaliel evidently assumed the moon could not be seen on the next evening because the skies were overcast.

4. One may not carry a staff and money on Yom Kippur. Rabban Gamaliel demands that R. Yehoshua demonstrate publicly that he accepts Rabban Gamaliel's authority.

5. That is, every subsequent court potentially possesses the same status as the court of Moses. Because we do not know who was on Moses' court, we can never say that a later court is inferior.

CHAPTER 11. AUTHORITY OVER THE CALENDAR

1. A deficiency of 11 days (365–354) over 19 years produces 209 missing days, which works out to about seven extra months.

2. The fixed calendar of Hillel II required periodic adjustments, and these were a source of controversy.

3. The story also appears in Yerushalmi Nedarim 6:8, 40a. Additional literature: Isaiah Gafni, *Land, Center and Diaspora: Jewish Constructs of Antiquity* (Sheffield: Sheffield Academic Press, 1997), 106–12; Alon, *The Jews in Their Land*, 1:237–48.

4. Rabbi suggests that the Babylonians violate the privileges of Jerusalem just as building a temple in the diaspora would violate sacrificial law. "Nehunyon" seems to refer to "Honyo" (Onias), the high priest who fled Jerusalem and built a temple in Egypt (Bavli Menahot 109b). The rabbis considered that temple an idolatrous shrine.

5. The sense is: You follow Hananiah's intercalation, as if your Torah reads, "These are the set times of Hananiah." But the verse says, "of the Lord," and we inhabit his holy land.

6. Hananiah's place of residence, a city in Babylonia.

7. But you follow Hananiah as if your version of Isaiah reads, "Torah shall come forth from Babylonia."

8. They themselves tell me that they have become great scholars (the kids have become goats). But I was there and saw how trivial their abilities.

9. The text is difficult here. Another possible reading is: "Since [he says] that if they do not know [how to calculate as accurately] as he, they

should listen to him. But since they do know how to calculate [as accurately] as he, he should listen to them."

10. Probably R. Hananiah was persuaded of his error. But the pronoun might refer to R. Yehuda, who hastened to correct the situation.

11. The high priest had to remain awake throughout the night of Yom Kippur. Priests and sages read to him from the lesser-known books of the Bible to keep him attentive.

12. That is, since he built them up with his first proclamation, he can no longer discredit them.

13. Hananiah was a Levite, so they derisively suggest that he play a musical instrument.

14. See Joshua 22:10–34. Reuben, Gad and half of the tribe of Manasseh built an altar in their territory on the west of the Jordan. Pinhas the Priest and the Israelites charged them with turning to foreign gods. They explain that they built the altar as a sign of their faith lest in the future the Israelites consider them aliens that "have no share in YHWH" (Josh 10:25–27).

PART III
CHAPTER 12. CONFLICT IN THE ACADEMY

1. See David Goodblatt, *Rabbinic Instruction in Sasanian Babylonia* (Leiden: Brill, 1975); Jack N. Lightstone, *The Rhetoric of the Babylonian Talmud, Its Social Meaning and Context* (Waterloo, Ontario: Wilfred Laurier University Press, 1994).

2. For descriptions of the Geonic academies, see Robert Brody, *The Geonim of Babylonia and the Shaping of Medieval Jewish Culture* (New Haven, Conn., and London: Yale University Press, 1998), 35–53.

3. See Catherine Hezser, *The Social Structure of the Rabbinic Movement in Roman Palestine* (Tübingen: J.C.B. Mohr, 1997), 195–214.

4. The Yerushalmi mentions the benches simply to describe the setting (G). The Bavli relates that the benches were added at that time (g).

5. It also relates to the theme of lineage.

6. To facilitate comparisons I have labeled the corresponding paragraphs in the two stories with the same letter: upper case for the Yerushalmi; lower case for the Bavli. Because the Bavli has supplemented and expanded the Yerushalmi's account (or another similar version), the labeling of the paragraphs in the Yerushalmi is not consecutive. Additional literature: Devora Steinmetz, "Must the Patriarch Know 'Uqtzin? The

Nasi as Scholar in Babylonian *Aggada*," *Association for Jewish Studies Review* 23 (1998), 163–90; Robert Goldenberg, "The Deposition of Rabban Gamaliel II: An Examination of the Sources," *Persons and Institutions in Early Rabbinic Judaism*, ed. William Scott Green (Missoula, Mont.: Scholars Press, 1977), 9–48; Alon, *The Jews in Their Land*, 119–31, 308–22.

7. The story also appears in Yerushalmi Taanit 4:1, 67d.

8. This question was debated throughout rabbinic times. Post-talmudic codes compromised by ruling that the evening prayer is technically optional but has become an accepted practice by the people and therefore must be considered obligatory.

9. The functions of these offices are not completely clear. The *meturgeman* (or *turgeman*) was apparently a human loudspeaker, a sage who stood next to the teacher and yelled out his words to the assembly. The *hazzan* seems to have been an officer who directed the proceedings in the academy.

10. The text here is difficult and may be defective. The sages apparently interrupt the study-session, send the students home and criticize Rabban Gamaliel for constantly humiliating them.

11. He miraculously aged so that he looked appropriate for his new position; see the parallel Bavli version (d). Alternatively, this line can be understood as a straightforward description: "He was sixteen years old, and his entire head (prematurely) had become full of white hair," thus making him look older and more distinguished.

12. The phrase also appears in Mishna Yadaim 4:2 and Mishna Zevahim 1:3. These Mishnas mention that certain rulings were made "on the day they seated R. Eleazar b. Azariah in the assembly." This comment claims that the appointment of R. Eleazar described in E is the same day mentioned in these Mishnas.

13. The rows of students resembled the rows of the vines in a vineyard. The editorial comment suggests that the configuration of benches and a fence in G explains why the Mishna elsewhere uses the metaphor of a vineyard to describe the rabbinic assembly.

14. Apparently to inform him that R. Yehoshua, the offended party, had accepted Rabban Gamaliel's apology.

15. See the introduction. The water for the ritual of the red heifer must be taken from a stream or other "living" body of water, the ashes from the burned heifer. Cave water and ordinary ashes are unfit for ritual use.

16. And usher him back into office.

17. The second position in the hierarchy.

18. The sages are called shield-bearers because they wage the war of Torah; see the introduction to the story.

19. See note 9 of this chapter.

20. See chapter 10 herein.

21. The reference is to a similar story in which R. Yehoshua and Rabban Gamaliel answer R. Zadoq's question about a blemished firstling in opposite ways. Rabban Gamaliel again humiliates R. Yehoshua in the academy, and the people tell Hutspit to stop (Bavli Bekhorot 36a).

22. The merit of his illustrious ancestors will protect him. But Akiba has no such merit to ward off evil.

23. R. Eleazar applies this principle of temple law—that once an object or sacrifice takes on a certain level of holiness it cannot be reduced to a less holy state—to his situation. Once he has been promoted to the position of head of the academy he will not be demoted.

24. In context the phrase means "about seventy." The comment interprets the phrase to mean "I am [in appearance] as [if I were] seventy," a response to his white hair. This source is also quoted in the Passover Haggada.

25. The casks with ashes symbolize unworthy students, students whose insides (personal character) are as worthless as ash.

26. See note 12 of this chapter.

27. That is, whatever separates has the status of the majority from which it separates. Here Yehuda the Ammonite separated from the latter-day Ammonites, those already mixed with other nations. He therefore has the status of the majority, the mixture, not the minority, the Ammonites. Most nations may convert to Judaism.

28. Apparently he realizes that the presence of numerous students helps to resolve disputes. He therefore decides to change his ways.

29. Another example of the theme of lineage.

30. R. Akiba believes that the laundryman is a servant of Rabban Gamaliel who has come to wage the case for his reinstatement.

31. In this tradition R. Yehoshua asks his students what new teaching they heard that day in the study-house and "whose Sabbath was it" to preach—who gave the homily. They answer that it was the Sabbath of R. Eleazar b. Azariah. This comment explains R. Yehoshua's question in terms of the final compromise worked out in the story.

32. For a superb literary analysis of the Bavli, see Steinmetz, "Must the Patriarch Know *'Uqtzin?*" Steinmetz discerns a chiastic structure based on the following correspondences (I have modified her divisions slightly). Sections a/o: in a an anonymous student provokes the controversy; in o that

student is identified. Sections b/n: in b the academy consists of shield-bearers and conflict rages; in n a compromise is made to resolve the conflict. Sections c/m: in c R. Yehoshua's speech uses imagery of living and dead; in m R. Yehoshua speaks using imagery of sprinkling, a ritual that purified the living from contact with the dead. Section d/l: in d they depose Rabban Gamaliel who troubles R. Yehoshua; R. Akiba is mentioned; in l R. Yehoshua instructs the sages to reinstate Gamaliel; R. Akiba is mentioned. Sections e/k: e is set in R. Eleazar b. Azariah's house; he does not look like a head of the academy; k is set in R. Yehoshua's house; he does not look like a sage but like a smith. Sections f/j: in f they allow students to enter the academy; in j they allow the Ammonite proselyte to enter the congregation. Sections g/i: in g they add benches for the increased students; in i Torah increases as they formulate a new tractate and solve all their questions. Section h is the center of the chiasm and points to the main theme: Rabban Gamaliel held back Torah from Israel by his restrictive policies. The dream emphasizes the contrast between inside and outside, also an important theme of the story. Besides the chiastic structure, there are several tripartite units (d, e, n). The word "distress" (*tsaar*) is a keyword, appearing in sections d, h, k, l.

CHAPTER 13. LEADERSHIP OF THE ACADEMY

1. In this case the Babylonian storytellers expanded and transformed an earlier Palestinian story to such an extent that the literary antecedent can be discerned only with difficulty. The earlier story appears in Yerushalmi Bikkurim 3:3, 65c: "When R. Meir would go up and study in the house of assembly, all the people would see him and rise before him. When they heard this *tanna* recite [this tradition, Tosefta Sanhedrin 7:8, cited below], they wished to treat him [Meir] accordingly. He became angry and left. He said to them, 'I have heard that one increases [the level] of holiness but does not decrease.'"

2. For an example of the importance of spousal lineage, see chapter 20, section G1.

3. The redactional location of the story is worthy of note. The story appears in the talmudic commentary to Mishna Horayot 3:1, which reads as follows: "[a] A priest precedes a Levite, a Levite [precedes] an Israelite, an Israelite a *mamzer*, a *mamzer* a *natin*, a *natin* a convert, a convert a freed slave. [b] When [is this the case]? When they are all equal. But if the *mamzer* is a sage and the high priest an ignoramus, then the *mamzer*-sage precedes the high-priest-ignoramus." (A *mamzer* and *natin* are Jews of

tainted descent, who may not marry untainted partners.) Thus the first part of the Mishna gives primacy to lineage for "precedence," that is, receiving honor (a). The second half gives primacy to knowledge of Torah (b). But in contrast to the story, the Mishna rules that knowledge of Torah supplants lineage as the primary criterion. This too suggests that the story warns against applying the Mishna's principle to the contemporary academy.

4. The Tosefta actually speaks of the rabbinic court, but the Talmud applies it to the academy.

5. "Sage" seems to have been the title of an office in the rabbinic court or academy.

6. That is, each student rises as he passes and sits down immediately.

7. Additional literature: Louis Jacobs, "How Much of the Babylonian Talmud Is Pseudepigraphic?," *Journal of Jewish Studies* 28 (1977), 55–56; David Goodblatt, "The Story of the Plot Against R. Simeon B. Gamaliel II," *Zion* 49 (1984), 349–74 (Hebrew); Steinmetz, "Must the Patriarch Know *'Uqtzin?*, 163–90; Rubenstein, *Talmudic Stories*, 176–211.

8. Note the wordplay. Rabban Shimon b. Gamaliel "enacts" *(taqqen)* a teaching for his benefit; R. Natan and R. Meir fix *(netaqqen)* something for themselves.

9. Tractate Uqtsin is the last tractate of Mishna and deals with the purity of the stems of fruits and vegetables. The rabbis choose a difficult and obscure topic for the challenge. One question to consider is whether this is a fair test or not.

10. That is, "Who should lead the academic discussions? He who knows the whole Torah."

11. Another wordplay: what the rabbis mean to do *(na'aveid)* is to depose *(na'avrei)* the partriarch.

12. R. Yaakov b. Qudshai repeated Tractate Uqtsin and explained it.

13. For the translation "stymied," see Adiel Schremer, "'He Posed Him a Difficulty and Placed Him'—A Study in the Evolution of the Text of TB *Bava Qama* 117a," *Tarbiz* 66 (1997), 409–10 (Hebrew). Rashi comments "finished": when Rabban Shimon b. Gamaliel finished expounding Uqtsin he spoke to them.

14. Measure-for-measure punishment. They tried to reduce Rabban Shimon b. Gamaliel's honor by shaming him. He reduces their honor by banishing them.

15. That is, they removed the rabbis' names from the content of their traditions, as in J. This too reduces their honor by ensuring that they will have no place in enduring rabbinic memory.

16. Who showed them is unclear. Presumably the angels or deceased rabbis are meant.

17. That is, dreams are meaningless. Literally, "dreams neither bring up nor bring down."

18. That is, "Your family lineage is sufficiently great that you may occupy the rank of head of the court. But you cannot be the partriarch."

19. The story shifts to the next generation. Rabbi Yehuda HaNasi was the son of Rabban Shimon b. Gamaliel.

20. R. Yehuda HaNasi thus restores the name of R. Meir to his tradition.

21. Apparently the indirectness diminishes his honor somewhat. The tradition is not attributed to R. Meir alone (R. Meir said...) but to others as well (*They* said in the name of R. Meir...).

CHAPTER 14. THE SAGA OF RAV KAHANA

1. See Daniel Sperber, "On the Unfortunate Adventures of Rav Kahana: A Passage of Saboraic Polemic from Sasanian Persia," *Irano-Judaica*, ed. S. Shaked (Jerusalem, 1982), 83–100.

2. Recall that in the "Oven of Akhnai" (chapter 9 herein), Rabban Gamaliel ultimately dies for shaming R. Eliezer. And see the following story.

3. The manuscripts of the Bavli preserve two different recensions of the story. See Schremer, "'He Posed Him a Difficulty and Placed Him,'" 403–16; and Isaiah Gafni, "The Babylonian *Yeshiva* as Reflected in Bava Qama 117a," *Tarbiz* 49 (1980), 192–201 (Hebrew). Additional literature: Sperber, "On the Unfortunate Adventures of Rav Kahana."

4. This explains why he took such drastic action.

5. The Persians do not allow the Jews to administer capital punishment and will therefore consider Rav Kahana to be a murderer.

6. The text here is difficult and the meaning obscure. This translation is tentative.

CHAPTER 15. THE TRAGEDY OF R. YOHANAN
AND RESH LAQISH

1. Daniel Boyarin interprets their relationship as homoerotic attraction and argues that the spear is a phallic symbol. See *Carnal Israel: Reading Sex in Talmudic Culture* (Berkeley and Los Angeles: University of California Press, 1993), 212–19.

2. See the other chapters in this part.

3. See chapters 9 and 14 herein for other such deaths.

4. Additional literature: Boyarin, *Carnal Israel*, 212–19; Rubenstein, *Talmudic Stories*, 272–75.

5. On kinship ties through marriage to a sister see chapter 4, story A, sections F and Q, and chapter 9, section L.

6. His decision to dedicate himself to Torah sapped his physical strength. A common talmudic motif is that study weakens a man because he directs all his energy to the Torah.

7. This is a type of pseudo-Mishna based on Mishna Kelim 14:5: "The sword—when is it subject to impurity? When it is polished. And the knife? When it is whetted." Utensils, not raw materials, are subject to impurity. The question is at what point in the manufacturing process a sword or knife has the status of a utensil.

8. Or, "He went out of his mind."

CHAPTER 16. THE TRAGEDY OF HONI

1. On the origins of this nickname, see chapter 18 herein. However, the character of Honi the Circle-Drawer, the sage in this story, differs from the character of Honi the Rainmaker in chapter 18. Different storytellers have portrayed the character in disparate ways for their own purposes.

2. The psalm (in the rabbinic understanding) was sung by the Jews who returned to the Land of Israel from Babylonia after the first exile, which lasted seventy years (586–16 BCE; see Jer 25:11, 29:10).

3. The formula "Thus people say" is used to introduce popular proverbs. Rava means that the story of Honi exemplifies this saying.

PART IV
CHAPTER 17. R. SHIMON BAR YOHAI

1. Josephus, *Antiquities* 18:38, reports: "For he (Herod) knew that this settlement was contrary to the law and tradition of the Jews because Tiberias was built on the site of tombs that had been obliterated, of which there were many there. And our law declares that such settlers are unclean for seven days."

2. Both sections are chiastic: A begins with three rabbis sitting, mentions Yehuda b. Gerim and lists R. Yehuda's three praises. The corresponding half of the chiasm begins with R. Shimon's condemnations,

mentions Yehuda b. Gerim and lists the three Roman responses. In C, R. Shimon states that he will fix something and then quotes Rav's threefold description of Jacob. The corresponding half offers the three opinions on what Jacob did, followed by R. Shimon asking if there is something to fix.

3. Other versions of the story appear in *Genesis Rabbah* 79:6; *Pesiqta deRav Kahana* §11; *Qohelet Rabbah* 10:8 (26b). Additional literature: Lee Levine, "R. Simeon b. Yohai and the Purification of Tiberias: History and Tradition," *Hebrew Union College Annual* 49 (1978), 143–85; Ofra Meir, "The Story of R. Shimon bar Yohai and His Son in the Cave—History or Literature?" *The Poetics of Rabbinic Stories* (Tel-Aviv: Sifriat Poalim, 1993), 11–35 (Hebrew); Rubenstein, *Talmudic Stories*, 105–38.

4. *teruma* is "heave-offering," the tithe of crops, fruit and dough given to priests.

5. *dimos* = *dismissus*. This is the Latin technical term for a judicial pardon.

6. This is the only hint of his reason for hiding. Perhaps there was a persecution and he fled for his life. The storytellers evidently assumed that their audience was familiar with the life of R. Shimon b. Yohai and knew why he concealed himself in a cave.

7. Alternatively, "We should institute a legal remedy" *(taqqana)*.

8. In context the verse means, "He encamped before the city." This midrashic reading takes "encamped" *(vayihan)* as "he was gracious" *(vayihon)*.

9. That is, those above ground, the Samaritan, should die, and the corpse he had buried should rise up.

10. Apparently an assembly of sages had accepted R. Shimon's purification process. The scribe participated in the assembly but now casts aspersion on the decision.

11. *Ben Gerim* means "the son of proselytes." The name is clearly symbolic, a combination of "Jew" *(yehuda = yehudi)* and "Gentile" *(ben gerim)*. At issue is the Jewish attitude to Gentile culture.

12. In the academy R. Shimon and his son survive on minimal subsistence, bread and water, and have minimal contact with others, only the sages of the academy and the wife/mother. They withdraw from sophisticated Gentile culture (markets, bathhouses) to the Jewish culture of Torah in the academy. The withdrawal to the cave is more extreme. See note 14 of this chapter.

13. The expression "women are simpleminded," a legal maxim that appears elsewhere in the Bavli, means that women are naive. Like children, they easily can be deceived and tricked.

14. The existence in the cave illustrates life devoted exclusively to study of Torah. Without agriculture, food and drink come from natural, if miraculous, sources. Carobs, moreover, are generally considered animal fodder in talmudic sources. The rabbis preserve their clothes by staying naked most of the time, submerged up to their necks, resembling carrots or tubers. They don their clothes only for prayers, since one cannot pray while naked, and the rapid series of verbs implies that they shed them as quickly as possible. The scene shows the necessary conditions for devoting one's life exclusively to Torah. The question is whether it is tenable.

15. That is, "We sinned with our destructive gaze. But even if we are judged as completely wicked, our sentence could not be longer than twelve months."

16. He intends to place the myrtles on the table or in the house to provide a pleasant fragrance. Some commentaries draw a parallel between the two myrtles and two Sabbath lamps.

17. The man is so caring about the commandments that he takes one myrtle for each verse commanding Sabbath observance, not just one myrtle for the Sabbath.

18. The phrase "Their minds were set at ease" is omitted in several manuscripts. This leaves open the question of their reaction. Were they mollified by this answer or equally disdainful?

19. A similar dialogue appears in the story of Nahum of Gamzu. See chapter 34 herein.

20. Jacob comes "whole" after surviving his encounters with Esau and with the angel against whom he wrestles all night.

21. See note 8 of this chapter. Significant is the association of Jacob (= Israel) with markets, coins and bathhouses, which R. Yehuda attributed to the Romans. The exegesis thus connects to the question of the Jewish attitude toward—and even appropriation of—Gentile culture.

22. Priests (kohanim) are forbidden to come into contact with graves or corpses except under certain circumstances.

23. See note 4 of this chapter.

24. How this purity test works and the significance of the lupines are not clear. Apparently the loose ground indicates the presence of a corpse. This part of the story was probably borrowed from the Yerushalmi and garbled in the transmission process.

25. A cemetery cannot be purified. The old man charges that R. Shimon bar Yohai improperly ruled the area pure.

26. The vote is not mentioned explicitly, but we must infer that the sages voted to accept R. Shimon's determination of purity. R. Shimon now

charges that the old man, who participated in the decision, should not impugn his ruling and reveal the dissension among the sages. Even prostitutes, who are jealous and competitive, nonetheless help beautify one another, if only to receive similar treatment in return. Others who see the old man criticize R. Shimon will consider the squabbling sages worse than prostitutes.

CHAPTER 18. HONI THE CIRCLE-DRAWER

1. For additional literature, see William Scott Green, "Palestinian Holy Men: Charismatic Leadership and Rabbinic Tradition," *Aufstieg und Niedergang der Römischen Welt* II.19.2 (Berlin and New York: de Gruyter, 1979), 619–41; Jacob Neusner, *Judaism: The Evidence of the Mishna* (Chicago: University of Chicago Press, 1981), 307–28.

2. The story appears here, Mishna Taanit 3:9–12, because it illustrates this principle. In E the people ask Honi to pray for the rains to stop, but he refuses to do so.

3. The title *me'agel*, usually understood as circle-drawer, also means rolling or leveling and is used of the plastering of roofs (see Mishna Makkot 2:1). A roof-repairer would be especially interested in heavy rains, which force people to fix their roofs more often on account of the damage.

4. According to the Talmud, this was the "lost and found" location on the Temple Mount. Finders brought lost objects there for their owners to claim.

5. Honi declines to pray for rain to stop. He will do so only when a large stone erodes, that is, never. Note too the structural parallel. In both B and E the people make a request of Honi, first to pray for rain to fall, then to pray for it to cease. First he instructs them to bring in the ovens lest they soften in the rain, then he directs them to see if a stone wears away in the rain. These exchanges bracket the tripartite unit, D1–D3.

6. *Mithatei.* The meaning of this word is not completely clear.

7. Adar falls around late February or March. Because the first rains typically fall in late October or November, by Adar the situation is acute. This version probably mentions Adar because in the Mishna's account (section B) Honi directs the people to bring in their Passover ovens, and Passover falls in Nisan, the month that follows Adar.

8. The meaning of this idiom, apparently an expression of respect, is unclear. The sense seems to be that Honi is such an accomplished miracle-

worker that the people fear lest he direct his abilities at them. Exodus 33:20 states that one cannot see God's face and live.

9. A *log* equals the bulk of six eggs, about .55 of a liter.

10. Rashi, however, explains that it is a bull for the confession of sins. However, *hoda'ah* generally refers to thanksgiving, and the nature of Honi's prayer is oriented to gratitude, not the confession of sin.

11. Elijah swore to King Ahab that there would not be rain except at his command, and it did not rain until the third year of the drought (1 Kgs 17:1—18:1). Perhaps a prophet had made a similar oath in Honi's time, or God had decreed a drought. To strongarm God for rain would then cause the violation of the oath or decree.

CHAPTER 19. R. YEHOSHUA B. LEVI
AND THE ANGEL OF DEATH

1. See Peter Brown, *Society and the Holy in Late Antiquity* (Berkeley and Los Angeles: University of California Press, 1982).

2. For other miraculous stories featuring R. Hanina bar Papa, see Bavli Qiddushin 39b and Yerushalmi Peah 8:9, 21b.

3. A type of skin disease. The Talmud lists the following symptoms: "his eyes water, his nostrils run, spittle comes out of his mouth, and flies afflict him."

4. Literally, "attach himself to them."

5. The reward for studying Torah should provide (super)natural protection against suffering, including suffering from disease.

6. Thus he entered Paradise without the Angel of Death taking his life.

7. According to rabbinic law, one who swears under mistaken assumptions may be released from an oath by appealing to a sage (see chapter 20, section J4 for another example). Here God rules that if R. Yehoshua b. Levi treated oaths lightly by swearing and then asking to be released, then here too his oath not to return need not be respected. He can be released from the oath and forced to return with the Angel of Death to die in standard fashion. But if he took oaths seriously and never asked to be released, this oath too should be respected and he should not be forced out of Paradise.

8. The Angel of Death needs the knife to bring death to human beings.

9. On R. Shimon b. Yohai, see chapter 17 herein.

10. The rainbow is a sign that God will not destroy the world (Gen 9:12). The existence of a great sage is likewise a guarantee that catastrophic destruction cannot occur, for the sage's merits will protect against divine wrath. Therefore, if a rainbow is seen, it proves that no supremely righteous man is alive at the time. R. Shimon bar Yohai apparently knows that R. Yehoshua b. Levi is a sage of great piety. He reasons that if the rainbow was seen in the lifetime of the man standing before him, then that man cannot be extremely righteous and therefore cannot be R. Yehoshua b. Levi.

11. In fact the rainbow was never seen during R. Yehoshua b. Levi's life.

12. R. Yehoshua b. Levi did not want to appear to be bragging about his piety by implying that no rainbow was seen due to his own merits.

13. Literally, "with his studies in his hand."

14. As did R. Yehoshua b. Levi, and to jump into Paradise without suffering death.

15. That is, I am as pious as R. Yehoshua b. Levi and deserve the same privilege.

16. As did R. Yehoshua b. Levi (section A). Thus R. Yehoshua b. Levi was in fact more pious than R. Hanina bar Papa.

17. So R. Hanina bar Papa was extremely pious, even if he did not attain the level of R. Yehoshua b. Levi. The pillar of fire is a sign of his great holiness.

PART V
CHAPTER 20. RABBIS AND WIVES

1. Additional literature: Jonah Fraenkel, *Aspects of the Spiritual World of the Aggadic Narrative* (Tel-Aviv: Hakibbutz Hameuhad, 1981), 99–115 (Hebrew); Shulamit Valler, *Woman and Womanhood in the Stories of the Babylonian Talmud*, trans. Betty Rozen (Atlanta, Ga.: Scholars Press, 1999), 51–72; Boyarin, *Carnal Israel*, 142–66; Tal Ilan, *Mine and Yours Are Hers: Retrieving Women's History from Rabbinic Literature* (Leiden: Brill, 1997); Judith R. Baskin, "Silent Partners: Women as Wives in Rabbinic Literature," *Active Voices*, ed. Maurie Sacks (Urbana and Chicago: University of Illinois Press, 1995), 19–40.

2. Note the irony. Rav Rahumei "regularly" came home once each year! Moreover, the name *Rahumei* derives from the root meaning "love." But Rav Rahumei is not exactly a devoted lover.

3. Note the wordplay *aḥit/iḥbit*. When a tear fell from her eye, the roof fell from under him.

4. The Mishna, A1–A2, does not mention scholars specifically.

5. Because he was such a holy man.

6. A mourning ritual: in a house of mourning the bed of the deceased, and sometimes all the beds, are overturned. Mourners customarily sit on the floor or on benches. The choice of this ritual hints at a measure-for-measure theme: Yehuda b. Hiyya neglected his bed and so his bed was overturned.

7. The story reflects the folk belief that something uttered cannot be taken back and may come to pass. A rather different version of this story appears in Yerushalmi Bikkurim 3:3, 65c: "Yehuda b. Hiyya was accustomed to go up and ask after the welfare of R. Yannai his father-in-law every Sabbath eve....Once he went up late. He [R. Yannai] said, 'It is not possible that Yehuda my son-in-law changed his routine.' He said, '[But] it is [also] not possible that sufferings should afflict that righteous body. It stands to reason that our Yehuda b. R. [Hiyya] is no more.'"

8. R. Hiyya's lineage was therefore inferior. It was not fitting that Rabbi's son marry into that family.

9. "Twelve" is a stock number in rabbinic sources and should not be taken literally. Read: "many years."

10. The first revelation, at the Reed Sea, proposes that the people and God be united ("married") when they reach the Holy Land and Mt. Zion. In the second passage, just a few chapters later in Exodus, God instructs the people to build the Tabernacle so that he may dwell among them while they journey through the Sinai desert. Thus God, as it were, changed his mind and made the "marriage" earlier.

11. According to Mishna Yevamot 6:6, a husband whose wife has not become pregnant for ten years must take measures so as to fulfill the commandment of procreation. He could either marry a second wife or divorce her and remarry.

12. They will say that he procreates with his wife and keeps the other woman purely for his sexual pleasure.

13. Similar versions of this story appear in *Genesis Rabbah* 95 and *Leviticus Rabbah* 21:8.

14. Bisa, Hama and Oshaya were all sages and apparently all lived long lives.

15. Someone who swears under mistaken assumptions can ask a sage to annul the oath, that is, to rule that the oath was not valid in the first place. Here R. Akiba annuls the oath because Ben Kalba Savua swore under the mistaken impression that his daughter was about to marry an ignorant shepherd. Had he known that she married a great sage (or a man who was to become a great sage), he would not have sworn.

CHAPTER 21. GOD AS MARRIAGE-MAKER

1. The sources are collected in the studies listed in the following note.

2. The translation is based on the critical text edited by Mordechai Margulies, *Midrash vayiqra rabba* (reprint; New York, 1993), 164–65. Additional literature: M. D. Herr, "Dialogues Between Sages and Roman Dignitaries," *Scripta Hierosolymitana* 22 (1971), 145–49; F. Böhl, "Die Matronenfrage im Midrasch," *Frankfurter judaistische Beiträge* 3 (1975), 29–64; R. Gershonzon and E. Slomovic, "A Second Century Jewish-Gnostic Debate: Rabbi Jose ben Halafta and the Matrona," *Journal for the Study of Judaism* 16 (1985), 1–41; Tal Ilan, "Matrona and Rabbi Jose: An Alternative Interpretation," *Journal for the Study of Judaism* 25 (1994), 18–51. Ilan disagrees with other scholars and explains *matrona* as the proper name of a Jewess, not the title of an aristocratic Roman woman.

3. The midrash takes the "parched land" as the dry ground upon which the Israelites trod after God split the Reed Sea. R. Yose connects this to the arranging of marriages since the beginning of the verse states that "God restores the lonely to their homes."

CHAPTER 22. RABBIS, HUSBANDS AND WIVES

1. Rabbinic law gave the sages the power to annul oaths under certain circumstances. But such annulments were not always granted. See chapter 20, note 15.

2. Hammat-Tiberias, located near Tiberias in the Galilee.

3. Literally, "By such and such that woman will never enter...."

4. Sages perceiving what has transpired by means of the holy spirit is a common motif in rabbinic stories. See chapter 17, story A, section f.

5. On whispering charms and other forms of magic in ancient Jewish society, see Daniel Sperber, *Magic and Folklore in Rabbinic Literature*

(Ramat Gan: Bar-Ilan University Press, 1994); and Morton Smith, *Jesus the Magician* (San Francisco: Harper & Row, 1978).

6. The reference is to the ritual of the suspected adultress, the Sotah (Numbers 5; Mishna Tractate Sotah). A man who suspects that his wife has been unfaithful can force her to drink the "waters of bitterness" in order to establish her innocence. A scribe writes an oath including the name of God on a scroll and dissolves it in water. The woman then drinks the potion. If guilty, she suffers a horrible death; if innocent, she emerges unscathed. Thus God allows his name to be erased in order to reconcile a couple.

CHAPTER 23. BERURIA

1. *Midrash Mishlei* 31:10, ed. Burton Vizotsky (New York: Jewish Theological Seminary, 1990), 190–91.

2. This maxim is also quoted in chapter 17, story B, section B.

3. The story is found in Rashi's commentary to Avodah Zarah 18b.

4. Additional literature: David Goodblatt, "The Beruriah Traditions," *Journal of Jewish Studies* 26 (1975), 68–85; Boyarin, *Carnal Israel*, 167–96; Rachel Adler, "The Virgin in the Brothel and Other Anomalies: Character and Context in the Legend of Beruriah," *Tikkun* 3/6 (1988), 28–32, 102–5; Tal Ilan, "The Historical Beruriah, Rachel, and Imma Shalom," *Association for Jewish Studies Review* 22 (1997), 1–8. On women in general, see Judith Romney Wegner, "The Image and Status of Women in Classical Rabbinic Judaism," *Jewish Women in Historical Perspective*, ed. Judith Baskin (Detroit, Mich.: Wayne State University Press, 1991), 68–93. Beruria is also mentioned in Tosefta Bava Qama 4:17; *Sifre* Deuteronomy §307; Bavli Pesahim 62b, Avodah Zarah 18a-b.

5. The commentaries explain that idle chatter with women either distracts time from the study of Torah or from productive labor, or leads to licentiousness.

6. Note the irony. He learns Torah by speaking to a woman, but the Torah he learns advises that one not speak with women. Had he spoken more with women he might have known not to speak with women....

7. The Oral Torah was supposed to be recited aloud. This aided the process of memorization.

8. A Christian may be intended, given the content. The Christian charges that Jews have no reason to rejoice since God has abandoned them, as indicated by the destruction of the temple and the persecutions

following the Bar Kokhba revolt. Beruria turns the charge around. That he loses an argument with a woman adds to the insult. See R. Travers Herford, *Christianity in Talmud and Midrash* (1903; reprint, Clifton, N.J.: Reference Book Publishers, 1996), 237–39. Herford suggests Beruria's insult may be patterned on Matthew 23:15, "Woe to you, teachers of the law and Pharisees, you hypocrites. You travel over land and sea to win a single convert, and when he becomes one, you make him twice as much a son of Hell *(geena)* as you are." See too Galatians 4:27, where Paul invokes Isaiah 54:1 in his rejection of Jewish law.

PART VI
CHAPTER 24. ALEXANDER MACEDON AND THE WORLD COURT

1. The Bavli brings the story in order to explain the significance of a date mentioned in *Megilat Taanit*, the "Scroll of Fasts," a list of significant dates from the Second Temple Period (see the introduction to chapter 1). *Megilat Taanit* designates the twenty-fourth of Nisan as the day on which "*dimosnaei* were removed from Judah and Jerusalem." (This is the Bavli's version. The surviving manuscripts of the scroll have a different date.) Most scholars explain *dimosnaei* as tax-farmers commissioned by the Roman authorities who were known to extort as much as possible from the local population. The Bavli seems not to have understood the foreign word and to have lost the tradition of the importance of the date. It connects the *dimosnaei* to the foreign nations mentioned in the story who came to make trouble for the Jews before Alexander Macedon.

2. See too chapter 21 herein.

3. Additional literature: On Alexander in rabbinic sources, see A. A. Halevi, *Sha'arei ha'aggada* (Tel-Aviv: Devir, 1982), 115–37; Richard Freund, "Alexander Macedon and Antoninus: Two Greco-Roman Heroes of the Rabbis," *Crisis and Reaction: The Hero in Jewish History*, ed. Menahem Mor (Omaha, Neb.: Creighton University Press, 1995), 19–72.

4. Alexander's native land was Macedonia, hence the rabbinic name Alexander Macedon.

5. Because Jewish law prohibits agricultural labor in the Sabbatical year, food was particularly scarce then. The abandoned fields of the Gentiles provide a much-needed source of crops.

RABBINIC STORIES

CHAPTER 25. ALEXANDER MACEDON
AND THE FARAWAY KING

1. The story of King Midas makes a similar point. The miserly King Midas starves to death because everything he touches turns to gold, making it impossible for him to eat.

2. Jonah Fraenkel, *Aspects of the Spiritual World of the Aggadic Narrative* (Tel-Aviv: Hakibbutz Hameuhad, 1981), 145–48 (Hebrew). Additional literature: Hezser, *Form, Function and Historical Significance of the Rabbinic Story in Yerushalmi Neziqin*, 66–77. Parallel versions: *Genesis Rabbah* 33:1; *Leviticus Rabbah* 27:1; *Pesiqta deRav Kahana* 9:1.

3. Literally, "the extreme king," what we might call "the king at the end of the earth." The parallel version in *Genesis Rabbah* 33:1 reads, "The extreme king beyond the mountains of darkness."

4. Literally, "May that man's (=your) breath expire!"—a mild expletive.

5. The storyteller interprets the verse as "You save man with the beasts" or "You save man on account of the beasts."

CHAPTER 26. ANTONINUS AND RABBI

1. In some sources the Roman is not designated emperor and could be any high-ranking official.

2. For a survey of the theories, see Luitpold Wallach, "The Colloquy of Marcus Aurelius with the Patriarch Judah I," *Jewish Quarterly Review* 31 (1940/41), 260.

3. At least this is what later rabbinic sources suggest. These sources refer to Rabbi Yehuda and his descendants as *Nasi*, a biblical term meaning "prince" or "chieftain" (see Lev 4:22). The Church Fathers and Roman sources call the leaders of the Jews patriarchs. That R. Yehuda HaNasi received this title and authority from Rome actually is not stated explicitly in any source. Scholars have arrived at this conclusion based on a great deal of circumstantial evidence. See Lee Levine, "The Jewish Patriarch *(Nasi)* in Third Century Palestine," *Aufstieg und Niedergang der Römischen Welt* II.19.2 (Berlin and New York: De Gruyter, 1979), 650–66, and *The Rabbinic Class of Roman Palestine in Late Antiquity* (New York: The Jewish Theological Seminary; Jerusalem: Yad Izhaq Ben-Zvi, 1989), 33–37.

4. See Wallach, "The Colloquy of Marcus Aurelius," 261–63. For another example see Bavli Tamid 31b–32b where Alexander the Great asks

ten questions of the "elders of the south." See Luitpold Wallach, "Alexander the Great and the Indian Gymnosophists in Hebrew Tradition," *Proceedings of the American Academy of Jewish Religion* 11 (1941), 47–83.

5. The Bavli follows the account of Antoninus and Rabbi with stories of Gentile rulers who converted.

6. Additional literature: Louis Ginsberg, "Antoninus in the Talmud," *Jewish Encyclopaedia* (New York: Funk and Wagnalls, 1901), 1:656–57; Luitpold Wallach, "The Colloquy of Marcus Aurelius with the Patriarch Judah I," *Jewish Quarterly Review* 31 (1940/41), 259–86, which includes a list of all relevant sources; Martin Jacobs, *Die Institution des jüdischen Patriarchen* (Tübingen: J.C.B. Mohr, 1995), 125–54; Shaye J. D. Cohen, "The Conversion of Antoninus," *The Talmud Yerushalmi and Graeco-Roman Culture I*, ed. P. Schäfer (Tübingen: J.C.B. Mohr, 1997), 141–72; Hezser, *The Social Structure of the Rabbinic Movement in Roman Palestine*, 441–46.

7. That is, God summons the "heavens" (= the soul) and the "earth" (= the body) for the final judgment after death.

8. *Genesis Rabbah*, ed. J. Theodor and H. Albeck (Berlin, 1912-36; reprint, Jerusalem, 1965), 320–21. I have followed the version of the Vatican 30 manuscript with minor emendations. The tradition also appears in Bavli Sanhedrin 91b.

9. A wordplay. The word *mi-ne'urav*, "from youth," is interpreted as "from its awakening" based on the similar word *ne'or*, "to awaken."

10. Likewise the soul animates the fetus. A fetus could not survive without a soul for three days.

11. This is the time when God (or an angel) takes note of the fetus while still in the womb, perhaps determining its sex. It apparently occurs soon after conception.

12. The context in Job relates to the formation of the fetus in the womb (Job 10:10–11). This verse mentions God's providence *(peqida)* over the spirit (soul), understood as ensoulment. Hence ensoulment takes place before birth.

13. Literally, "leaders, commanders" *(dukas* = dux).

14. Cf. the version of Bavli Avodah Zarah 10a: "Antoninus said to Rabbi. The notables of Rome are distressing me. He [Rabbi] brought him to a garden. Every day Rabbi would uproot one radish from the vegetable bed and give it to him. He [Antoninus] said, 'This means that he is telling me to kill one of them each day and not to provoke them all at once.'"

15. To study Torah. This is suggested by the talmudic context, which collects several stories of Gentile kings and aristocrats who converted to Judaism.

16. In order that there be no witnesses that he visited Rabbi each day.

17. That is, "He is an angel."

18. The rabbis identified Rome with Edom, the descendants of Esau.

19. And not to Antoninus, who treated the Jews benevolently.

CHAPTER 27. JESUS AND HIS DISCIPLES

1. The Roman emperor Constantine converted to Christianity in 312 CE. But it would take many years before Christianity became the religion of the majority of the inhabitants of the Roman Empire.

2. See, however, Jacob Neusner, *Judaism in the Matrix of Christianity* (Philadelphia: Fortress Press, 1986), who claims that the later rabbinic documents are grappling directly with the ascent of Christianity. See too Robert Goldenberg, *The Nations that Know Thee Not: Ancient Jewish Attitudes Toward Other Religions* (New York: New York University Press, 1998), 96–98. There are also polemical passages in many rabbinic works that seem to be responding to Christian theology and biblical interpretations. See Mark Hirshman, *A Rivalry of Genius: Jewish and Christian Biblical Interpretation in Late Antiquity*, trans. Batya Stein (Albany, N.Y.: State University of New York Press, 1996).

3. Bavli Sanhedrin 104b.

4. This story clearly reflects the traditions of Jesus as a healer.

5. In times of persecution, however, Jewish law mandates that one sacrifice oneself rather than violate the commandments. See chapter 37 herein.

6. This tradition perhaps picks up on the common biblical metaphor of worshiping idols as "going awhoring" or committing adultery (see Exod 34:15, Lev 17:7, Num 15:39).

7. For another mention of Jesus, see chapter 4, story A, section R3. Additional literature: R. Travers Herford, *Christianity in Talmud and Midrash* (1903; reprint, Clifton, N.J.: Reference Book Publishers, 1996); Jacob Z. Lauterbach, "Jesus in the Talmud," *Rabbinic Essays* (New York: Ktav, 1951), 473–570; Stephen Gero, "The Stern Master and His Wayward Disciple: A 'Jesus' Story in the Talmud and in Christian Hagiography,"

Journal for the Study of Judaism 25 (1994), 287–311; Richard Kalmin, "Christians and Heretics in Rabbinic Literature of Late Antiquity," *Harvard Theological Review* 87 (1994), 155–69; Daniel Boyarin, *Dying for God: Martyrdom and the Making of Christianity and Judaism* (Stanford, Calif.: Stanford University Press, 1999), 24–34. See too the references in note 2 of this chapter. Parallels to A-C: Yerushalmi Shabbat 14:4, 14d; Avodah Zarah 2:2, 40d–41a; Bavli Avodah Zarah 27b. Parallels to D-H, Bavli Avodah Zarah 16b–17a. Parallels to a-h, Bavli Sotah 47a and Yerushalmi Hagiga 2:2, 77d (the latter is a different version that does not mention Jesus by name).

8. The version in the Yerushalmi reads, "...came to heal him. He (Yaakov) said to him, 'Let me speak (invoke) for you in the name of Jesus b. Pandera'" (Yerushalmi Avodah Zarah 2:2, 40d–41a).

9. This interpretation of "fence" as a rabbinic fence (=edict) involves a wordplay based on *gader* (fence) and *gezeira* (edict).

10. *dimos* = *dismissus* = "you are dismissed," an authentic Roman legal term.

11. *Notsri* is the common rabbinic term for a Christian. This designation probably derives from Nazareth *(Natseret)* or Nazarene (a man of Nazareth).

12. In context the verse pertains to a "foreign" woman, a seductress or whore.

13. The Talmud first relates the story of Gehazi and Elisha; cf. 2 Kgs 5:1–26. In the rabbinic version Gehazi turns to heresy after being rebuked by Elisha.

14. On Yannai (Janneus), see chapter 2 herein. Josephus mentions that Janneus, who died in 76 BCE, massacred 6,000 people who objected to his serving as high priest on the Festival of Sukkot; *Antiquities* 13:373; *War* 1:89. Yehoshua b. Perahia is one of early rabbis mentioned in Mishna Avot 1:6; he lived in the second half of the second century BCE. The rabbinic chronology is clearly at odds with the conventional dating of Jesus' life.

15. On Shimon b. Shetah, see chapter 18 herein.

16. The word *aksania* means both "inn" and "innkeeper (fem.)." Jesus thought that Yehoshua b. Perahia was admiring the hostess. Yehoshua understands Jesus' misinterpretation as evidence of lecherous propensities.

17. The ban, somewhat analagous to excommunication, could be instituted against those who troubled the rabbis or rejected rabbinic authority. The shofar (ram's horn) was part of the ceremony. See also chapter 9, section H.

18. The *Shema*, composed of biblical passages (Deut 6:4–9, 11:13–21, Num 15:37–41), is one of the most important prayers in the Jewish liturgy. Its recitation may not be interrupted. Yehoshua therefore could not speak to Jesus until he completed the prayer.

19. Literally, "A master stated." This idiom is used to introduce rabbinic traditions.

20. Jesus. See note 11 of this chapter.

21. Therefore they were especially careful to solicit testimony for his innocence lest the authorities think that he did not receive a fair trial.

CHAPTER 28. ONQELOS THE CONVERT

1. Bavli Megilah 3a: R. Yirmia—some say R. Hiyya bar Abba—said, "Onqelos the Convert formulated the Aramaic translation *(targum)* according to the words (literally: from the mouth) of R. Eliezer and R. Yehoshua."

2. See Schürer, *The History of the Jewish People in the Age of Jesus Christ*, 1:100–5; 3:493–98. The Yerushalmi also mentions a convert named Aqilas who translated the Torah into Greek. In Yerushalmi Qiddushin 1:1, 59a, we find: "Aqilas the Convert translated before R. Akiba." Cf. Yerushalmi Megilah 1:2, 71c: "R. Yermiah said in the name of R. Hiyya bar Ba: 'Aqilas the Convert translated the Torah before R. Eliezer and R. Yehoshua.'" Note that the Bavli tradition cited in the previous note is parallel to this Yerushalmi tradition. However, while the Yerushalmi refers to the Greek translation, the Bavli speaks of the Aramaic translation. The Yerushalmi tradition is primary and presumably more accurate.

3. For another tradition about Onqelos, see chapter 4, story A, sections Q-R. Additional literature: Schürer, *The History of the Jewish People in the Age of Jesus Christ*, 1:100–5; 3:493–98; L. Rabinowitz, "Onkelos and Aquila," *Encyclopaedia Judaica*; A. E. Silverstone, *Aquila and Onkelos* (Manchester: Manchester University Press, 1931).

4. Some manuscripts read "Qalonimos."

5. The image is that of a Roman procession marching according to rank.

6. A *mezuza* is the casing placed on the doorpost of the house that contains a brief scriptural text, in accordance with Deuteronomy 6:9.

NOTES

PART VII
CHAPTER 29. HILLEL, SHAMMAI AND CONVERTS

1. Of course, the Pentateuch claims to be the revelation of God to Moses on Mt. Sinai. But so too does the Mishna (Mishna Avot 1:1). How do we know that these claims are true and not inventions?

2. Additional literature: on conversion in general, see Gary G. Porton, *The Stranger within Your Gates* (Chicago: University of Chicago Press, 1994); Bernard Bamberger, *Proselytism in the Talmudic Period* (reprint; New York: Ktav, 1968); Johanan Wijnhoven, "Convert and Conversion," *Contemporary Jewish Religious Thought*, 101–6. On this story, see Yizhak Buxbaum, *The Life and Teachings of Hillel* (Northvale, N.J.: Jason Aronson, 1994), 130–44, and David Kraemer, "The Formation on the Rabbinic Canon," *Journal of Biblical Literature* 110 (1991), 619–20. On humility, see Bernard Sternberg, "Humility," *Contemporary Jewish Religious Thought*, 429–33.

3. Tadmor is the Hebrew name for Palmyra, a city in central Syria. In the third century CE Palmyra became an important power and conquered parts of Palestine, Egypt and Persia.

4. Literally, "Convert me on the condition...." That is, "I wish to convert but to learn only the Written Torah, not the Oral Torah."

5. That is, Hillel identified a different symbol with each letter.

6. Thus the Gentile knows how to read Hebrew because Hillel taught him. One relies on Oral Tradition to know how to read the Written Torah. There is no reason to accept the truth of one but not the other.

7. A measuring rod or stick with which builders measured length. The image suggests that Shammai always holds such an implement in his hand and uses it often.

8. Some interpreters see a double meaning here. The word *regel*, meaning "leg," evokes the Latin *regula*, a law or principle. The convert asks for the Torah standing on one *regel*; Hillel articulates the one *regula* on which the Torah stands.

9. A logical inference *a minori ad maius*, from the lighter (less significant) to the weighty (more significant). See chapter 8, note 6.

10. Note the pun. The convert is lowly (*qal*) because he is not loved by God or called God's firstborn. Therefore he is the "light" (*qal*) side of the *qal va-homer* inference with respect to the native-born Jew.

CHAPTER 30. THE COMMANDMENT
OF THE FRINGES AND ITS REWARD

1. *Sifre* Numbers §115 (128–29). Text cited according to manuscript Vatican 32. A version of the story, differing only in minor details, appears in Bavli Menahot 44a.

2. The following discussion is indebted to Warren Zev Harvey, "The Pupil, the Harlot and Fringe Benefits," *Prooftexts* 6 (1986), 259–64, and Alon Goshen-Gottstein, "The Commandment of Fringes, the Prostitute and the Homiletical Story," *Rabbinic Thought*, ed. Marc Hirshman and Tsvi Groner (Haifa: University of Haifa Press, 1989), 45–58 (Hebrew). The Bible often uses the expression "go a whoring" of sin, especially "to stray" after idolatry (see Exod 34:15, Lev 17:7, etc.).

3. Literally, "whose reward is not at its side." In fact, that wearing the fringes will merit a reward is not explicitly specified in Numbers 15:37–41 or anywhere else. But the man's explanation why he withdraws, a somewhat strained exegesis of Numbers 15:41, nonetheless reads into the verse a promise of reward and punishment (F). The expression "at its side" may also be interpreted as "near at hand," that is, imminent, not deferred to the distant future or the next world.

4. The phrase "cities by the sea" connotes a distant land in rabbinic usage.

5. Note the threefold repetitions of "and the top one was of gold" (D1, D2, D3) and "When…" (C, D1, E).

6. Saul Lieberman, *Greek in Jewish Palestine* (New York: Jewish Theological Seminary, 1942), 140, translates the Hebrew *gappa shel romi* as "Love of Rome," taking *gappa* as *agapé*. He explains that this was a designation for the goddess Isis. Thus the prostitute swears by a pagan goddess while the Jew swears by the temple service. She subsequently swears by the temple service too, the first step in her process of conversion (G).

7. The full verse reads, "I am the Lord your God, who brought you out of the land of Egypt to be your God; I am the Lord your God." What is the point of repeating "I am the Lord your God" at the end of the verse? R. Natan interprets it as a promise of reward.

8. Perhaps she is attracted by his looks and not committed to Judaism. She evidently produced the text and explained what had happened.

NOTES

CHAPTER 31. THE POWER OF RIGHTEOUSNESS

1. That is, the fates of Jews are not determined by the stars (horoscopes).

2. A Persian, probably Zoroastrian, sage. Ablet is mentioned in several talmudic sources.

3. When the man placed his knife in his bag, he happened to kill a snake that had crawled into it and otherwise would have bitten him.

4. On the significance of shame in the Bavli, see chapter 9 and chapters 12–14 herein.

5. An "unusual death" is a premature or accidental death. Even the most righteous eventually die. The point is that they do not die prematurely ("an unusual death") nor do they live merely a normal lifespan ("death itself") but enjoy extreme longevity.

6. Apparently to store it until she should need it.

7. The "poor man at the door" is a common motif that regularly appears in stories when a character is threatened by death. See chapter 9, section L, for another example. The threshold often functions as a liminal space and place of danger and marks transitions from one state to another.

CHAPTER 32. THE HONOR OF PARENTS

1. See also chapter 32, story B, section c.

2. Additional literature: Gerald Blidstein, *Honor Thy Father and Mother: Filial Responsibility in Jewish Law and Ethics* (New York: Ktav, 1975).

3. She could not fix her shoe or tie it up since it was the Sabbath.

4. That is, that is the way she wishes to be honored, so you must permit her.

5. Deuteronomy 5:16 promises "long life" as reward for honoring parents. The rabbis interpreted the phrase in terms of the world to come.

6. Rabbinic tradition discouraged Jews from leaving the Holy Land to settle in the diaspora. Because living in the Land of Israel was considered an act of piety, leaving it was akin to sin. The rabbis also wished to maintain a high Jewish population in Israel.

7. The high priest's breastplate, described in Exodus 28:20, had twelve precious jewels, one for each tribe. Jasper was the jewel for the tribe of Benjamin.

8. A red cow was required for the purification ritual prescribed in Numbers 19. Such cows were extremely rare and were worth a tremendous amount of money.

9. The contextual meaning of the verse is slightly different. R. Shabtai probably means to contrast the reward for Jews, which rabbinic tradition generally assumes will materialize in the next world, with the reward for Gentiles, which is given immediately.

10. Since they needed it for the ritual. See note 8 of this chapter.

11. Gentiles are not obligated to observe the Torah's laws, yet Damma was rewarded for doing so. How much the more so, argues R. Hanina, will Jews be rewarded for honoring their parents. The rabbis generally believed that it was a greater act of piety to observe commandments that God had imposed than voluntarily to observe the commandments.

CHAPTER 33. THE PURSUIT OF TORAH

1. Bavli Berakhot 63b.

2. On the intercalation, see chapter 11 herein.

3. Literally, "the season of Tevet," the winter solstice.

4. They violated the Sabbath by washing and anointing Hillel.

5. Literally, "a load of flour upon his shoulder."

6. They did not recognize him. The drafting of citizens to perform labor on behalf of the city or emperor was a type of tax in antiquity. Here, ironically, R. Eleazar b. Harsom owns the cities. The servants inadvertently try to conscript him to work for the good of his own possessions. His own wealth, therefore, eventually draws him away from Torah, despite his best effort to free himself from it.

7. Why he did not wish to reveal himself is unclear. Some textual witnesses omit this line, and some add, "He gave them a great deal of money in order that they leave him be."

8. "Wicked" (rasha) is the literal translation. A contextual translation might be "passionate" or "carnal."

9. Note the tripartite structure and the parallel between the beginning and ending.

10. On the importance of shame and the connection between Torah and ethical behavior, see chapter 9 herein.

NOTES

PART VIII
CHAPTER 34. NAHUM OF GAMZU

1. The Yerushalmi story also appears in Sheqalim 5:6, 49c. Additional literature: David Kraemer, *Responses to Suffering in Classical Rabbinic Literature* (New York: Oxford University Press, 1995), 111–12; Yaakov Elman, "The Suffering of the Righteous in Palestinian and Babylonian Sources," *Jewish Quarterly Review* 80 (1990), 315–40.

CHAPTER 35. SUFFERING

1. Additional literature: David Kraemer, *Responses to Suffering in Classical Rabbinic Literature*, and *Reading the Rabbis: The Talmud as Literature* (New York: Oxford University Press, 1996), 124–41; Yaakov Elman, "Righteousness as Its Own Reward: An Inquiry into the Theologies of the Stam," *Proceedings of the American Academy of Jewish Religion* 57 (1990–91), 35–67.

2. That is, "I can't bear my sufferings."

3. Literally, "restore his soul." R. Hanina apparently spoke a healing spell. For another example of a spell, see chapter 22, story A.

4. That is: "I could heal others while I was well. But now that I am sick I am not in a position to heal myself."

5. Those who do not break but yield and bend like lilies in the wind. Suffering does not break their spirit. The rabbis interpreted the Song of Songs as an allegory of God's love for Israel.

6. Rabbinic sources regularly characterize Abraham and Joseph as "righteous" *(tsadiqim)*. Abraham was tested by the command to sacrifice his son Isaac; Joseph was tested by the seductive wife of Potiphar to see whether he would resist sinning.

7. A proverb. Someone who helps others break out of jail cannot extricate himself once imprisoned. Similarly, although R. Yohanan could heal others, while weakened by illness he could not heal himself.

8. R. Yohanan's beauty was legendary. See chapter 15 herein.

9. This maxim is adapted from a Mishna dealing with sacrifices: the Torah describes both an animal offering (an expensive sacrifice) and a meal offering (an inexpensive sacrifice) as pleasing to God. What matters is not the size or expense of the sacrifice but the intention with which it is brought. Similarly, whether one studies and teaches a great deal of Torah or a small amount of Torah is all the same in the eyes of God if done with the proper intention.

10. The two tables are Torah (eternal riches) and wealth (earthly riches). The point of this adage is that R. Eleazar merited becoming a master of Torah and should not lament his poverty.

11. According to the commentaries, R. Yohanan tied the bone around his neck as a token or charm.

CHAPTER 36. THEODICY AND TORAH

1. Additional Literature: Jonah Fraenkel, "Hermeneutic Problems in the Study of the Aggadic Narrative," *Tarbiz* 47 (1978), 166–72 (Hebrew); Kraemer, *Responses to Suffering in Classical Rabbinic Literature.* On rabbinic theodicy in general see Byron L. Sherwin, "Theodicy," *Contemporary Jewish Religious Thought*, 959–70; Joseph Blenkinsopp, "The Judge of All the Earth: Theodicy in the Midrash on Genesis 18:22–23," *Journal of Jewish Studies* 41 (1990), 1–12; Elman, "Righteousness as Its Own Reward: An Inquiry into the Theologies of the Stam," and "The Suffering of the Righteous in Palestinian and Babylonian Sources."

2. The calligraphy of Torah scrolls requires decorative "crowns" be placed above various letters. Moses asks God what purpose these crowns serve.

3. From giving the Torah now, without the crowns.

4. *Hazor laahorekha.* This phrase can be translated, "Turn to the future."

5. Students sat in a hierarchical order according to their abilities (see chapter 14 herein). Moses sits in the back with the most inferior students.

6. Literally, "Thus it came up in my thought."

7. R. Akiba was tortured to death, his flesh raked by iron combs and (according to this tradition) then sold in the market. See chapter 37, story B, section N.

CHAPTER 37. STORIES OF MARTYRDOM

1. Medieval Jewish tradition gave the woman the name Hannah based on 1 Samuel 2:5, a verse from the biblical Hannah's prayer: "While the barren woman bears seven; the mother of many is forlorn."

2. 2 Maccabees 7. The story is retold at length in 4 Maccabees 8–14. Another rabbinic version appears in *Lamentations Rabbah* 1:16.

3. See the Introduction, p. 15.

NOTES

4. See Daniel Boyarin, *Dying for God: Martyrdom and the Making of Christianity and Judaism* (Stanford, Calif.: Stanford University Press, 1999), 102–14.

5. Additional literature: Gerson Cohen, "Hannah and Her Seven Sons," *Encyclopaedia Judaica* 7:1270–71; idem, "The Story of Hannah and Her Seven Sons in Hebrew Literature," *Mordecai M. Kaplan Jubilee Volume*, ed. M. Davis (New York: Jewish Theological Seminary, 1953), 109–23 (Hebrew); *The Third and Fourth Book of Maccabees*, ed. Moses Hadas (New York: Harper, 1953), 127–35; Kraemer, *Responses to Suffering in Classical Rabbinic Literature*, 110–12, 167–71; Hyam Maccoby, "Sanctification of the Name," *Contemporary Jewish Religious Thought*, 849–54; Boyarin, *Dying for God*, 93–126. See also chapter 1, story B, the martyrdom of Lulianus and Pappus, and chapter 38, story B, sections B1–B2.

6. That is, "If you are so concerned for your own honor that you want me to pretend to bow, lest others see me reject your commands, how much the more so should I be concerned for the honor of God and obey him!"

7. Presumably because she and her sons are reunited in the next world.

8. *Mekhilta d'Rabbi Ishmael, Neziqin*, §18, ed. Jacob Lauterbach (Philadelphia: Jewish Publication Society, 1935), 141–42.

9. A Roman official; the Latin would probably be "Tineus Rufus." Scholars have attempted to identify him with various historical figures.

10. The *Shema* is a prayer composed of several scriptures beginning with Deuteronomy 6:4–9.

11. Literally, "May that man's (=your) breath expire!" In our idiom, "Go to Hell."

12. The rabbis interpreted the term "muchness" (*me'odekha*) in terms of money and possessions.

13. The story also appears in Yerushalmi Sotah 5:7, 20c.

14. Note the wordplay: Akiba warns not to abandon or "avoid" (*mevatlin*) Torah, while Pappos, who does "avoid" Torah, is arrested for meaningless or "void" (*beteilin*) matters. Pappos thus realizes that he gained nothing by desisting from Torah study.

15. You must proclaim your faith even under such circumstances?

16. The full verse reads, "Hear O Israel! The Lord our God, the Lord is *one*" (Deut 6:4). It is customary to draw out the word "one" (*ehad*) both to emphasize God's unity and to avoid confusing the similar word "other" (*aher*).

17. Three statements proclaim Akiba's good fortune ("Happy are you…"): once while alive (M), once at his death (P), once at his approach to the next world (Q). These correspond to the three challenges to Akiba's policies: Pappos challenges his wisdom in continuing to teach Torah (J); the students challenge his proclaiming his faith while being tortured (O); and the angels challenge the justness of his death (Q). This contrast in perspectives effectively communicates the didactic point.

PART IX
CHAPTER 38. STORIES OF ELISHA B. ABUYA

1. This interpretation is suggested by the tradition's context in Tosefta Hagiga 2:3, for the relevant Mishna, Hagiga 2:1, prohibits or restricts study of portions of Torah. See Alon Goshen-Gottstein, "Four Entered Paradise Revisited," *Harvard Theological Review* 88 (1995), 69–133. Following Gershom Scholem, many scholars see the *pardes* as a term for mystical speculation or praxis.

2. In context the verse relates to vows. One's mouth should not lead one to sin by uttering and then not fulfilling a vow, which would anger God and invite punishment.

3. It should be clear that the story is not a historical account of the real Elisha b. Abuya but a later interpretation of a text.

4. The guttural pronunciation of the *reish* in talmudic times resembled the *aleph* more closely than today.

5. Ironically, Elisha is misled when a rabbinic tradition (Torah!) about the nature and posture of angels in Heaven conflicts with his vision. (The problem is that the tradition claims that there is "no sitting" on high, but Metatron is seated.) The sense of "no back" derives from Ezekiel's vision in which the animals bearing the chariot of God have faces on all four sides, hence no backs (Ezek 1:1–28).

6. Apparently to prove to Meir that there are not two gods. It is unclear if Metatron is at fault for not rising and thereby creating a mistaken impression. One manuscript adds here, "They said to him [Metatron], 'Why did you not rise before him?'" On the other hand, the punishment of Elisha suggests that the fault was the human's.

7. Measure-for-measure punishment. Elisha caused Metatron to be burned with fire, so Metatron burns out Elisha's merits.

8. Elisha has no merits and no possibility to repent. His sins will therefore damn him in the next world.

9. A play on the name *Aher*, which means "other, another." As noted in the introduction, this incident explains the tradition that Elisha "cut the shoots" of the Tosefta.

10. This theology of transferring merits and sins is completely exceptional in rabbinic literature. It may appear here to justify Elisha's loss of merit: it sometimes happens that individuals do not receive reward for their merits, so Elisha's loss of merit is not extraordinary. Note that Elisha's (or Akiba's) interpretation is far superior to that of Meir, who offers the commonplace idea that God created everything.

11. Isaiah refers to the righteous, Jeremiah to the wicked.

12. If Torah can be compared to various types of vessels, then it must be comparable to worthless clay vessels as well.

13. This interpretation clearly relates to the theme of the story, as evident from Meir's immediate rejoinder.

14. It is forbidden to ride a horse on the Sabbath. Meir nonetheless follows because he covets Elisha's Torah.

15. One may not travel more than 2,000 cubits from one's city or place of lodging on the Sabbath.

16. To solicit the study-verse of a child was a common method of seeking an oracle, a type of divine guidance, in an age after the cessation of prophecy. See chapter 4, story A, section C. The study-verses confirm for Meir what the heavenly voice told Elisha, that God wants no part in Elisha's repentance.

17. The dissection is modeled on Judges 19:29–30. This is the one heinous sin attributed to Elisha in this story. Otherwise he is portrayed sympathetically, even tragically. His earlier sins, such as soliciting a prostitute and riding on the Sabbath, simply seek physical or material comfort.

18. Meir intends to bring about punishment for Elisha's sins so that the reward may follow. Printings of the Talmud in fact add, "It is better that he be punished and enter the world to come," to clarify his motive. While Meir succeeds in effecting the punishment—and presumably the reward will eventually follow—he also causes great pain to his master, which troubles R. Yohanan.

19. The "guard of the gate" of Gehenom, the rabbinic conception of Hell, is not mentioned in other sources. The sense here seems to be that R. Yohanan personally escorted Aher from his punishment, and none dared interfere because of his stature. This line appears to be a later gloss.

20. The context concerns the fate of the wicked man.

21. Apparently a warning that he better support Elisha's daughters or suffer divine punishment.

22. One should separate God's wisdom (Torah) from "their wisdom," the baleful advice of sinning masters.

23. It is possible to learn Torah (incline your ear) and yet shun the evil ways of the master (forget your father's house).

24. Proverb 22:17 and Psalm 45:11 contradict Malachi 2:7. The solution is that a minor should not learn from a sinner, but an adult is able to distinguish the Torah from the deeds. This comment is a later gloss.

25. The term for "sins" here is *sarah*, literally, "rot, spoil, stink." This choice of term continues the vegetable imagery.

26. The same motif appears in chapter 9, section G.

27. Thus God calls Meir "his son" and cites a Mishna that contains Meir's words. To repeat traditions in the name of a sage bestows a type of immortality, namely perpetuation in the Oral Torah of the rabbinic community. God first not mentioning Meir's name and then restoring it parallels both God rejecting and then saving Elisha and Rabbi Yehuda HaNasi rejecting and then supporting the daughters.

28. For example, "not for the sake of Heaven" (A2, D3), "Alas for things lost and not found" (A1, A2), "They (came and) said to R. Meir" (A, C1, C2, C3), "desiring to visit" (C1, C2, C3), "Years later" (C1, D).

29. The midrash turns on the preposition *me-* (of *me-reishito* = than-the-beginning), which means both "than" and "from." While Meir has forgotten (or not learned) the explanation of Akiba and offers a banal paraphrase of the verse, Elisha knows Akiba's tradition and offers a creative midrash. This contrast establishes Elisha as the superior in Torah and as Meir's true master. Note that Elisha's midrash relates to the subject of the story: will he receive reward for the good deeds he performed before he sinned?

30. Again Elisha's midrash takes *me-* as "from" instead of "than." And again it is superior to Meir's, which simply offers three parables exemplifying the simple meaning of the verse. Elisha not only employs a midrashic novelty, but he presents himself as a real-life application of the interpretation. Meir gives hypothetical parables, Elisha a true illustration.

31. See note 15 of this chapter. Again Elisha demonstrates his proficiency: he counted the paces of his horse to measure the Sabbath limit while simultaneously engaging in conversation. Meir would have violated the Sabbath were it not for Elisha's punctiliousness.

32. Note the extended wordplay on *hazar*: R. Eliezer and R. Yehoshua are *hozrin* (turning) words of Torah; Meir claims that a sage who forgets his Torah can *lahazor* (return) and learn it anew; finally Meir asks Elisha why he does not *hazar* (repent).

33. The Holy of Holies, the inner chamber of the temple, was considered God's terrestrial residence. Elisha thus violates the Sabbath—which celebrates God as creator of the universe—on the holiest day of the year at the holiest place on earth. It is perhaps significant that Elisha states that he *cannot* repent, not that he does not wish to, which argues for a sympathetic view of Elisha. (C1 returns to this issue.) The impossibility of repentance means that Elisha will die both with merits, on account of his former study of Torah, and unexpiated sins. This narrative strategy allows the story to ponder the question of the inviolability of the merit of Torah.

34. The Galilee *(qineret)*.

35. Elisha's weeping is ambiguous: does he weep in order to repent, as Meir seems to think, or because all others can repent, even on their deathbed, except for him? The next scene is likewise ambiguous: was he punished because he did not repent or because his repentance was rejected, as the voice from the temple decreed?

36. A sign of posthumous punishment.

37. The Mishna rules that honor of one's master takes precedence over honor of one's father, "because his father brought him into this world but his master, who teaches him wisdom, brings him into the world to come" (Mishna Bava Metsia 2:11). Meir thus informs his students that Elisha retains his status as Meir's master despite his sins. Note that C1 portrays Meir visiting Elisha in this world, C2 describes Meir in this world visiting Elisha's burning grave, a sign of Elisha's condition in the hereafter, and then C3 reports that Meir will visit Elisha when they are reunited in the world to come. Meir treats Elisha as his master in all circumstances and in both worlds.

38. This Mishna rules that one may save a Torah scroll and phylacteries from fire on the Sabbath despite the usual prohibition against carrying from a private to a public domain. While saving the holy contents, one may save the outer casings as well. So too, Meir explains, Elisha contained Torah within a profane or even sinful body. He too is saved together with the Torah he possesses. The analogy is particularly apt because Meir stops the fire burning on Elisha's grave, and because Elisha is a Sabbath breaker, while this Mishna permits breaking the Sabbath when fire breaks out.

39. The psalm speaks of the wicked man. Rabbi rejects Elisha's daughters because of their father's sins.

40. Bavli Ketubot 72a and Shabbat 32b.

41. Note that the interpretations do not expound every part of the verse, but only a few choice phrases. This is typical of rabbinic midrash that decontextualizes words and phrases from their full context.

42. A *karmelit* refers to a domain that is neither public nor private, such as an alleyway or field. While carrying within a *karmelit* was forbidden by the rabbis, it does not violate Pentateuchal law.

CHAPTER 39. THE POWER OF REPENTANCE

1. Some versions read, "She said" instead of "He thought/said."
2. The verse implies that the mountains and hills may be displaced or ruined. They must pray that this not happen to them.
3. For the heavenly voice stated "*Rabbi* Eleazar…" (E).

CHAPTER 40. A SINNER'S GOOD DEED

1. From *pantos* (completely) and *kakos* (evil). See Saul Lieberman, *Greek in Jewish Palestine* (New York: Jewish Theological Seminary, 1942), 31 n. 18; Michael Sokoloff, *A Dictionary of Jewish Palestinian Aramaic of the Byzantine Period* (Ramat Gan: Bar Ilan University Press, 1990), 437. Others derive the name from *penta* (five) and *kakos* (evil), "Mr. Five Sins," based on the following line.
2. That is: "I need money, so I am forced to become a prostitute.…"
3. Lieberman proposes an emendation: "I sold my drum and the items belonging to my drum" (*Greek in Jewish Palestine*, 32 n. 22).

BIBLIOGRAPHY

Alon, Gedaliah. *The Jews in Their Land in the Talmudic Age (70–640 C.E.).* Translated by Gershon Levi. Jerusalem: Magnes Press, 1980.

Boyarin, Daniel. *Carnal Israel: Reading Sex in Talmudic Culture.* Berkeley and Los Angeles: University of California Press, 1993.

———. *Dying for God: Martyrdom and the Making of Christianity and Judaism.* Stanford, Calif.: Stanford University Press, 1999.

Buxbaum, Yizhak. *The Life and Teachings of Hillel.* Northvale, N.J.: Jason Aronson, 1994.

Cohen, Arthur A., and Paul Mendes-Flohr, eds. *Contemporary Jewish Religious Thought.* New York: The Free Press, 1987.

Elman, Yaakov. "Righteousness as Its Own Reward: An Inquiry into the Theologies of the Stam." *Proceedings of the American Academy for Jewish Research* 57 (1990–91), 35–67.

———. "The Suffering of the Righteous in Palestinian and Babylonian Sources." *Jewish Quarterly Review* 80 (1990), 315–40.

Fraenkel, Jonah. *Darkhei ha'aggada vehamidrash* (The Methods of the Aggada). Masada: Yad Letalmud, 1991.

Hezser, Catherine. *Form, Function and Historical Significance of the Rabbinic Story in Yerushalmi Neziqin.* Tübingen: J.C.B. Mohr, 1993.

Jastrow, Marcus. *A Dictionary of the Targumim, the Talmud Babli and Yerushalmi and the Midrashic Literature.* Reprint. New York: Jastrow Publishers, 1967.

RABBINIC STORIES

Kraemer, David. *Responses to Suffering in Classical Rabbinic Literature.* New York: Oxford University Press, 1995.

Rubenstein, Jeffrey. *Talmudic Stories: Narrative Art, Composition, and Culture.* Baltimore, Md.: Johns Hopkins University Press, 1999.

Schiffman, Lawrence H. *From Text to Tradition: A History of Second Temple and Rabbinic Judaism.* Hoboken, N.J.: Ktav, 1991.

Schürer, Emil. *The History of the Jewish People in the Age of Jesus Christ.* Revised by G. Vermes, F. Millar, et al. Edinburgh: T. & T. Clark, 1973–87.

EDITIONS OF RABBINIC WORKS

Avot d'Rabbi Natan. Edited by Solomon Schechter. Vienna, 1887.

Genesis Rabbah = Midrash bereshit rabba. Edited by J. Theodor and H. Albeck. 3 vols. Reprint. Jerusalem, 1965 [Berlin, 1912–36].

Lamentations Rabbah = Midrash eicha rabba. Edited by Salomon Buber. Reprint. Hildesheim: Georg Olms, 1967 [Vilna, 1899].

Leviticus Rabbah = Midrash vayiqra rabba. Edited by Mordechai Margulies. Reprint. New York, 1993 [Jerusalem, 1953–60].

Mekhilta d'Rabbi Ishmael. Edited by H. Horovitz and I. Rabin. Reprint. Jerusalem, 1960 [Breslau, 1930].

Sifre to Numbers = *Sifre al sefer bamidbar vesifre Zuta.* Edited by H. S. Horovitz. Reprint. Jerusalem: Wahrmann, 1966 [Leipzig, 1917].

Talmud bavli. New York: M. P. Press, 1976. Manuscript readings from Raphaelo Rabbinovicz. *Diqduqei Sofrim: Variae Lectiones in Mischnam et in Talmud Babylonicum.* 12 vols. Reprint. New York, 1960.

Talmud yerushalmi. Facsimile of first edition, Venice 1523–24.

Tosefta. Edited by Saul Lieberman. 4 vols. New York: Jewish Theological Seminary, 1955–88.

Tosephta. Edited by M. S. Zuckermandel. Reprint. Jerusalem: Wahrmann, 1970 [Pasewalk, 1880].

INDEX OF BIBLICAL
AND RABBINIC SOURCES*

*Page numbers follow comma after chapter and verse.

RABBINIC STORIES

INDEX OF BIBLICAL AND RABBINIC SOURCES

SUBJECT AND NAME INDEX

"Scroll of Fasts," 25
Shabtai, R., 197
Shammai, 181–85
Shema, 6, 219
Shemaya, Rav, 203
Shimon b. Gamaliel, 58, 104, 105, 106, 107–8
Shimon b. Laqish, 1, 109, 111, 114–16, 236
Shimon b. R. Yehuda HaNasi, 104, 108
Shimon b. Shetah, 31–32, 128, 129, 130–31, 132
Shimon bar Kosiba. *See* Bar Kokhba
Shimon bar Yohai, 103, 121–27; education of, 125–27; martyrdom, 222; as miracle-worker, 123–24; wedding, 143; and Yehoshua b. Levi, 134–35
Shmuel, 126, 142, 191, 198
Sin, 229–44
Siqra, Abba, 44
Suffering, 210–14; Nahum of Gamzu, 207–9
Sukkot, 25

Tannaim, 3, 96, 258n35; and calendar, 85–87
Tarfon, R., 194, 195
Temple of Jerusalem: destruction of, 48–50; rebuilding, 34–37, 61–63
Titus, 40, 45, 46
Torah, 1–2, 215–17, 231–360; accessibility of, 97; Babylonian vs. Palestine Torah, 109–13; and family, 139–45; and rabbinic

academy, 105–6; study of, 8–9, 74, 200–3; women and, 151–53; Written and Oral Torah, 1–2, 182, 183
Tosefta, 3, 13
Tur Malka, destruction of, 41, 51–53

Ula, Rav, 198

Vespasian, 10, 38, 39, 40, 42, 44, 45, 48–50

Women: and Torah, 151–53; see also Marriage and family

Yaakov, R., 240
Yaakov b. Qudshai, 105, 107
Yaakov b. Sisi, 98–99
Yaakov of Kefar Sakhnia, 172, 173
Yannai, King, 31–32, 174
Yehoshua, R., 50, 82–83, 86–87, 96, 98, 99–100, 102–3, 239
Yehoshua, b. Hananiah, 61, 62–63
Yehoshua b. Levi, 133–35
Yehoshua b. Perahia, 174
Yehuda, R., 54, 82, 125, 198, 216; and Akavia b. Mehalalel, 68, 69
Yehuda the Ammonite, 272n27
Yehuda the Baker, 240
Yehuda b. Betera, 91
Yehuda b. Gerim, 125, 127
Yehuda b. R. Hiyya, 140, 142
Yehuda HaNasi, 2, 3, 90, 140, 142, 143; and Antoninus, 163–68; editor of Mishna, 2, 3; and Elisha b. Abuya, 231, 235, 242; repentance, 245–46
Yerushalmi, 4, 13; calendar, 88–89

Other Volumes in This Series

Other Volumes in This Series

John and Charles Wesley • SELECTED WRITINGS AND HYMNS

Meister Eckhart • THE ESSENTIAL SERMONS, COMMENTARIES, TREATISES
AND DEFENSE

Francisco de Osuna • THE THIRD SPIRITUAL ALPHABET

Jacopone da Todi • THE LAUDS

Fakhruddin 'Iraqi • DIVINE FLASHES

Menahem Nahum of Chernobyl • THE LIGHT OF THE EYES

Early Dominicans • SELECTED WRITINGS

John Climacus • THE LADDER OF DIVINE ASCENT

Francis and Clare • THE COMPLETE WORKS

Gregory Palamas • THE TRIADS

Pietists • SELECTED WRITINGS

The Shakers • TWO CENTURIES OF SPIRITUAL REFLECTION

Zohar • THE BOOK OF ENLIGHTENMENT

Luis de León • THE NAMES OF CHRIST

Quaker Spirituality • SELECTED WRITINGS

Emanuel Swedenborg • THE UNIVERSAL HUMAN AND SOUL-BODY
INTERACTION

Augustine of Hippo • SELECTED WRITINGS

Safed Spirituality • RULES OF MYSTICAL PIETY, THE BEGINNING OF WISDOM

Maximus Confessor • SELECTED WRITINGS

John Cassian • CONFERENCES

Johannes Tauler • SERMONS

John Ruusbroec • THE SPIRITUAL ESPOUSALS AND OTHER WORKS

Ibn 'Abbād of Ronda • LETTERS ON THE SŪFĪ PATH

Angelus Silesius • THE CHERUBINIC WANDERER

The Early Kabbalah •

Meister Eckhart • TEACHER AND PREACHER

John of the Cross • SELECTED WRITINGS

Pseudo-Dionysius • THE COMPLETE WORKS

Bernard of Clairvaux • SELECTED WORKS

Devotio Moderna • BASIC WRITINGS

The Pursuit of Wisdom • AND OTHER WORKS BY THE AUTHOR OF THE
CLOUD OF UNKNOWING

Richard Rolle • THE ENGLISH WRITINGS

Francis de Sales, Jane de Chantal • LETTERS OF SPIRITUAL DIRECTION

Albert and Thomas • SELECTED WRITINGS

Robert Bellarmine • SPIRITUAL WRITINGS

Other Volumes in This Series

Other Volumes in This Series